Practical Research and Evaluation

Practical Research and Evaluation

A Start-to-finish Guide for Practitioners

Lena Dahlberg and Colin McCaig

Los Angeles | London | New Delhi
Singapore | Washington DC

First published 2010

SAGE Publications Ltd
1 Oliver's Yard
55 City Road
London EC1Y 1SP

SAGE Publications Inc.
2455 Teller Road
Thousand Oaks, California 91320

SAGE Publications India Pvt Ltd
B 1/I 1 Mohan Cooperative Industrial Area
Mathura Road, New Delhi 110 044
India

SAGE Publications Asia-Pacific Pte Ltd
33 Pekin Street #02-01
Far East Square
Singapore 048763

Library of Congress Control Number: available

British Library Cataloguing in Publication data

A catalogue record for this book is available from
the British Library

ISBN 978-1-84787-003-2
ISBN 978-1-84787-004-9

Typeset by C&M Digitals (P) Ltd, Chennai, India
Printed in Great Britain by MPG Books Group, Bodmin, Cornwall
Printed on paper from sustainable resources

Contents

Notes on Contributors

Tamsin Bowers-Brown is a lecturer teaching on the BA Education Studies degree at Sheffield Hallam University. Tamsin teaches Education Policy, Research Methods and the Sociology of Education as well as conducting research into class inequality and educational achievement.

Lena Dahlberg is a lecturer at Dalarna University and Director of the Gerontology Centre at Dalarna Research Institute, Falun, Sweden. She was awarded her PhD in Political Science at Stockholm University in 2004, and worked at Sheffield Hallam University from 2004–2009. She has published widely within the area of social gerontology. Her particular research interests are social exclusion among older people, and the interaction of the state and the voluntary sector in supporting family caregivers.

Joanne Davies is a research fellow in the Centre for Education and Inclusion Research at Sheffield Hallam University. As an experienced qualitative and quantitative researcher, Joanne is responsible for the planning, delivery and management of research projects.

Scott Fernie is a lecturer at Heriot-Watt University with an overriding interest in management studies. As well as challenging undergraduate and postgraduate students to think more critically about management and methodology, Scott is also engaged in research that challenges the rhetoric and reality of management in seeking to encourage and develop social change within the workplace.

Guillaumette Haughton has worked as a researcher in various academic social science departments, and in private research consultancy. She is presently a PhD Researcher in the Department of Town and Regional Planning at the University of Sheffield, undertaking research into governance processes and public participation in relation to urban river corridors.

Jason Leman is lecturer in Strategic Development and Evaluation at the Learning and Teaching Institute at Sheffield Hallam University. Having had several years experience carrying out a range of survey work he is now responsible for the institution's internal student survey.

Colin McCaig is a senior research fellow in the Centre for Education and Inclusion Research, Sheffield Hallam University. He has over a decade of experience in educational research, mainly in the field of policy analysis and has published widely on Labour Party education policymaking, widening participation and access to higher education, and the impact of informational and communications technology in further education.

Karen Smith is a research fellow within the Caledonian Academy at Glasgow Caledonian University. She conducts research into higher education policy and practice and is currently working in the area of transformational change. She has published in the areas of undergraduate dissertation supervision, transitions to university, transnational teaching and the language of higher education policy. She has recently co-authored a student guide to writing dissertations in the social sciences.

Maria Smith is a senior lecturer in the Learning and Teaching Institute at Sheffield Hallam University. She has many years experience of contract, consultancy and institutional research and is particularly interested in equality issues within higher education.

Anna Stevens is a research associate at Sheffield Hallam University's Centre for Education and Inclusion Research. As an experienced quantitative researcher she manages large-scale surveys and undertakes statistical analysis in a variety of educational and social research settings.

ONE

Practitioner Research and the Research Process

Lena Dahlberg and Colin McCaig

By the end of this chapter, you should be acquainted with:

- the meaning of the term 'practitioner-researcher';
- which environments practitioner-researchers are likely to work in, the challenges they may face and how to tackle them;
- the different phases of the research process.

Introduction

In our knowledge society, there is an expectation that practice should be evidence based. The emphasis on evidence and knowledge means that practitioners need to keep themselves updated with the research development in their area and may even find themselves in a position in which they have to undertake research to inform their practice. The main objective of this book is to provide a user-friendly handbook of social science research methods for the busy professional who has benefited from little, if any, formal research methods training and yet needs to know how research works. It is a practitioner-researcher handbook to research that aims to:

(1) enable readers to carry out small-scale research or evaluation projects of their own;
(2) enable readers to better understand research or evaluation reports; and
(3) provide readers with the basic understanding of research necessary to commission pieces of research or evaluation for others to carry out.

The first part of this chapter will discuss the specific roles of practitioner-researchers and the environment in which they are likely to carry out research. It will also discuss the advantages of practitioner research, and the potential challenges and how to deal with them. In the second part of this chapter, we will give an overview of the research process from start to finish, from the first idea to the dissemination of findings. This overview will serve as an outline of the chapters to follow and their positions in the research process.

Practitioners undertaking research or evaluations may have some public sector and voluntary sector roles, for example, within the areas of education, health, social services and community. When this group of people are involved in research and evaluation, this is likely to take place within their own organisations, professions and practice. This is the group generally referred in the literature as 'practitioner-researchers'.

This book will also be useful for university and college lecturers with limited research experience or training. Lecturers may engage with research and evaluation either to inform their own teaching or enhance their academic credentials. As such, university and college staff can be seen as practitioner-researchers, particularly if the subject of their research is teaching and learning in educational environments. This book will also be of use to postgraduate research students, particularly because many of the examples used herein are of relatively small-scale and limited research projects carried out under time pressure and with limited resources. Whatever the background and approach of the readership, this book aims to provide both practitioner-researchers and others with insight into research basics so that they can carry out a small-scale research study on their own.

Yet another practitioner group with a clear interest in research is the commissioners of research. It is they that set the frame for research. This group of readers will have an interest in research issues in general. Specifically for this group this book will provide an insight into how to prepare research briefs and review proposals.

Naturally, many practitioners may be interested in research without wishing or having the chance to undertake or commission research or evaluations. They may see themselves more as users of research than as researchers or commissioners, ensuring that their practice is evidence-based. This book will better equip users of research, allowing them to understand the research and evaluation process and outcomes, but also to be more critical of research and evaluations, that is, to be able to identify what is rigorous and what is weak in studies they come across. A deeper understanding of research will also enable practitioners to consider how research and evaluations can be used, and how findings can be applied in their own practice.

Practitioner Research

Your Role as a Practitioner-Researcher

In this book, we refer to 'practitioner-researcher' as anybody who combines his/her position within practice with conducting research concerning that practice. (S)he can be involved in research of any kind of design. It can be a research study, a piece of action research or an evaluation (see Box 1.1). The study may be carried out by means of qualitative or quantitative methods or by a combination of different kinds of methods. Practitioner-researchers may be emphasising theory or, more often, applications of research. Nevertheless, practitioner-researchers share the common characteristic that they are well placed to work in a participative or collaborative style, including engagement with both colleagues and service users (Fuller and Petch, 1995), and they are likely to undertake studies small in scale. As noted by Jarvis (1999), though, practitioners who have become practitioner-researchers do not always regard themselves as such and their role has not received much attention.

Box 1.1   Characteristics of practitioner research

Drawing on Shaw (2005), it can be argued that practitioner research is likely to have some, though not necessarily all, of the following characteristics:

- Direct data collection and management or reflection on existing data.
- Aims and outcomes set by professionals.
- Intended practical benefits for professionals, organisations or service users.
- A substantial proportion of the inquiry undertaken by practitioners.
- Focus on professionals' own practice and/or that of their immediate peers.
- Small-scale and short-term.
- Usually self-contained, that is, not part of a larger research programme.
- Data collection and management typically carried out as a lone activity, that is, a kind of 'own account' research.

Practitioner-researchers may find themselves within various fields within the public or voluntary sectors, but it should be noted that practitioner research has not advanced in parallel throughout different services. For example, documented work on practitioner research is substantially greater in fields such as education than it is in social and health services. Draper argues that the role of practitioner-researcher within nursing would have been unthinkable in the early 1990s and that nursing 25 years ago was 'undeniably and unashamedly a practical profession' (2000: 43). So, why has practitioner research not developed simultaneously in all social fields? Fox et al. (2007) have identified two reasons for this. First, in health and social care there is a predominance of experimental research and a perception that research using randomised controlled study designs is of highest quality. Second, bureaucratic structures within health and social care are slow to change and it takes time to accept that research that is carried out in unusual and creative ways is not automatically poor research. Another explanation is offered by Yerrell:

It is not surprising that nursing research has had little impact in a context where a highly educated medical workforce is dealing with less abstract concepts compared to an arguably less educated nursing workforce that hangs on to complex abstract notions of caring health beliefs and patent-centredness. (2000: 37)

Practitioner-researchers may have different intentions for their research. It may be something that is a requirement of their post (either in order to provide information for policy decisions or as a response to the increasing expectation that practice should be evidence-based), part of a course of study, career development or personal interest (Fox et al., 2007; Jarvis, 1999). Before embarking on research, practitioner-researchers need to understand the subject, the context and the implications of the social change that may follow from research. In doing so, practitioner-researchers will work towards enabling an attitude to research that is both critical and impartial. Being critical implies acknowledging that there is not one single 'truth' out there, that is, that many different 'truths' may be held by individuals and groups. Being impartial implies that findings are not presented as 'the only truth' that inevitably leads to a single, irreversible solution. Practitioner-researchers usually have no organisational authority to implement change and they need to be perceived as being trustworthy and without implementing an agenda of their own (Fox et al., 2007).

The role of practitioner-researcher is to take on board and understand different views of the organisation, although it should be noted that not all of these may be overtly discussed or mentioned. Often research brings these undiscussed issues out in the open, which can be threatening and make people anxious. Therefore, it is important that the practitioner-researcher clarifies both who the stakeholders are in the research project and considers the culture of the organisation. Fox et al. identify three main groups of stakeholders:

(1) The commissioner – the person(s) who asked for the research to be undertaken.
(2) Service providers – those who are involved in delivering the service that is going to be researched and who are potentially affected by the findings.
(3) Service users – people for whom the service is tailored and who should benefit from improvements. (2007: 62)

Other stakeholders may include boards of trustees, elected members of a council or managers in the organisation. Stakeholders have in common vested interests in the outcomes of research, although they are likely to have different interests. To give an example of what this could mean in practice, some stakeholders may want to cut costs by shutting down an inefficient service, while others may be dependent on this service as a user but would like to see improvements in certain aspects of it, and yet others may have invested many years in working in and developing the service and wish to preserve it as it is.

Practitioner-researchers carrying out research need to consider the environment or organisational culture in which they find themselves, whether this is a social service department, a school, a community centre, a town planning department or a leisure centre. Fox et al. simply define 'organisational culture' as 'how things are around here' and argue that the organisational culture needs to be considered in terms of:

(1) Decision-making – how decisions are made and implemented, and what the goals are and who sets them.
(2) Power – who has the power in the organisation with regard to, for example, budgets, meetings, key stakeholders, and information access and dissemination. (2007: 61)

The organisational culture also has a lot to do with how research is perceived and acted upon. When was research last discussed or a report circulated? When where research findings last acted upon? Does the person responsible for research promote research in general or only their own research? Does this person have a good relationship with the manager? Who has the power to block or protect research? The culture has implications for your role as a practitioner-researcher. It is worth thinking through whether and how your relationships would change if you begin to call yourself a researcher, and whether it would change your team. In other words, you need to think about the implications of undertaking research within the organisation.

Advantages of Practitioner Research

Why should practitioners undertake or even be interested in research? Many fields of the public sector have had to meet with demands for professional accountability. There have been increased expectations that practice should be informed by research, that is, being evidence-based, and the use of performance indicators, quality assurance and evaluations has been introduced. At the very least, this means that there is a case for practitioners to develop a degree of 'research-mindedness' (Fuller and Petch, 1995).

Researchers are usually 'outsiders' with a neutral or detached view on what is being researched. This is not the case when it comes to practitioner-researchers, as they tend to undertake research on their own practice, involving their own professions and collecting data within their own organisations. With this come both advantages and disadvantages.

Among the major advantages of practitioner research (compared to external research) are those relating to specific knowledge and organisational culture, for example, that a practitioner will know the most relevant and meaningful questions to ask, that the research is undertaken by somebody who understands the field, that the research is sympathetic towards values within specific practices and that the research benefits practice and promotes change. It has also been argued that practitioner research is more ethical than academic research since it has more potential to 'give voice to the voiceless' (McWilliam 2004: 114; compare with Shaw, 2005). For practitioner-researchers and their peers, practitioner research has the additional advantages that it may raise the standing of the profession, increase professional skills and promote reflective learning (Fuller and Petch, 1995; Fox et al., 2007).

Challenges of Practitioner Research and How to Deal with Them

The insider position of practitioner-researchers is, however, linked with some potential problems. First, practitioner-researchers may be seen as biased, less trustworthy and with vested interests – both by academics and by people within the organisation (Fox et al., 2007). With regard to scepticism from academics, it has been argued that practice is to practitioners what disciplines are to academics, that is, that academics are as keen to be informed by and contribute to their disciplinary knowledge as practitioners are keen to be informed by and contribute to their professional knowledge. The difference is that vested interest – or 'interestedness' in McWilliam's (2004) terminology – in a discipline is seen as legitimate, while vested interest in practice is not, as it is the practice that is under scrutiny in the research study or evaluation. Nevertheless, both internally and in relation to other researchers it is important that practitioner-researchers are seen as impartial and objective. Therefore, they need to show that they do not have any agenda beyond carrying out good quality research, that is, that they are not seeking to achieve any particular finding (Fox et al., 2007).

Second, the practitioner-researcher's role within the organisation may be a barrier to research. Even with the best intentions, research participants may continue to see the researcher as the nurse, teacher or social worker. Consequently, as a practitioner-researcher you need to be clear about your role and to be reflective. You need to consider your role as a practitioner-researcher, that is, to consider your researcher role in relation to your practitioner role and the environment in which you work. You also need to be sensitive to power and politics in the environment – power and politics can be either a hindrance or a support for your study and for the implementation of your findings (Fox et al., 2007).

A third potential problem with practitioner research is that it may raise ethical issues. Practitioner-researchers have a dual role; they deal with colleagues and clients as practitioners, but it may not always be ethical to use this role to act as researchers (Jarvis, 1999). It may also be difficult, or even impossible, to maintain anonymity and confidentiality (Fox et al., 2007). In order to tackle ethical problems that may follow from practitioner research, you need to think through all foreseeable ethical issues before the project starts. However, it may be not be possible to avoid ethical dilemmas occurring while the study is underway. Then, it is important to communicate these dilemmas with people concerned, so that they can make an informed decision on whether to participate or withdraw from the study (for further discussion on ethics, see Chapter 4; for a further discussion of the role of practitioners in action research, see Chapter 7).

Fourth, practitioner-researchers often have to combine this role with normal duties, which places considerable time-constraints on both research and practice. As with all research, it is important to stay focused on the study. In common with other types of researchers, practitioner-researchers are likely to come across interesting issues that may be worth further exploration, but if these issues are not part of the purpose of the study, they must wait for another study that puts them in focus. Therefore, revisit the purpose of your study regularly and stay focused on the study. You also need to be aware of the scale of the study, that is, to be clear about what you can achieve and what impact this may have on the environment in which the study is taking place. Furthermore, it is important that you receive the support that you need to undertake the study. Clearly, you need appropriate time and resources set aside for this. Research cannot be fitted around other tasks and undertaken in an hour here or there. Time and resources need to be negotiated with practitioner-researchers' line managers and the research commissioners.

Additional constrains may result from the fact that many practitioner-researchers find themselves working in a practice-oriented environment, which does not necessarily promote or support research, such as a busy clinic or school. At a minimum, practitioner-researchers ought to receive supervision/intellectual guidance and support from their manager. In research, frequently things do not go according to plan and it is important to have support and somebody to discuss alternative strategies with. To undertake research in isolation is difficult, and it will be even more difficult if your experience in undertaking research is limited. If you are inexperienced as a researcher, support in formulating specific research questions and designing the project may also be needed (Fuller and Petch, 1995; for more details on research design, see Chapter 3).

A final challenge for practitioner research is that it often meets with criticism from traditional, academic research. It is a relatively new field that challenges traditional beliefs about the nature of knowledge. McWilliam (2004: 113) argues that practitioner research is sometimes seen as a theory-free zone and it has been argued that it may be difficult to frame clear policy for larger populations because of the difficulty of extrapolating from a large number of small-scale, 'me-focused' studies. She continues:

> To its critics, it [practitioner research] continues to be a blot on the landscape of inquiry, a bastardisation of sciences, either pure or applied. Thus any claim it might make to parity of esteem with other 'legitimate' methods of inquiry remains both dubious and troubling – dubious because of its lack of scientific pedigree, troubling because of its challenge to the 'impracticality' of social science as practised with in the academy.

Despite such criticism, high quality practitioner research is, of course, legitimate within the profession and/or specific organisation and of value to the

Figure 1.1   The research process

stakeholders. Fox et al. (2007: 86) recommend practitioner-researchers to develop skills in arguing for and defending their position. They also recommend them to 'lead the way' and write: 'the greater the quality and quantity of practitioner research that is put in the public domain, the easier it will be for others to follow' (Fox et al., 2007: 86). The other side of this coin is that new practitioner-researchers need to familiarise themselves with the growing practitioner research literature.

The Research Process from Start to Finish – Outline of the Book

Research and evaluation projects include a number of phases and this book is designed to cover this by taking the reader through each of these phases, from idea to completion. Figure 1.1 illustrates the research process and identifies the chapters that will provide useful guidance in relation to each phase of the process.

Before embarking on presenting and discussing different phases of a research or evaluation project, this book will introduce its readers to central themes and concepts within research and evaluation. In Chapter 2, Lena

Dahlberg and Colin McCaig discuss what characterises science and research, and the differences: between different types of research, evaluations, action research and development work; between explorative, descriptive/empirical and theory/hypothesis testing studies; and between qualitative and quantitative research.

Usually, research projects and evaluations start with a question or problem. This may be both broad and vague. To make it possible to illuminate the problem through research, the problem has to become specific and focused, that is, it has to be developed into one or several research questions. Research questions are closely linked to the purpose of the research study. The identification of research questions and the purpose of the study is part of the planning of the study.

When planning a study, significant consideration also has to be made to the research design. Research design links the initial problem and the purpose of the research to methods of data collection and data analysis, that is, to how the study will be carried out whether through one research method (such as a survey) or a combination of different methods (for example, a series of interviews coupled with observations of practice). This is not only a matter of choosing methods, such as interviews, questionnaires, focus groups or a combination of these, it is also about deciding on how many respondents to include in the study (sample size), how to get in contact with potential respondents (recruitment or sampling), how to analyse the data and so on. All these decisions are crucial to the project and are closely linked to which conclusions the researcher will be able to draw at the end of the study.

In Chapter 3, Colin McCaig discusses the concept of research design as an underlying and linking logic to the whole research process from idea to completion. He advises on how to assess the purpose of the project and define the research question(s) and how to choose appropriate methodologies to attain the information that is required. This chapter also covers other key factors involved in successful research design, such as resource constraints (most importantly budget and time management issues), supervision and the needs of the audience for the final research findings.

Every research or evaluation project will have to take ethical considerations into account. These must be considered throughout the project – from the planning stage via data collection and analysis to dissemination. Broadly speaking, there are two main aspects of ethics that will apply to projects in any area of social science research: research integrity and protection of the participants. For some research projects, approval from an ethical committee is required. Other projects have to go through a research governance process. Maria Smith discusses issues related to ethics and research governance in Chapter 4.

Most pieces of research begin with an idea or problem, closely followed by a need to obtain funding for the project – perhaps with the exception of research undertaken as part of a university course and some internally funded studies. Therefore, researchers often will write their research design in the form of a research proposal. Proposals can be reactive and written in response to specific invitations to tender or they can be pro-active and submitted to research funding organisations offering open calls for research projects. In pro-active proposals, researchers have a greater opportunity to develop their own thoughts in defining the problem and designing the project. Commissioners of research will often have to write a brief outlining the research. In the brief, they usually have to provide similar information as would be expected in a proposal, although without the same the level of detail. In Chapter 5, Colin McCaig and Lena Dahlberg present the process of developing proposals and briefs, and they give advice on how to write these kinds of documents.

It is essential to find out about and build on previous research when planning a research study or an evaluation by carrying out a review of existing literature. The literature review will provide information that will support the planning of the project, since this is how researchers demonstrate what is already known, identify the gap(s) in knowledge and make an argument for why this particular piece of research is important. When making conclusions on basis of the data, the researchers will link back to what was found in the review. More substantial literature reviews can be seen as pieces of research in their own right. For example, this is the case in so called 'systematic reviews', which aim to locate, critically review and synthesise the best available research relating to a specific topic. Literature reviews are discussed by Tamsin Bowers-Brown and Anna Stevens in Chapter 6. They outline the purpose and process of conducting a literature review, and give advice on how to make an effective and analytical literature search. Importantly, their chapter also covers critical review and appraisal of publications.

A specific form of research, common among practitioner-researchers, is action research. Its emphasis on collaboration between practitioners and researchers on context-specific problems makes it particularly attractive as a problem-solving approach. Scott Fernie and Karen Smith present different forms and explore the central issues of action research in Chapter 7. They also explain the basic assumptions that underpin action research and make clear the distinctive nature and benefits of action research.

Once the research or evaluation project is underway, one or several research methods will be used to collect and analyse data. Studies can use qualitative or quantitative methods or a combination of both. In Chapter 8, Maria Smith and Tamsin Bowers-Brown introduce different qualitative research methods with a main focus on in-depth interviewing and focus groups. They describe what semi-structured interviewing and focus groups are and in which contexts they can be most appropriate. They also discuss the merits of unstructured interviewing, observation, diaries and documentary analysis. In Chapter 11, Jason Leman offers an equivalent introduction to quantitative research methods. He examines different aspects of quantitative data collection, including postal, face-to-face, telephone and online surveys.

In Chapters 9 and 10, issues relating to qualitative research are further developed. In Chapter 9, Joanne Davies describes the process of carrying out the most common qualitative research methods. This includes the selection of participants and groups that need to be represented to answer the research question, how to design appropriate topic guides and carry out a qualitative interview or focus group. Once the data is gathered, it needs to be managed appropriately and analysed in a systematic way. This is discussed by Joanne Davies and Karen Smith in Chapter 10. They also present the process of studying, reducing analysing and interpreting the data.

Quantitative research methods are further discussed in Chapters 12 and 13. In Chapter 12, Jason Leman presents issues relating to sampling (who to ask) and questionnaire design (what to ask). In Chapter 13, Guillaumette Haughton and Anna Stevens illustrate how to enter and clean data, code open-ended questions and comments, and merge datasets. They also explain how to analyse the data and report the findings, for example, in tables and graphs.

Research projects and evaluations do not end once the data has been analysed and conclusions drawn. There is a final and important task left: to disseminate the findings. This can be done in a number of ways and the choice of dissemination form should be based on types of clients/funding organisations, the context of the project, and target audience. Commonly, research and evaluation findings are disseminated via written reports and/or oral presentations. However, research findings have the potential to reach a broader audience via the public media. In Chapter 14, Colin McCaig and Lena Dahlberg will guide the reader in how to effectively disseminate research findings in these different ways.

Further Reading

Jarvis, P. (1999) *The Practitioner-Researcher: Developing Theory from Practice*. San Francisco, CA: Jossey-Bass.
A theoretical approach to the idea of the practitioner-researcher, knowledge and the nature of reflective practice is found in Jarvis' book. This book also includes an introduction to small-scale research.

Fox, M., Martin, P. and Green, G. (2007) *Doing Practitioner Research*. London: Sage.
Fox and colleagues provide an excellent introduction to practice-research, especially with regard to practitioner-researchers' role and the environment in which they undertake research. They discuss a range of issues that may arise when you research or evaluate your own organisation or practice.

(Continued)

(Continued)

Jarvis, P. (2000) 'The practitioner-researcher in nursing', *Nurse Education Today*, 20 (1): 30–5.

Although findings from practice research are sometimes reported in academic journals, practitioner-research as such is not often discussed in these fora, perhaps due to the nature of the topic. An exception is *Nurse Education Today*, which in 2000 published an article by Jarvis with comments by four other academics. Despite the fact that these articles focus on practice research in nursing, they are relevant to a broader audience.

TWO

Introduction to Research and Evaluation Basics

Lena Dahlberg and Colin McCaig

By the end of this chapter, you should have an understanding of:

- what characterises research;
- the difference between basic and applied research;
- different types of evaluations;
- what characterises action research;
- what characterises development work;
- what empirical and non-empirical research is;
- the differences between theoretical, descriptive and explorative research;
- inductive and deductive approaches to research;
- the differences between qualitative and quantitative research.

Introduction

This chapter introduces the central themes and concepts of social science research and evaluations. The chapter starts by introducing what research is and the requirements it should meet. Thereafter, the differences between alternative research approaches are described. This includes a discussion of basic/pure versus applied research; evaluation; action research; development work; empirical versus non-empirical research; theoretical, descriptive and explorative research; and inductive and deductive approaches to research.

Finally, there will be a discussion of methodological issues. Following a brief introduction of the concepts of methodology and methods, the differences between qualitative and quantitative research are discussed, including differences in data collection and analysis as well as the underlying assumptions of qualitative and quantitative research.

What Is Research?

The mission of research is to provide us with knowledge. Research describes and explains phenomena surrounding us. A minimalist way of describing research is to say that it 'offers ordered knowledge based on systematic inquiry' (Stoker and Marsh, 2002: 11). This means that it applies scientific procedures to the collection and analysis of information (Clarke, 1999).

Requirements of research vary between disciplines. Also, as we shall see, qualitative and quantitative researchers have often got different views on these requirements. As a starting point, a few requirements will be discussed, including that social science research should seek to:

- contribute to theoretical development;
- be based on empirical data, that is, on observations of society;
- build on previous research, that is, be cumulative;
- be objective;
- enable generalisations; and
- be both valid and reliable.

Research studies and evaluations may have smaller or larger elements of theory and empirical data (for more on this, see Different Kinds of Research and Evaluations later in this chapter). Regardless of how theoretical or empirical a study is, it is essential that it builds on previous research. In the planning of a research or evaluation project, the researcher should undertake a literature review. This will ensure that the planned project builds on rather than duplicates previous studies. Perhaps at least part of the answer is already out there? Even if the answer to your particular research question is not to be found in the literature, previous research would still inform and improve your research or evaluation project (for more information on literature reviews, see Chapter 6).

There is also a norm that research provides us with knowledge that is objective and true. Objectivity may sound uncontroversial, but there is a debate about whether or not research can be objective. This debate relates to the avoidance of bias. As will be shown later in this chapter, some researchers argue that this is impossible. For example, objectivity can be compromised if there are close links between the researcher and the studied phenomenon. Let us say that a practitioner-researcher is evaluating a service that (s)he is involved in delivering, such as an English course for immigrants attending a community centre, a residential care unit for older people or a nursery group. Evaluating a service that you are working in and/or responsible for, means that you as a practitioner-researcher may be biased and therefore interpret the findings in a more positive light than an external evaluator would. Objectivity can also be compromised when research is used as means for political or financial power, for example, to establish evidence supporting a certain policy or agenda. The rule of thumb here should be that, if the researcher has a bias or vested interest, this should be declared when findings are presented. Thereby, the reader can take this into account when judging the credibility of the findings.

The requirement that research and evaluations should seek to enable generalisations means that it should be possible to apply research findings in other circumstances and settings than those studied. In other words, the group included in the study (often called the 'sample') should be representative of a larger population, although the potential to make generalisations varies depending on the design of the study, for example, whether it uses qualitative and quantitative methods (see the section on differences between qualitative and quantitative research later in this chapter).

Finally, to be able to draw conclusions from the data, it is essential that the findings are valid and reliable (see Chapter 3 for more on this), that is, that they represent the 'real world'. 'Validity' refers to how well the research question is operationalised into questions (called 'variables' in quantitative research). Do specific questions/variables capture the broader research question or phenomenon that you want to study? Are you studying what you intended to study? 'Reliability' concerns errors in measurement in the collection and analysis of data. How trustworthy is the measurement and the study? Would the same findings be obtained if somebody else did the study? The relationship between reliability and validity has been described in the following way:

> Loosely speaking, 'reliability' is the extent to which a measurement procedure yields the same answer however and whenever it is carried out; 'validity' is the extent to which it gives the correct answer. (Kirk and Miller, cited in Teorell, 2001: 15)

To a large degree, the requirements of research and evaluations have to do with trustworthiness. For us to take account of research and evaluation findings, they have to be believable. They have to be based on a systematic way of asking questions, and the method has to be transparent and justified so that we can judge how credible the research study or evaluation is.

Different Kinds of Research and Evaluations

Basic versus Applied Research

Although practitioner-researchers are rarely, if ever, involved in basic research, it may be useful to be familiar with the concept. Basic research – or pure research – is research 'for research's own sake'. This means that it is not driven by commercial or practice purposes; it develops basic knowledge without regard to any practical applications. One example of basic research would be a project that explores how cells work, without focusing on developing a new drug or treatment. Of course, findings from such a project could at a later stage be utilised to develop applications. Another example of basic research is the early research on genetics, which today has a variety of applications including assisting forensic investigations and methods for identifying and treating diseases.

For most practitioner-researchers basic research is far from the reality; they are likely to be involved in research or evaluations closely linked to their practice. The problem would be identified in practice and the findings would feed into practice. This is commonly called 'applied research', such as a study on orthopaedic injuries among older people (Dahlberg and Herlitz, 1997). In this study, older people's recovery and their experiences of various forms of services and support were examined through a combination of questionnaires and qualitative interviews. The findings were disseminated to social service practitioners, who could then use the findings in their efforts to develop services and meet the needs of older people.

Evaluation

Evaluation is a form of applied research and it uses standard research methods to identify the effectiveness of some sort of practice, such as how often a new bureaucratic process is used, or how a new health and safety directive is being implemented by professionals on the ground. Robson argues:

> ... evaluation research is essentially indistinguishable from other research in terms of design, data collection techniques and methods of analysis. (2002: 204)

The difference compared to research in general, is that the aim of evaluations is to study how effectively existing knowledge is used in practice rather than to provide new knowledge. Robson continues: 'An evaluation is a study which has a distinctive purpose; it is not a new or different research strategy' (2002: 202). Evaluations involves 'judging the value, merit or worth of something' (Clarke, 1999: 1) or, as clarified by Stufflebeam and Shinkfield: 'The most important purpose of evaluation is not to prove, but to improve' (1985, in Clarke, 1999).

There are different types of evaluations. These can be categorised in different ways (see Robson, 2002). Commonly, evaluations are categorised in terms of whether they focus on the process or on the outcome. Process evaluations aim to detect strengths and weaknesses in a programme or project process, while outcome evaluations aim to establish how well a programme, project or intervention works in practice. In outcome evaluations, the evaluator may take into account how parts of the programme or project influence the outcome as well as implementation issues (Clarke, 1999; Robson, 2002). If you as a practitioner-researcher undertake a process evaluation of, for example, a respite care service, you may focus on how informal carers are recruited to the service and in what way such care is delivered. An outcome evaluation, conversely, may focus on the extent to which the service enables carers to continue caring for their relatives.

Another distinction is between formative and summative evaluations. Formative evaluations are done to provide feedback for those trying to improve something. They are intended to help in the development of the programme. By comparison, summative (or impact) evaluations aim to determine the effectiveness and impact of a programme (Clarke, 1999; Robson, 2002). While a formative evaluation of respite care would inform service deliverers on how to improve the service, a summative evaluation would make recommendations on whether or not the service should continue. Following Robson (2002) a number of basic evaluation questions are listed in Box 2.1.

Box 2.1   Basic evaluation questions

- What is needed?
- Does what is provided meet the clients' needs?
- What happens when it is in operation?
- What are the outcomes?
- How do costs and benefits compare?
- Does it meet the required standards?
- Should it continue?
- How can it be improved?

Robson (2000: 46)

Evaluations can be conducted by external or internal evaluators. External evaluators are independent researchers who are commissioned to carry out an evaluation on behalf of the service providing or funding organisation, while internal evaluators are employees who carry out evaluations within their own organisation (Clarke, 1999). Often, practitioner-researchers find themselves in the role of an internal evaluator (see Chapter 1, for more information on the role of practitioner-researchers working within their own organisation).

Action Research

In action research, research and implementation go hand in hand. Actions are taken and evaluated leading to findings that are, in turn, acted upon. As the research continues, these new actions are studied and evaluated. Action research is future-oriented and aims to improve service and practices. Often, action research involves people at different levels – practitioners as well as service users and the wider community. It is specific to the context in which it is carried out and enables practitioner-researchers to identify qualities in their practice. Action research involves a cycle of planning, acting, observing and reflecting (Lewin, cited in Robson, 2002). The process of action research is explained in further detail in Chapter 7.

Development Work

Development work has an even greater emphasis on the implementation of findings. Usually, development work is discussed in terms of research and development (R&D). The aim of R&D is to develop a service or a product. Often, this development is based on the need of the clients. Their opinions can be gathered via, for example, focus groups, surveys or interviews. For instance, as a practitioner-researcher in a school setting, you may hold a focus group with students to identify what they expect and would like to see in terms of support from their teachers. The findings would inform the development of how courses are delivered.

Practitioners' own experiences are an alternative starting point for development work. In some projects, practitioners from different organisations meet and have structured discussions on certain aspects of their service delivery, for example, social workers and youth workers can meet to discuss how to address the problem of child abuse. In these discussions, practitioners can learn from one another and can use this new knowledge in the development of their own services. These discussions can be taken a step further, whereby practitioners evaluate one another's work. Then, knowledge gained can be used to improve both their own services and the services evaluated.

Empirical versus Non-empirical Research

Another distinction is made between empirical and non-empirical research, that is, whether or not the study is based on empirical observations. An example of a non-empirical science is mathematics. Mathematicians do not necessarily have to study reality to be able to draw conclusions. Instead, they can improve the knowledge of their subject through abstract, theoretical calculations.

Most research is empirical meaning that it is based on observations of reality, which can take the form of analysing data derived from social actors, such as survey responses or interviews, which tell the researcher what people think. Empirical research could be, for example, focus groups with parents of children attending nursery to identify which activities they would like the children to be involved in, a survey on how satisfied older people are with received home help or qualitative interviews with patients to explore their experiences of a specific treatment. Research undertaken by practitioner-researchers is nearly always empirical, as practitioner-researchers usually are involved in research closely linked to their practice. Similarly, evaluations are empirical by definition, as they focus on an existing service or programme.

Theoretical, Descriptive and Explorative Research

Research and evaluations – undertaken by practitioner-researchers or others – can be more or less linked to theory. In short, theory is a group of ideas related to a research area. These ideas are interlinked and their function is to assist in explaining as much of the available data as possible and to predict new observations.

To test or develop a theory, a number of hypotheses are defined. A hypothesis is an assumption about how phenomena are related. This assumption or hypothesis can be tested in research studies or evaluations. For example the 'substitution theory' assumes that extensive welfare states substitute and crowd out service provision by voluntary organisations (see Dahlberg, 2005). From this theory, one could derive the following testable hypotheses:

(1) In areas where the welfare state provides extensive services, limited services are provided by voluntary organisations.
(2) When the provision of welfare state services increases, services provided by voluntary organisation decreases.

These hypotheses can then be tested in empirical studies: the first hypothesis can be tested in a study comparing different areas, while the second can be tested in a longitudinal study.

Sometimes, it is argued that it should be possible to test (and falsify) a theory. Then, it is important that the theory is worded in a way that enables observations of as many of its implications as possible and that it is phrased in a concrete way. For example, King et al. write:

> Vaguely stated theories and hypotheses serve no purpose but to obfuscate. Theories that are stated precisely and make specific predictions can be shown more easily to be wrong and are therefore better. (1994: 20)

An illustration of the process can be found in Box 2.2. It is a very simplified example that is often given in introductions to research theory and methods, sometimes to show the weakness of this kind of thinking, as of course there are black swans!

Observation: Every swan I have ever seen is white.

Hypothesis: All swans are white.

Test: A random sample of swans from each continent where swans are indigenous identifies only white swans.

Conclusion: The research indicates that swans are always white, wherever they are observed.

Verification: Every swan any other scientist has ever observed in any country has always been white.

Theory: All swans are white.

Prediction: The next swan I see will be white.

While some research tests hypotheses and theories, other research generates hypotheses. A small piece of research may not have the capacity to test a hypothesis, but may generate new ideas and new hypotheses, to be tested in future research projects.

Not all research aims to develop theory. In areas where there is some knowledge available, but where this has not yet been presented as theories, research will be descriptive. Descriptive research aims to describe one or a few aspects of a phenomenon in detail, but has no ambitions of testing or developing theory. In areas where there is even less available knowledge or gaps in knowledge, the research is explorative. Explorative research has the purpose of gathering as much information as possible about a specific area or about specific aspects of a phenomenon. This information will form the basis on which future research can be undertaken.

Inductive and Deductive Approaches to Research

Related to the issue of theory is whether an inductive or deductive approach to research is applied. These approaches are illustrated in Figure 2.1. In an inductive approach to research, the study starts with the collection of empirical data. This data collection is flexible in that questions can change and new questions can be introduced at any time, as and when the researcher becomes familiar with the context and the phenomenon that is studied. The analysis contributes to an understanding of the reality and generates theories. It is a bottom-up approach to research. By comparison, a deductive approach is a top-down approach. When applying a deductive approach, the researcher uses theory as a starting point. A number of hypotheses are derived from the theory and these are tested empirically (as described above).

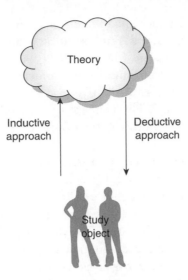

Figure 2.1   Inductive versus deductive approaches

It should be noted that inductive/deductive approaches are ideal models. Such models are more apparent at the starting point of any research project than later on. In practice, there is often an interaction between observations of reality and analysis of findings, on the one hand, and the development of theories, on the other.

The chosen (inductive or deductive) approach does not determine which method should be used. Neither does it determine whether the method should be qualitative or quantitative. Nevertheless, inductive approaches are typically used in qualitative research, while deductive approaches tend to be more common in quantitative research. This leads us on to the issue of methods in general and qualitative versus quantitative research methods in particular. What are qualitative and quantitative methods? What is the difference? Why does it matter? This will be discussed in the following section of this chapter, but first the concepts of 'method' and 'methodology' will be introduced.

Qualitative and Quantitative Research Methods

This section focuses on differences between qualitative and quantitative research. An overview of these differences is given in Table 2.1 (detailed information on different qualitative and quantitative methods and how to use them are provided in Chapters 8–10 and 11–13, respectively; see also Chapter 3 for research design).

After the researcher has identified which problem is to be examined, (s)he needs to decide on which method(s) to use to carry out the study. This is part of a process called 'research design' (discussed in Chapter 3). The term 'method' refers to a set of tools used to examine a phenomenon and the characteristic of these tools can be more or less qualitative or quantitative. 'Method' is not the same thing as 'methodology'. The concept of methodology also includes the underlying assumptions of methods, for example, philosophical assumptions (discussed below).

It should be noted that much discussion about the differences between qualitative and quantitative research is shallow and based on stereotypes. Some researchers express a very strong defence of their own choice of methods and an equally strong critique of other methods. In practice, qualitative and quantitative methods are not opposites, but rather different ends of a continuum. By focusing on differences between qualitative and quantitative research, we risk contributing to a simplified view. Nevertheless we think that it is important that practitioner-researchers have an awareness of what characterises qualitative and quantitative research.

Table 2.1   Qualitative versus quantitative research

	Qualitative research	Quantitative research
Kind of descriptions	General and detailed descriptions, difference in kind	Numerical descriptions, quantifications, difference in number/degree
Cases	Few cases	Many cases
Examples of methods	Focus groups, in-depth interviews, diaries, observations/ethnography, content analysis	Questionnaire surveys, observations, content analysis
Ontology/perception of reality	No reality exists outside our perceptions	The reality is independent of our perceptions
Epistemology/theory of knowledge	Knowledge is subjective, bias cannot be avoided	Aim to collect objective data
Generalisation to population at large	Limited potential	Possible (if accurate sampling)
Understanding and explanation	Understand meaning (e.g. of behaviour)	Describe and explain (e.g. behaviour)
Theory development	Inductive approach	Deductive approach

Basic Differences between Qualitative and Quantitative Methods

Research and evaluation methods can be either qualitative or quantitative. One way of describing the difference between qualitative and quantitative methods is to say that qualitative methods deal with difference in kind, while quantitative methods deal with difference in numbers/degree. While qualitative approaches use general descriptions to describe or explain phenomena, quantitative approaches use numerical means and rely on counting and statistical analysis.

Another way of describing the difference is to say that qualitative data collection involves 'the intensive studies of but a few cases', while quantitative data collection involves 'the extensive studies of many cases' (Teorell, 2001: 17).

Examples of Qualitative and Quantitative Methods

Qualitative methods include, for example, in-depth interviews, focus groups/group interviews and diaries. To give one example: in research on transport and commuting, qualitative methods can be used to investigate people's attitudes to public transport, their thoughts on its viability as an alternative to the car, and their opinions on timetables, bus routes, fares and so on. With qualitative methods, participants are given the chance to elaborate on topics that are relevant to them and the study would result in a detailed description of the topic. Qualitative methods also allow participants to talk more freely, which enable them to share ideas (for example on how to improve a service or find a solution to a problem), including ideas that could not be anticipated by the researchers.

Surveys – in the form of postal questionnaires, online surveys, structured interviews – are a common quantitative method. In the transport example, quantitative methods could be used to gather information from a large group of people. They could still give their opinions on various aspects of public transport, although this would be in the form of ticking a box or choosing a value from a rating scale. With quantitative methods, systematic variations across different groups (such as men–women, people of different ages or ethnicities, people living in different areas and so on) can be identified. Perhaps the service needs to be targeted differently to different groups? Perhaps some groups are significantly less satisfied with the service or even discriminated against? Perhaps some areas are insufficiently served by bus routes?

Some research methods can be used in both qualitative and quantitative research, for example, observations and content analysis. An ethnographic study based on observations would require the researcher to gather qualitative data trying to reveal the underlying meaning of phenomena for people involved. At the same time, observations can be used to gather quantifiable data, for example by registering the number and kind of statements people make in a meeting. Content analysis is sometimes used in political studies. Then policy documents can be studied in order to identify, for example, the development of a certain policy or the occurrence of certain themes. Content analysis can also include counting, for example, the number of times during a specific period that different political parties are covered in media or the number of words each party devotes to social housing in their election manifestos.

Underlying Assumptions about Knowledge

However, there is more to the difference between qualitative and quantitative research than this. Often (but not always), qualitative research and quantitative research are based on different philosophical assumptions, such as different perceptions of reality and different views on what we can know about the world and how we can know it. Philosophical assumptions that concern our perception of reality are often referred to as 'ontology', while assumptions on how we can research the world are referred to as 'epistemology', that is, the theory of knowledge (Marsch and Furlong, 2002).

Qualitative research is often based on a 'relativist' ontology, which acknowledges that both researchers and respondents are conscious actors who attach subjective meaning to their actions and their situation. Relativist ontology assumes that there is no single reality apart from our perceptions of it. All of us experience the reality from our own point of view, which means that all of us experience a different reality. Consequently it is – at an epistemological level – assumed that it is impossible to avoid bias and be objective. The aim of research is not to present the 'truth' but to ensure that different versions of the truth are accurately recorded and reported (Clarke, 1999). Following this assumption, it is essential to describe the context in which people live their lives, form opinions, take action and so on (Devine, 2002; Stoker and Marsh, 2002). You have to study a phenomenon in its context in order to fully understand it, and ideally the researcher should experience what it is like to be part of the context studied. Accordingly, many anthropologists using qualitative methods have lived for long periods in the community they study.

In qualitative methods, explanation is a matter of understanding and interpreting actions, opinions or experiences, not a matter of drawing conclusions about relationships and regularities between statistical variables (Devine, 2002). Qualitative researchers often find quantifications simplistic and limited as this looks at a small part of a reality that cannot be isolated without losing the essence of the phenomenon.

Quantitative research is based on rather different philosophical assumptions. It is often based on a different ontology, a 'realist' ontology, assuming that there is a single, objective reality that exists independently of human perception. At an epistemological level, it is assumed that the researcher can be separated from the researched phenomena (Clarke, 1999). Therefore, researchers attempt to create conditions in which objective data can be collected (Devine, 2002). One example of an environment conducive for collecting entirely objective data is a laboratory. In laboratories, researchers attempt to control everything that may influence the outcome, thereby providing researchers with the opportunity to carry out experiments to see what impact each factor has on the object studied. In 'real world' settings, efforts are made to keep interaction between the researcher and the respondent to a minimum in order to avoid bias (Devine, 2002). This is why surveys, where respondents are asked to complete question- naires on their own and return them, are seen as more objective than qualitative surveys where the researcher asks questions and records the answers from a respondent sitting in front of them.

What Conclusions Can Be Drawn?

Differences between qualitative and quantitative methods have implications for how to interpret data and the potential of making generalisations, that is, to apply findings to different groups or different settings than those studied. In order to make generalisations, the sample has to be very similar to the population from which it is drawn, in those aspects that are relevant to the study (Mark, 1996). For example, you may undertake a study on homeless people. By selecting your sample well, the group included in your study could represent a larger population of homeless people. If you have a large sample of people with various back- grounds (such as men and women of different ages and with different ethnic backgrounds – or other aspects that you believe are important to your research question), you have a greater potential to generalise your findings than if you have a small sample of people with similar background (such as a few white men in their 30s). In other words, if the sample size is large enough, if the selection of the sample has been well thought through and carried out, and if there is a large or unbiased response rate, quantitative researchers can generalise their findings and make statements for a larger population (see Chapter 12, for sampling in quantitative research).

By comparison, large-scale qualitative research is very time-consuming and expensive. Therefore, qualitative research nearly always has fewer participants. The process of selecting study participants is as important and rigorous in qualitative research and evaluation as in quantitative research and evaluation (for selection methods, see Chapters 9), but due to the smaller sample size qualitative researchers cannot be sure that the sample is representative of the larger popula- tion. Consequently, the potential for generalisations is limited in qualitative research. In fact, the aim of qualitative research is rarely to generalise. Instead it provides rich and detailed descriptions of the studied phenomenon and will be able to 'tell the story' from participants' points of view. In qualitative research, purposive and strategic selection of cases is made in order to maximise the chance of including as many aspects of the studied phenomenon as possible.

Although qualitative researchers have to be tentative about making generalisa- tions from a small sample of the population, they can corroborate one in-depth study with other research to establish similarities and differences and this would work as a test of confirmation. Qualitative research findings can also be further researched via quantitative methods leading to generalisations at a later stage (Devine, 2002). Finally, as stated by Devine:

> As it is, it is rarely the case that a sample of interviewees is so unrepresentative or the interpretations so misleading that suggestion about the wider incidence of certain phenomena is wholly specious. (2002: 207)

So, What Is the Difference?

Differences between qualitative and quantitative research methods should not be overestimated. In practice, the distinction is rather blurred and most research has both qualitative and quantitative elements. Qualitative research usually somewhere down the line includes quantified qualifications. Similarly, quantitative research cannot be carried out without qualitative considerations, for example, in preparations of scales, instruments and questionnaires. Neither do the philosophical assumptions necessarily differ. Many researchers use both qualitative and quantitative methods, and strive towards objectivity at the same time as they realise that completely unbiased and objective data can be difficult to accomplish.

Primarily, the difference concerns the methods of collecting and analysing data, and whether data is quantified or not. This difference is important, though, as it has consequences for the possibility of drawing conclusions and making generalisations, as discussed above.

What Is Best – Qualitative or Quantitative Methods ...

The answer to this question is that it depends on what problem you are interested in studying. The choice of methods is usually (and should be!) based on what would be the most suitable way of answering a particular research question; the choice of method(s) follows from the aim and objectives of the study (see Chapter 3). When deciding whether to use qualitative and quantitative methods – or a combination of qualitative and quantitative methods – the practitioner-researcher needs to consider their strengths and weaknesses. There is, to put it simply, a choice between gathering deep and particular information (by means of qualitative methods) or broad and general information (by means of quantitative methods).

Through qualitative research detailed, and often more valid, information can be gathered (George, 1979; King et al., 1994; Mays and Pope, 1995), not the least when the goal of the study is to explore people's experiences, practices, values and attitudes in-depth and to establish the meaning for those concerned (Devine, 2002). Quantitative research has the advantage of determining how common a phenomenon is, detect associations between measured variables and make generalisations. Qualitative methods are suitable for generating and developing theories, while quantitative methods are often useful in testing theories (George and McKeown, 1985).

Let us assume say that you want to study social exclusion. If you are interested in how common social exclusion is among different groups of people, you are likely to use quantitative methods. Thereby you can measure the prevalence of social exclusion in the population and identify differences between different groups (men and women, age groups, ethnic groups, people in different areas, people living alone or together with somebody, people with different labour market status and so on). However, social exclusion is a multi-facetted concept and people have different views on what it means. Quantitative methods would not get you very far if you are interested in what social exclusion means to people. To obtain a deep and nuanced knowledge on the meaning of social exclusion you would be better off using qualitative methods such as in-depth interviews or focus groups. Of course, you may be interested in both these aspects. Then, a combination of methods would be advisable.

... or a Combination of Both?

The strengths and weaknesses of qualitative and quantitative methods suggest that many research questions are best answered by means of a combination of qualitative and quantitative methods. Combining two or more different research methods is often referred to as 'triangulation' of methods.

There are two main approaches to combining qualitative and quantitative research methods. The researcher can start by using qualitative methods to generate hypotheses. These hypotheses can then be tested in a quantitative follow-up study and data gathered at this stage can lead to generalisations. The other approach is to start with a quantitative study to generate data and then carry out a qualitative study to explore deeper meanings.

By combining different methods – whether mainly qualitative or mainly quantitative – the researcher will be able to address many different aspects of a research question. It also increases the validity of the research, since one method serves as a check of another method (Read and Marsh, 2002).

Conclusion

This chapter has introduced readers to basic requirements of research and what characterises research, and to different kinds of research and evaluations. Also, this chapter has given readers some insight into the differences between empirical and non-empirical research, between theoretical, descriptive and explorative research, and between inductive and deductive approaches to research. Finally, qualitative and quantitative research methods have been discussed, along with the benefits of triangulating different kinds of methods.

Further Reading

Robson, C. (2002) *Real World Research. A Resource for Social Scientists and Practitioner-Researchers*, 2nd edn. Oxford: Blackwell.
Robson provides a comprehensive guide for applied social scientists and practitioner-researchers. It covers the whole research process, from proposal and design via data collection and analysis to dissemination and intervention.

Clarke, A. (1999) *Evaluation Research. An Introduction to Principles, Methods and Practice*. London: Sage.
Clarke's book provides insights in different kinds of evaluations and their advantages and disadvantages. Clarke also presents evaluation principles and methods, and discusses examples of contexts (criminal justice and crime prevention, health care, and schools) in which evaluations have been conducted.

THREE

Research and Evaluation Design

Colin McCaig

By the end of this chapter you should be able to:

- understand the notion of hypotheses derived from a conceptual understanding of the subject at hand;
- develop appropriate research questions;
- understand the importance of validity;
- understand the difference between qualitative and quantitative approaches to research design;
- design research within constraints.

Introduction

Research and evaluation design can be characterised as the logic that links an initial question or problem to the methods of data collection and analysis, and thus also the conclusions drawn. This chapter will briefly introduce some concepts that are dealt with in more detail throughout this book, covering different methods of approaching research and evaluation design along the way: the importance of understanding the purpose of the research; the need for conceptual understanding of the subject of the research; formulating research questions (including the specific requirements of evaluations); the differing methodological approaches employed by qualitative and quantitative researchers (and when to combine them); and the importance of validity. The chapter will conclude with a discussion of other key factors involved in successful research design, such as resource constraints (that is budget and time management issues), supervision and the needs of the audience for the final research findings.

Research Design as Strategic Overview

A research design can be seen as an overarching strategy for unearthing useful answers to problems. Only after a strategy or design has been identified can social researchers think about the tactical considerations of how the data can be gathered to answer the research questions, such as what specific questions to ask, who to ask and how to ask them:

> The strategy is a roadmap, an overall plan for the systematic exploration of the phenomenon of interest; the methods are the specific tools for undertaking the exploration. (Marshall and Rossman, 2006: 40)

Designing research implies that researchers stand back from the immediate needs of employers, supervisors, awarding bodies or other funding bodies for whom you will carry out the research. In this sense the research design is larger or 'purer' than the research proposal (discussed in Chapter 5), which is often concerned with more pragmatic issues such as the time/cost of aspects of the research (how many days to develop and pilot a questionnaire, how many interviews can be feasibly carried out in the time available and so on) and the relationship with funders or stakeholders, who will have their own reporting requirements and meetings' schedules. The design stage is where you can think through strategic approaches to investigating social issues and problems in the abstract. Once the design is arrived at, it then fulfils another function as the basis and core of the proposal and the work to follow.

Practitioner-researchers may not always have the necessary time to develop a research design in isolation from the needs of clients. However the development of a plan of activity that logically and coherently relates problems to explanations via the application of appropriate research methods is a skill that all researchers should aim to master.

Evaluations often leave researchers less room for manoeuvre in terms of design. The problems or issues to be explored will be set by the process and outcomes of the programme being evaluated. Indeed the evaluation may well have been at least partially designed by the programme funding body. However, an evaluation still has to be designed on the same basis as any other piece of research. There must be a coherent and logical thread to the enterprise that links the problem, the hypothesis (or starting point of the enquiry), the research questions and methods, the data gathering stage, and finally the analysis and reporting stage.

Maxwell's interactive approach (see Figure 3.1) highlights the importance of five distinct yet overlapping elements that will govern the strategic approach the research takes: purpose, conceptual understanding, research questions, methods, and validity. Maxwell deliberately places research questions at the centre.

It is important not to see these elements as a tick-list of things to do, a linear pathway from inception to final report. Instead they need to be seen as a body

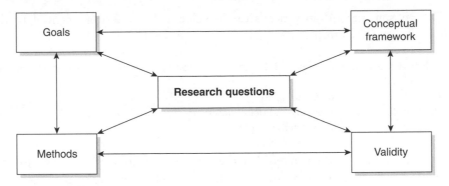

Figure 3.1   Maxwell's interactive model of research design
Source: Maxwell (1996: 5).

of principles behind your methodology that will always link back to the 'how' and 'why' questions that can otherwise be forgotten in the process of research. For instance, it is surprisingly easy to lose sight of the purpose of research or evaluation once you get mired in the difficulties of achieving access to a particular group of people, and it is tempting to then tailor the research questions to the achieved sample to ensure you get some useable data. The problem then is that you may have a collection of data that does not directly address the issues relevant to the sample that you intended but failed to achieve. Here we can see the importance of carefully designing a sampling strategy from the outset as opposed to taking an opportunistic approach by simply going for the easiest sampling method.

Of equal importance is the emphasis on conceptual understanding, the context set by previous empirical studies and theoretical literature in the field. Again the essence of the research has to be informed by context or it risks becoming disembodied from the work of other members of the research community. Part of the value of any research or evaluation is its comparability in some way to similar work, in that it shares the same understandings and refers back to the same body of previous research (even if only to highlight points of departure).

Research questions should flow logically from the purpose, not take the research into different directions. Practitioner-researchers need to be concerned with what they want to come to understand through the study, identifying what they *do not know* at the moment. Research questions should not be confused with specific questions that will be developed as part of an interview schedule or survey and be targeted at certain groups of respondents. Rather, as in Figure 3.1, research questions should form the basis of the whole design, linking the purpose and conceptual context with a methodology that produces valid research outcomes. Note also that the arrows in Figure 3.1 point both ways, as research questions that emerge during the research process feed back into the ongoing design (often a feature of exploratory qualitative research).

The chosen methodology needs to answer a set of questions central to the whole design, for example:

- What is the research relationship with people being studied (for example, are they co-workers)?
- How will the population be sampled?
- What data collection methods and data analysis methods will be employed?
- At which site(s) will the research take place?

These questions are interlinked. For practitioner-researchers carrying out (for example) an evaluation of a new procedure in their own workplace where the researcher has a pre-existent relationship with the subjects, an anonymised survey may be the most appropriate data collection method to minimise the 'researcher effect' (the impact a researcher has on the subjects of the research). The methods are thus partially determined by the setting. Another example, if the focus of the research is disabled young people in educational settings then the sampling method will need to accommodate a representative ratio of relevant disability groupings in the population and the fullest possible range of data collection options needs to inform the methodology; surveys would need to be offered in various sizes and formats (online and paper, Braille, large print, different coloured paper/screens, provision for assisted completion). Here, the validity of the research is closely tied up with the sampling and methodology chosen.

The next stage is to move from the strategic to the specific issues that form the subject of your investigation by exploring different elements of the research design.

Elements of Research Design: the Hypothesis

Research questions can be rephrased as hypotheses. Approaching research design implies some understanding of the key issues at a practical and/or theoretical level and the development of a hypothesis or 'hunch' about what, for example, leads certain social groups to behave in certain ways under certain conditions. The notion of hypothesis we employ in this chapter does not have to imply that the world is made up of 'facts' just waiting to be discovered by asking research questions (a positivist viewpoint): some qualitative research, for example, ethnography or participant observation research, starts from a relativist basis that refutes the notion that there are objective facts to be discovered in this way. However, as few such researchers go out into the field without any (at least subconscious) notions of what or who they are to observe based on an understanding of the issues affecting the subject group, they too can be said to have a loosely defined hypothesis for our purposes. Burroughs, for example, defines a hypothesis very loosely as an 'educated guess that one thing relates to or is caused by another'

(1975: 21), though he acknowledges that there can be examples where researchers come across a completely new set of social conditions that have been the subject of no previous observation or theorising.

The hypothesis, in this general sense, is what the research is designed to test – or, if you like, the research questions that the research is designed to explore. In evaluations and some contract research, the hypothesis may have already been developed by the funder; alternatively you may have your own hypothesis based on previous work. For example, to borrow again from Burroughs (1975), if you should find a Roman coin in your garden, that is good, but if you have hypothesised that you *should* find a coin in your garden based on the location of the property, geography, type of soil and so on, then finding it (by testing your hypothesis) is even more rewarding.

Hypotheses set the rules for the research design, outlining what is to be tested by stating things in a testable form, and this in turn implies the structure of the experiment. For example, if your hypothesis is that providing additional information and communications technology (ICT), such as interactive whiteboards and projectors, in college classrooms will encourage lecturers to use technology more often in their teaching, then your research design could include a series of qualitative interviews with lecturers asking if, how and why they have changed their practice. Alternatively you could administer a quantitative survey of students asking them if programmes are being delivered differently since the new technology was installed. Both these methods will test your hypothesis, albeit in different ways, though of course they may not prove that other factors have not had an effect too; for that you may need multiple hypotheses.

Hypotheses can be used at different levels and stages of the research. In the college example, previous research in this area may have led you to hypothesise that lecturers in post for 10 years or more are less likely to make use of the new technology than those in post for just a few years, and that some subjects (sciences, art and design for example) that are concerned with models and images offer more scope for the use of interactive video and graphics than others (such as philosophy or history) that are essentially about ideas. Another hypothesis may be that students of lower ability levels can be engaged by the use of interactive and visually stimulating classroom techniques, and thus derive more benefit from ICT in the classroom than higher ability students. Once you have developed a series of testable hypotheses you can think about the research questions and methods that will elicit usable answers in the form of data.

Elements of Research Design: Research Questions

This section looks at formulating research questions and assessing competing methodologies to best elicit answers. More is said in subsequent chapters about the most appropriate methodological approaches to take (Chapter 8 on qualitative methods, Chapter 11 on quantitative methods). Here, we look at the importance of identifying research questions that operationalise the general purpose of the enquiry. Research questions – what you want to understand – will influence every other part of the design, and often only emerge as the research progresses, especially in the case of qualitative research. In a research proposal, research questions explain what your research will unearth, but in the research design they also help to focus the study and give guidance on how to conduct it (Maxwell, 1996).

For example, the purpose may be to discover why some schools have difficulty recruiting high quality teachers. This can only be answered by framing individual research questions about schools' recruitment policies, the environment of the school (including such factors as pupil behaviour and attainment level), factors personal to applicants (how far they are willing to travel to work) and how general recruitment problems are, for example, does recruitment experience vary by region, school type or subject area. Then there has to be consideration of which groups will be asked each type of question (for example, those applying for teaching posts, existing teachers, head teachers, those responsible for initial teacher training).

Each of these questions is central to the entire purpose and conceptual understanding, linking methods that can produce valid findings (see below). In this sense, for Hammersely and Atkinson, research design is 'a reflexive process operating through every stage of the project' (cited in Maxwell, 1996: 2). As we have noted, in qualitative research key research questions may only emerge during the initial data gathering stage and the design will have to be revisited, in effect become a reiterative process rather than an essentially linear process (hypothesis, operationalisation, data collection, data analysis, validation) typical of quantitative research. This reiteration requires practitioner-researchers to build reflection time into the design (Flick, 2009).

For example, if the chosen methodology is to use interview and focus group evidence to unearth the reasons why the introduction of new administrative procedures throughout a health authority have not produced the anticipated improvement to front line services, a strong research design will have anticipated the need to allow time to revisit the problem and perhaps ask different research questions in different ways of different groups of staff and service users. However, employers or funding bodies, with an eye on the time and budget, may take some convincing of this need for flexibility, even if they recognise that the research is to some extent exploratory. They may consider your need to 'go back to the drawing board' a weakness of design, when in fact a design based on an intelligent expression of the purpose and a thorough conceptual understanding of the issues at hand needs to spell this out.

Elements of Research Design: Validity and Sampling

Validity is 'concerned with the integrity of the conclusions that are generated from a piece of research' (Bryman, 2008: 30). Validity is defined as: the correctness or credibility of an account, explanation or interpretation that you may come up with. In other words why should anyone believe your conclusions? Two main types of validity are discussed here in relation to research design: internal and external validity (for more on validity see Chapter 2). Closely related to research validity is sampling; sound sampling techniques can go a long way to ensuring validity (for more on sampling, see Chapter 9 and Chapter 12 on qualitative and quantitative data collection, respectively).

Internal and external validity apply in separate contexts and conditions. Internal validity relates to causal relationships so that the test ensures that only those variables tested are the cause of the findings, and not the cause of unforeseen variables. External validity relates to the generalisability of findings to other groups and populations so that the same test applied elsewhere by other researchers would achieve the same results.

You can have good internal validity without it being generalisable, for example, a finding about the relative educational attainment level of boys and girls in secondary schools may be valid with the specific population sampled in one school, but not valid in other schools with different teaching styles, environment or ability ranges. To an extent this is an issue of sampling and research design. Sampling comes into play when, to test a hypothesis or answer a research question, a sub-group of the population needs to be drawn where it is expensive and time-consuming to survey (or census) the whole population of school pupils. If your research is focused only in one school this is less of a problem (as long as your in-school sample is representative of the school's population), but if you wanted to extrapolate the findings more widely to say something about *all* school pupils the sample would have to be broadly representative of all pupils in the country to achieve external validity.

Validity essentially asks the question: how might the researcher be wrong? As validity requires the possibility of testability it relies on others being able to achieve similar results using the same methods on the same subjects. To this end quantitative researchers build in control groups or representative sampling methods to achieve validity. Qualitative research rarely enables directly comparable conditions, so qualitative researchers need to anticipate weaknesses regarding validity in their research design (Maxwell, 1996).

Triangulating qualitative research findings with quantitative findings and other qualitative research is an accepted method of ensuring validity where the sample size is insufficient to offer validity on its own. The term triangulation has been applied to research strategies intended to serve two distinct purposes: confirmation (of qualitative findings by quantitative data) and completeness (where some techniques can provide a more rounded picture than others). For example, survey data about the efficacy of a clinical intervention will only reflect the options respondents were obliged to choose from; qualitative interviews with the same cohort can provide a richer and broader understanding of how the intervention actually impacted on the sample. Equally a small set of qualitative findings can be triangulated with a survey of a cohort with similar characteristics. A research

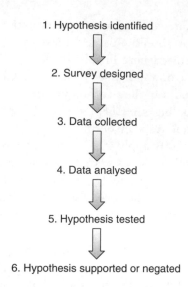

Figure 3.2   Quantitative linear research design process

design that incorporates analysis of qualitative and quantitative data related to a closely defined aspect of the research can provide both convergent validity and a broader understanding of one's subject matter (Breitner et al, 1993) (see below where I discuss mixed methods).

Elements of Research Design: Selecting Research Methods

Once you have settled on research questions, your research design needs to incorporate suitable methods to elicit data that will answer those questions (for more on selecting appropriate research methods, see Chapter 2). Quantitative research tends to follow a linear pathway in which each stage (hypothesis/research question, survey design, data collection, data analysis) depends on the successful completion of the previous stages (see Figure 3.2). Quantitative research is usually concerned with measuring variations, for example to what extent variance in *x* relates to variance in *y*. In the example on learning technology in colleges cited above, a quantitative research design might take the hypothesis about *y* (an increase in technology in the classroom leading to more use of it by lecturers) and use survey frequencies to illustrate variation by *x* (length of time lecturers have been in post) or by *z* (subject area). In quantitative research, theories are developed prior to the research, then tested and supported or proved false during the research.

In contrast, many qualitative research projects depend on an understanding of the processes in play that explain *how* or *why* variance in *x* causes variance in *y*. Therefore the design might incorporate a series of, for example, unstructured interviews, observations and focus groups to find out how and in what ways different groups react to the presence of x (a new bureaucratic procedure) in the context y (an accident and emergency unit). Qualitative research designs can anticipate complex scenarios involving differential engagement with the new bureaucratic procedure by, for example exploring specific meanings and contexts, identifying unanticipated phenomena, and understanding the processes that lie behind events and what connects them for each potential user of the procedure (Maxwell, 1996).

In this kind of research there is no simple 'test'. Therefore the design needs to allow researchers to revisit stages in the linear process outlined above. It is essentially an iterative process where new questions emerge, and new groups are identified as important to the process, which then have to be observed, interviewed or taken to focus groups. The aim of qualitative research is not to reduce complexity by breaking it down into variables but to increase understanding by including context; this implies that methods are chosen as appropriate to the issue being studied:

> The principle of openness implies that theoretical structuring of the issues under study is postponed until the structuring of the issue under study by the person being studied has emerged. (Hoffmann-Riem, cited in Flick, 2009: 41)

For Marshall and Rossman (2006) the key to qualitative research design is that it should be as flexible as it is concise and systematic, and fully integrated into an equally coherent research proposal. Practitioner-researchers should also see Chapter 5 on research proposals for more on the importance of presenting the research design in the most favourable light from the point of view of funders.

Combined or Mixed-methods

Many research methods books, including this one, tend to illustrate quantitative and qualitative approaches by highlighting the differences between them and in doing so they risk perpetuating the long tradition of mutual mistrust between advocates of either approach. While these methodological traditions clearly have their roots in quite different theories of knowledge (epistemologies) and seek to answer different kinds of questions in quite different ways (see Chapter 2), in practice many small scale pieces of research of the type likely to be undertaken by practitioner-researchers will combine quantitative and qualitative techniques in their methodology. As we noted (above and in Chapter 2) in relation to triangulation, both survey findings and interview data can be used to inform and support the other. However, practitioner-researchers that have previously only worked with one specific approach (for example, quantitative or qualitative) should note that it is important to have an understanding of the protocols and processes of each before embarking on a mixed-methods research design.

Combining approaches can give a research design an added dimension and offer far richer findings at the reporting stage. In some research and evaluation work qualitative interviews and/or focus groups are used to gain an understanding of the key issues and can be an invaluable aid to questionnaire design and thus enhance large-scale surveys (Drew et al., 2008). Conversely, qualitative methods can be used to follow up and explore survey findings in more depth or in specific contexts. For example, researchers may carry out a large-scale nation-wide survey of youth workers' attitudes to the impact of anti-social behaviour orders, whereby statistical analysis of the resultant dataset may show wide variations by region, level of training and mode of employment of youth workers. Anticipating some variation at the hypothesis stage, an intelligent research design will have incorporated sufficient time and money to select a set of local authority-based case studies where qualitative techniques such as in-depth interviews and focus group sessions with youth workers and interviews with key stakeholder and management figures are employed. All being well the result is a piece of research that can authoritatively reflect the views of reasonably representative segment of youth work practitioners, including all the key variables, and present a series of case studies that explore in-depth many of the concerns and perspectives of youth workers in their own words. While combined approaches are relatively common in research design for nationally based research, practitioner-researchers that have smaller budget (or indeed focus) can also employ combined methods in this way.

Constraints on Your Research Design

Resource constraints will apply to all research designs, and are particularly relevant to those that are considering combining methods, most obviously because of the additional time and labour costs that will be involved. If the quantitative survey is designed to inform the choice of case studies for in-depth qualitative work (in our youth work example), then time has to be allowed for a thorough analysis of the data to identify the key variables and research questions for the qualitative element of the research, for example. Even if you are able to design a research project that has quantitative and qualitative elements running concurrently, either more preparation time or more research staff will have to be built into the project (see Chapter 5 for more on the importance of resource constraints).

The time allocated for the research is another ever-present constraint on research design. Often this constraint is set by your employer (if a practitioner-researcher), the funding body or your research supervisor (in an academic environment) and this can take several forms. Practitioner-researchers will almost certainly have a limit set on the time they can spend away from their normal duties, either in the form of a block of time or in the allocation of time allowed per week or month for this task. In all cases, those sponsoring, funding or supervising research will also have a timeframe in mind, which will include a date by which they expect a report or presentation of the findings.

Research design will also usually have to accommodate other constraints, notably ethical and legal considerations, and those set by the interests of the funding body. Examples of the former may include restrictions on access to vulnerable groups and the use of data relating to them (children, patients and so on), which can limit the nature of your research (see Chapter 4 for guidance on this area). Examples of the latter may be the political context your employer or funder works within; for example, practitioner-researchers may not have *carte blanche* to criticise the organisation or profession they work within. Researchers based in more academic environments may come be constrained by the requirement that they work within a certain subject discipline or theoretical approach. The funder or supervisor may of course also constrain your research design by expressing a preference for quantitative or qualitative approaches at the outset.

The needs of the final audience for any study, be they direct line managers, funding bodies, academic boards or a physical audience of your peers, should form a natural constraint too. They will have certain expectations and the chances of your research or evaluation having any impact will depend to a certain extent on how you have carried through a piece of research from an identifiable purpose to a robust conclusion (see Chapter 14). One final constraint is set by the parameters of the original social issue or problem that inspired the research design in the first place. It is all too easy to lose sight of your original purpose by following research approaches that appear interesting but lead you further from your field of enquiry and fail to answer your original questions. The unifying factor in all these cases is that careful and intelligent research design has to be carried out within the context of a sophisticated understanding of what is doable in different circumstances.

Conclusion

This chapter has endeavoured to anticipate many of the themes of this book as they apply to the specific case of the research design in order to demonstrate the essentially strategic nature of the exercise. The importance of placing research questions at the centre of any research design, regardless of the data gathering tools methods employed or methodological approach has been reinforced by a series of examples that necessarily link questions to validity and thus also a considerations of methods and constraints practitioner-researchers and others will inevitably face.

Further Reading

Maxwell, J. (1996) *Qualitative Research Design: An Interactive Approach*. Thousand Oaks, CA: Sage.
This is an invaluable introductory source for those wishing to use qualitative research methodologies, drawing on traditional approaches to research design in the process of developing a model that places research questions at the centre.

Bryman, A. (2008) *Social Research Methods*, 3rd end. Oxford: Oxford University Press.
Bryman's book is a good overall introduction for those wishing to know more about quantitative methods or indeed employ a combined approach.

Robson, C. (2000) *Small-Scale Evaluation*. Thousand Oaks, CA: Sage.
Robson has produced an invaluable guide for those working specifically within the field of evaluation. Robson's book is particularly strong on the requirements of clients and constraining factors. It is a good point-by-point pragmatic guide for practitioner-researchers embarking on their first piece of work combined with a good survey of the theoretical underpinnings.

FOUR

Ethics and Research Governance

Maria Smith

By the end of this chapter you should be able to:

- know what research ethics and research governance ethical guidelines are;
- see how ethical issues affect the design and execution of research projects;
- understand the principles of informed consent and anonymity;
- recognise professional standards and what research misconduct is;
- know how to apply for formal ethical approval.

Introduction

This chapter will begin by describing what ethics and research governance are. The chapter will then discuss ethical considerations arising from the relationship between the researcher and the research participants. In particular it will focus upon the two main cornerstones of modern research ethics: informed consent and anonymity, including a discussion of when and if, research can be conducted without either of these and yet still remain ethical.

The chapter will then cover professional integrity including research misconduct. It will discuss the importance of researcher independence and potential conflicts of interest between researchers and project funders and also includes a section on intellectual property. Finally this chapter will present a discussion on formal procedures such as ethics committee approval, and there will be directions on how to find more specific guidelines for different types of research.

Ethics and Research Governance

Ethics in practitioner research are the moral principles that guide activity from inception to completion (including the publication of results). Research governance, conversely, is a code of practice that is applicable if you are conducting research in the field of health and social care. The regulations concern ethics, science, information, health and safety, finance and quality. This chapter is primarily concerned with the framework's position on ethics. The framework's section on ethics covers a lot of the same ground as ethics generally and therefore this chapter discusses the two areas largely as one subject. It is worth remembering that, although all research must adhere to general ethical guidelines, not all research must adhere to the ethical standards of research governance. In spite of this, research governance ethical guidelines will be useful to practitioner-researchers in any field.

It is worthwhile, at this early stage in the chapter, to make it clear which types of research are covered by research governance. Fortunately, it is a relatively simple distinction, although if you are uncertain, there is lots of information available, for example on the Department of Health's website (http://www. dh.gov.uk), that will clarify whether or not your proposed research falls under its remit and if so whether you need to apply for NHS ethical approval.

In summary, if you are conducting research that includes any of the following then you must adhere to the principles of research governance:

- patients or users of the NHS and anyone who is recruited to the research by virtue of their current or past treatment by or use of the NHS;
- anyone who is a carer or relative of those defined as a patient or user;
- NHS staff participating in the research by virtue of their professional role;
- any research on NHS property.

Ethics originate from a branch of philosophy that was developed by the Ancient Greek philosophers, Socrates and Aristotle. The Greeks saw connections between conducting oneself in the correct manner or 'doing the right thing' and achieving what they considered to be the most desirable outcome of all, human happiness. As such, it follows that the principle concern of modern research ethics is human happiness and well-being. Thus, it is important that all researchers take steps to ensure that their research does not cause unhappiness to any of its participants. Furthermore, the researcher must use a broad definition of what happiness is and consider not only how a project affects participants in terms of physical harm but also in terms of social and psychological well-being.

This is, of course, no simple task and there is no easy set of rules to follow. The new researcher soon finds that, in order to conduct research ethically, they must learn to think and reflect upon their project holistically and to see ethics as an integral part of the research, rather than as something that is tacked on at the end (Soobrayan, 2003). Indeed, researchers must weave ethics into the very design, fieldwork, analysis and dissemination of their work.

Informed Consent

Informed consent is, essentially, a term made up of two parts. For the first part, research should always be conducted openly, honestly and participants should be aware of what taking part in the research entails. For the second, participation has to be voluntary and participants must give their consent to being involved in your project. These two parts, when combined, are, essentially, what is meant by the term 'informed consent'.

Before you begin any fieldwork, it is important that you obtain the informed consent of your research participants. In particular, there are six areas that you must consider and make arrangements for.

1. Participant Understanding of the Elements of the Research

You must make it clear to research participants, at the outset of fieldwork, what their involvement entails. For example, if you are planning to conduct a focus group followed by one-to-one interviews with the same participants, you must inform them of this at the outset. It would be poor ethical practice to surprise them with news of the second part of the research half way through the focus group (although of course, there are times when the research design has to be adapted to changing circumstances). In addition and if possible, you should write down what is expected and give it to participants in the form of a 'participant consent' document to read and sign. Of course, some methods of research, such as online or postal questionnaires, make this type of informed consent impossible as there is no face-to-face interaction. In these circumstances, you should make it explicit what they are participating in with accompanying information in a clear and accessible language.

2. Participation Is Voluntary

Research participants should be made aware of the fact that they can refuse or withdraw consent at any point and furthermore, that they do not have to give an explanation for their withdrawal. If a participant withdraws from the research, then you must ask if you can keep and use the data that you have already gathered or if their withdrawal signifies that you no longer have their consent for any part of the research. If the latter is the case, then you must respect the wishes of your research participant and destroy the data that you have collected. Although, of course, it is unfortunately possible that you will already have used the data and made the findings available. If this is the case, then the ethical thing to do is to inform your research participant of this situation. On other occasions, you may come across examples of partial consent, for example, if you are conducting research with carers of very ill spouses or partners, research participants may feel that subject areas such as personal care or sexual relations are too personal to share with a researcher, but are happy to talk about issues such as transport or home adaptations. Some might agree to be interviewed but do not wish the interview to be recorded. Experienced researchers have all switched off the recorder at the end of an interview, only for the participant to reveal interesting information, or else snippets are disclosed during the interview but as an aside 'off the record' or 'just between you and me'. In situations like these, you must always ask if that particular piece of information can be included in the research.

3. How Long the Research Will Take

You must also ensure that you inform participants of the likely timescale of their participation. This maybe as simple as telling participants a date for their interview or how long a questionnaire will take to complete, noting that certain research participants, for example, some older people, may take longer to complete a questionnaire. Conversely, some projects require a more substantial commitment from participants, such as longitudinal studies or projects that need participants to complete diaries. In cases such as these, you must inform participants of the time period that this will entail. For a longitudinal study, there might be an expected date that you will return to conduct another interview or, for the completion of diaries, it might include how many days, weeks or months that they are expected to fill in the diary.

4. Participant Risks

The potential risks to participants can be wide ranging and can include physical harm/discomfort as well as emotional distress or embarrassment caused by questioning on sensitive issues. Research that is conducted thoughtlessly can also damage a person's social standing, their privacy, their values and beliefs as well as their relationships with their family, community or employer, for example, if you are conducting research about the career aspirations of young British Pakistani women, it would be unethical to do this in front of family members who might hold traditional views and thus disapprove of their responses. Research governance ethical guidelines state that risks in research must always be proportional to the potential benefit of the research (Department of Health, 2005). Of course, when we consider non-clinical research of the type covered by this book, potential risks and benefits can be difficult to quantify. However, the researcher still needs to ensure that participants are subjected to minimum risk and one way of achieving this is to gain informed consent at the outset of the research.

5. How the Results Will Be Used

It is important that participants are aware of how the findings will be used. For example, if you are planning to disseminate the results in a report that will be published on the Internet, writing a summary document that is distributed to the local community or presenting the findings at a practitioner conference then you must ensure that each research participant is aware of this and gives full and informed consent. In addition, if you are planning on combining the results of this research with data from another project and using that information to form the basis of a third project, this is also something that you must gain informed consent for. Furthermore, you must disclose if you are going to discuss the individual's research responses with colleagues or if there are any other team members who will see non-anonymised data from the project.

6. Nature of Any Compensation or Incentive

Some forms of research commonly use an incentive to encourage people to take part in the research. This is something that must be considered in relation to informed consent and participants must be told what they will receive and when they will receive it, before any fieldwork takes place.

Additional Considerations

Informed consent is harder to achieve with some groups of people than others. For example, certain vulnerable groups, such as frail older people or people with learning difficulties, may lack the capacity to consent to research on their own. If this is the case, then consent must be sought from someone close to that person, a gatekeeper, who can make an independent assessment of the participant's interests. Research with children is a particularly sensitive area and you will need both the consent of the child and a parent or carer. Furthermore, when you are conducting interviews with groups such as these you must provide relevant material in an appropriate written or pictorial form so that they can understand what you are asking of them. Additionally, if you are planning to interview vulnerable adults or children, it is likely that you will need to have a Criminal Records Bureau (CRB) check to demonstrate that you do not have a history that would make you unsuitable for work involving these groups (see Box 4.1).

Box 4.1   Criminal Records Bureau checks

The Criminal Records Bureau (CRB) is part of the UK Government's Home Office and provides information about criminal records for employers as well as some professional, licensing and regulatory bodies. It aims to ensure that anyone working with children or other vulnerable groups is suitable to do so. Therefore, for example, anyone planning to undertake face-to-face interviews with children must undergo a CRB

(Continued)

(Continued)

check. The self-employed or individual researchers cannot apply to have a check conducted on themselves so you must arrange for either your employer or funder to apply for you.

There are two types of checks available, standard and enhanced. The former looks at criminal records and, if relevant, at information on the Protection of Children Act List, the Protection of Vulnerable Adults List and information held under the Education Act 2002. Enhanced checks are generally conducted on people who are in charge of children or vulnerable groups, such as teachers or scout leaders, and look at the same information as standard checks but also at relevant information held by the local police.

There is a fee for CRB checks and the process does need to be built into your research timetable. Fortunately though, it does not take an unreasonable period of time and the CRB aims to process 90% of standard checks within two weeks and 90% of enhanced checks within four weeks.

Further information and guidance on the application process is available on the CRB's website at http://www.crb.gov.uk.

Some forms of research extend over a period of time and, as such, consent becomes something that is ongoing. You may wish to develop a system of review, so that as the project progresses, you will still have the full and informed consent of your research participants. This might be achieved, for example, by asking participants to read and sign a shortened or adapted version of the participant consent form each time you ask them to take part in a new stage of the research.

Research in some communities may also require that any information regarding consent is translated into languages that can be understood by your research participants. If a participant is not able to read or understand the information, this information should still be provided in a written format as they may wish to consult with others before giving their consent. When conducting research, it is also important that you are fully prepared and aware of any cultural, ethnic or religious issues that you will need to consider when conducting fieldwork to ensure that you do not threaten or offend participants through ignorance or insensitivity.

Finally, you should take special care when conducting research over the Internet (for example when using comments gathered in chatrooms, weblogs or discussion boards, information submitted via email) as obtaining informed consent, security of data, negotiating a participant consent document and the boundary between the private and the public can all become problematic. Therefore, researchers who adopt this medium should spend some time familiarising themselves with the current ethical debates on Internet research before beginning any fieldwork (British Sociological Association, 2002).

An area that is related to informed consent is user involvement, which is the participation of representatives from your target research group in aspects of your work. Examples include conducting discussion groups to help formulate questionnaires or setting up a steering group with representatives whose skills and experience will help direct your research. This type of involvement is stipulated by research governance ethical guidelines and must be demonstrated to some funding bodies. For example, the Big Lottery research programme particularly looks for innovative ways of involving and empowering research participants.

This collaborative approach is also important in action research and there should be a transparent sharing of information between the participants and the researcher-practitioner. Of course, action research, although different from other methodologies, also requires the informed consent of all participants (Mockler, 2007: 95; see also Chapter 7 of this volume).

Covert Research

The emphasis on informed consent in ethics is, of course, a reflection of current mores in our society and therefore research that is conducted without this type of consent is generally held in low esteem. However, covert research used to be a much more popular method than it is today and produced some of Social Science's most respected and famous research. For example, Erving Goffmans (1991) 'Asylums' (a study of life for people with mental health problems incarcerated in hospitals) and William Foote Whyte's (1993) 'Street Corner Society' (a study of an Italian slum in Boston) were both the result of covert research involving a considerable period of participant observation.

If you are thinking of adopting a covert approach, it would be wise to consider whether or not the information you wish to gather could be obtained by other means. The Economic and Social Research Council (ESRC) states:

> Covert research may be undertaken when it may provide unique forms of evidence or where overt observation might alter the phenomenon being studied. The broad principle should be that covert research should not be undertaken lightly or routinely. It is only justified if important issues are being addressed and if matters of social significance which cannot be uncovered in other ways are likely to be discovered. (ESRC, 2005)

Therefore, covert research should only be undertaken after all other methodologies have been explored and found to be inadequate.

Anonymity

It is usually a requirement of research ethics that the identity of individuals (and sometimes groups or organisations) who have participated in research is not revealed.

As such, no research material, in any shape or form, should be published or disseminated that makes participants, actually or potentially, identifiable without their consent, nor should research data be shared with colleagues unless it is anonymised. It is helpful to distinguish between anonymity and confidentiality, as the two terms are often used interchangeably although they do have separate and discrete meanings. Anonymity refers to hiding the identity of the person who provides information, although the information itself can be disclosed. Confidentiality, in contrast, means that the information itself cannot be revealed. Therefore, anonymity is more likely to come up as an issue when conducting research. The principles of anonymity apply across all media, whether you are writing a report, giving an oral presentation or placing a summary on a web page. You should remember that ensuring anonymity quite often depends upon context and what is already known by the audience. For example, if you are conducting research with excluded pupils in schools, you should not disseminate the findings back to teachers (in a way that reveals the school involved) as they are likely to be able to identify the pupils who took part in the research.

Another potential threat to anonymity occurs when reporting on small groups within your sample as this can easily lead to identification of participants. For example, if you are conducting research in a workplace that largely employs men and only a handful of women, reporting on findings from the women and men separately would make it relatively easy to trace particular responses back to the women who had made them.

Ensuring the anonymity of research participants is a legal requirement stipulated in the Data Protection Act 1998 (DPA), which protects the rights of individuals in respect of data held about them. The DPA came about as a result of growing concerns about how new technologies could store information on individuals and how this could be used (although the range of the DPA is not limited to electronic methods). The DPA has a major influence on the conduct of ethical research as it is now a legal requirement to either comply with the DPA or else anonymise data to the degree that it is impossible to reconstruct an individual's identity from the information held.

Complying with the DPA is not as daunting as it may sound and its main principles are largely covered by the ethics of informed consent. However, it is worth specifically mentioning the seventh principle of the DPA that states that you must ensure that any non-anonymised data that you store is completely secure and not accessible by others. For example, paper copies of documents or audio recordings should be kept in locked cabinets and electronic data should be stored on password protected files. If you transfer data from one place to another, for example from your computer at work to a computer at home on a mobile device (such as a USB memory stick) you should make sure that the data is encrypted so that no-one else will be able to read your files. Box 4.2 gives a brief summary of the Act, although you may wish to investigate further. Specifically, many universities have useful web pages devoted to how the DPA affects research, which you can easily find through an Internet search engine by, for example, searching 'DPA anonymity'.

Box 4.2   Data Protection Act 1998

All organisations that hold personal data about people must comply with the Data Protection Act (DPA). The DPA covers how information about living and identifiable people is used and is intended to protect the rights and privacy of people and to ensure that any data held about them is only processed with their knowledge and consent. The DPA places obligations on those who process personal information in the form of eight principles.

The data must be:

(1) fairly and lawfully processed (the participant knows how and by whom their data will be used);
(2) processed for one specified purpose (for example, research);
(3) adequate, relevant and not excessive for the specified purpose;
(4) accurate and up to date;
(5) not kept longer than necessary;
(6) processed in accordance with the individual's rights;
(7) secure, that is, manual data should be kept in a locked facility and computer files should be password protected;
(8) not transferred to countries outside of the European Economic area unless that country has adequate protection for the individual.

In addition, Section 7 of the DPA gives an individual the right to be informed by someone using personal data about him or her including what data is held, the purposes for which it is held and the people to whom it may be disclosed.

There are a number of exemptions to the DPA when data is collected for research purposes, although the exemptions are a complex legal area. Generally speaking, data that is gathered for research is exempt from the second and fifth data protection principles. Therefore, your data can be processed for purposes other than those for which it was originally obtained and can be kept indefinitely. However, this is only the case if the data is not processed and used to support measures or decisions that affect individuals or cause damage or distress to an individual. Therefore, it is possible for researchers to keep data, questionnaires and interviews transcripts and revisit this information when working on similar research in the future. It is important to remember, however, that this is not a blanket exemption from the DPA and most of the data protection principles still apply. It is also good ethical practice to consider the legal issues every time research data is collected and processed.

If you do not comply with the DPA, for example by passing on your data to third parties without the consent of your research participants or by storing data in a non-password protected computer file or network, you are legally obliged to anonymise your data, preferably as soon as possible after collection and before any analysis is undertaken. In addition to removing all direct identifiers such as names, addresses or similar personal information, you may wish to go further and remove indirect identifiers, such as places of work and geographical location.

Anonymising qualitative data is more complex than anonymising quantitative data. If you remove identifiers, it may result in a distortion of the data and so you may want to consider the replacement of identifiers with pseudonyms. If you do use pseudonyms, though, do take care to choose ones that are not culturally or ethnically sensitive and as such minimise the possibility of causing distress to your research participants. Another option would be to replace names with letters or numbers. How you choose to anonymise your data should be discussed with your participants and they should be informed that the process of anonymisation could result in a measure of distortion being introduced. Unfortunately, it is possible that a researcher may come across information that means that you must override the pledge of anonymity given to participants. This might include uncovering abuse of vulnerable people such as children or discovering other criminal or immoral activity.

Also, some types of research lend themselves well to a non-anonymised approach. In particular, oral historians and especially those studying groups that have been historically marginalised, argue that anonymising the identity of participants may actually go against the wishes of the participants themselves. When oral history became popular in the 1970s many historians argued that giving a voice to certain groups, such as racial minorities, women or people in poverty, gave them a place in history that they had previously been denied. Furthermore, their involvement in the research process restored dignity and self-confidence. As such, oral historians generally give participants the opportunity to state whether or not they are willing to have their identities revealed. This approach was adopted by Anne Grinyer, who conducted research with the families of young adults diagnosed with cancer. She felt that the use of pseudonyms might not be appropriate when the young adult had died, as they might now be doubly 'lost' as a result of the research not referring to them by their real name. Grinyer asked her participant families if they wanted anonymity but only a quarter responded that they did (Grinyer, 2002).

However, given that anonymity is now seen as an integral part of ethical research and is the usual and expected way of conducting research, if you are thinking of adopting a different approach it would be sensible to consider carefully whether the research and/or the participants will actually benefit if anonymity is waived. Additionally, permission to reveal identity must always be sought from the research participants and preferably, at the beginning of the project, so that participants are aware that all they are saying can be traced back to them as individuals. Of course, if participants decide to 'opt in' to revealing their identity half way through the project, this too is acceptable. However, the researcher has certain responsibilities and it has also been suggested that people who give their consent to having their identities revealed do not necessarily fully understand the impact that this will have on their lives once their words and ideas are placed into the public arena (Janovicek, 2006). Therefore, it is very important that you gain informed consent from participants and discuss the likely effects that the waiving of anonymity could have on participants before the research begins. However, it is worth emphasising once more that the identification of participants is unusual in modern research.

Professional Integrity and Quality

It is important, that as well as conducting yourself ethically throughout your research project you also adhere to certain professional standards. Of course, mistakes and errors are, to some degree, inevitable. However, it is important to minimise the risk of error in your research and conduct yourself honestly and professionally. Examples of unprofessional research activity, or research misconduct, are:

- The fabrication or the invention of data, such as filling in additional questionnaires to 'make up the numbers' or inventing data with particular 'desirable' responses.
- The falsification of data through distortion or misrepresentation such as rejecting 'undesirable' results or misrepresenting the findings of other researchers to 'fit in' with your own findings.
- Plagiarism, the unattributed copying of other people's work (see Box 4.3 on intellectual property).
- Deception, which is the failure to declare a conflict of personal interest or giving misleading statements when applying for research funding.
- Non-compliance, which is the wilful failure to comply with statutory obligations concerning the use of human subjects.
- Facilitating misconduct by collusion or concealment which is failing to challenge or deliberately ignoring unethical research practices among colleagues or students. (Sheffield Hallam University, 2004).

Box 4.3   Intellectual property

Intellectual property (IP) is the name given to different types of knowledge including ideas, tunes, blueprints or databases. It is both similar and dissimilar to property. It is similar in that it can be valuable, although it may be that you have to invest money and time into its development in order to realise that value. It is dissimilar in that, when a person trespasses in a house and steals items, if they are

(Continued)

(Continued)

caught and made to return the items, that is the end of the matter. However, if someone hears a tune, then they will always know that tune and no matter how many sanctions are applied, that tune can never be reclaimed in the way that stolen property can (Doctorow, 2008).

IP can apply to research in a number of ways. For example, if you develop a research proposal and submit it to an authority such as a council or charity and they do not fund your research but take your ideas and carry out the research themselves, then they are using your IP. However, if, conversely, you have a funder for your research that helped to develop the research questions, then the issues involved may be different. Indeed, that funder may have some claim to the IP rights of the research. In order to clarify such issues, it is worthwhile establishing who owns which ideas or outputs before the research begins.

It is also worthwhile mentioning two other aspects of IP: plagiarism and copyright. Plagiarism comes from the Latin word for 'kidnapper' and means using the ideas or words of others without acknowledging the source and/or passing them off as your own. Copyright is less concerned with the referencing of work and more to do with its actual use. If you use too much of another's original work, or distribute it too widely, even if the source is properly acknowledged, this may be a copyright infringement. Copyright law is complicated but generally, whoever writes an article or book owns the copyright to it (journal articles are an exception although practice is changing and some publications now only require a licence to reproduce). Copyright also extends to photographs, diagrams and pictures so you must always get permission from the author before you reproduce.

To conduct research professionally it is necessary to begin with an open mind, to not bring your own personal or political agenda to work and to be impartial. If you are undertaking the research with the aim of finding particular 'results', not only do you run the risk of being disappointed, you are also in danger of biasing your research by trying to make your research 'fit' in with what you already hold to be true. Of course, you cannot 'switch off' your personality when conducting fieldwork or analysing results but by recognising your own beliefs and experiences and how they could impact upon your research, you are going a long way towards conducting yourself both ethically and professionally.

Research misconduct can also creep into a project due to pressure from others who have a vested interest in promoting particular outcomes and downplaying others. Political interference can be very difficult to deal with, especially if it comes from an individual or body who has some form of power over you, such as your employer or the funder of the research. The researcher is left in the quandary of trying to please the other party and yet struggling to fulfil the ethical requirements of the research. This type of pressure can take a number of shapes and forms and might include being asked to interpret results in a particular way that distorts the data or being asked to use other (more politically acceptable) research findings and calling them your own. Action researchers are particularly vulnerable to this sort of difficulty as the boundaries between researcher, participant and funder are often blurred (see Chapter 7 of this book). To minimise the possibility of this sort of interference, you should at the outset of all research projects have open and honest discussions with interested parties about what they wish to achieve from the research. This will enable you to marry the sometime conflicting needs and expectations of third parties with your ethical and professional considerations.

Researchers may also find themselves under pressure to relax the ethics around informed consent and anonymity and once again, interference of this sort should be resisted. It is not unknown, for example, to be put under pressure to reveal the identity of particular participants, so that a third party can 'intervene' and improve things for the research participant concerned. For example, if you are conducting research about employees and discover instances of bullying in the workplace, a manager may wish to know who has reported this, so they can 'solve' the situation for the participant. However, in such a situation, this would not be ethical and the researcher should relay the request to the participant, explaining the consequences of waiving their anonymity. Under no circumstances should identities be revealed without the express permission of the research participant.

Researchers also have responsibilities towards those that are funding their research. Not only must they not accept conditions that may run contrary to professional integrity, they also have a responsibility to deal honestly with funders of research or other interested third parties. This might include being truthful about the advantages or disadvantages of different methodologies and approaches to the research and also being honest about the progress and development of the project.

Formal Procedures: Applying for Ethical Approval

Before you begin your research, you must consider whether you need to obtain approval from an ethics committee to conduct your research. You will not need to apply for approval on all projects, however, you should always check with the relevant authorities that this is the case as rules and procedures will vary from organisation to organisation.

Which particular ethical committee(s) you apply to is dependent both upon what type of project you are doing and your place of employment. All ethical approval submissions require that you complete a form and provide enough information to demonstrate that you have thought about and then made appropriate arrangements to ensure that your project is conducted ethically. Obtaining ethical approval can be a lengthy process and depending on which body you apply to, and whether or not you are granted immediate approval, it can take a substantial period of time from weeks to months. This time frame is something that you need to build into the design of your project and you need to be prepared to wait for approval before you begin any fieldwork.

As discussed earlier, certain categories of research are covered by the research governance code of practice and as such you must apply for ethical approval through the National Research Ethics Service (NRES). The exact nature and form of this application depends on a number of contextual variables and furthermore, the process is also subject to regular change. It is a complicated process and there are a number of interested parties that you must obtain permission from before you can proceed with your research. The interested parties might include the site where the research is taking place (for example, a hospital), the sponsor (possibly the funder of the research or your employer) as well as the regional NHS ethics committee.

However, a new single streamlined online system was introduced in January 2008. This system enables you to enter the information at the Integrated Research Application System (IRAS), and collates the information submitted by researchers and sends the appropriate forms to the appropriate regulatory bodies. The website is open to anyone seeking ethical approval for a research project, and has extensive advice and guidance to help you through the process. The IRAS form can be found on the NRES website (http://www.nresform.org.uk).

Practitioner-researchers should always personally approach the site's research and development's office or representative before undertaking the application process. Otherwise you risk going through the process of application, which generally takes from three to six months, only to be turned down by the site at the last hurdle. While NHS ethical committees are legally bound to process applications within a certain timeframe, site research and development offices are not bound by the same rules, and some are slower than others. Therefore, it might be wise to ask colleagues about their experiences and build this into your timetable.

If your research does not need NHS ethical approval, the process of seeking ethical approval is generally a lot easier. If you work in a large organisation, such as a town or city council department for housing, education, social services or similar, there will almost certainly be established procedures for ethical scrutiny and a few simple enquiries should guide you to the appropriate authority. Similarly, most universities have established ethics committees of their own to which employees can submit their research proposals for ethical scrutiny. Within each university there are usually a number of research ethics committees that cover different subject areas. If you work in a smaller organisation that does not have established procedures for ethical scrutiny, you may wish to consider whether there is a similar procedure that you will have to go through.

If there is no particular procedure that you must go through to ensure that your project is conducted in an ethical manner, then you may consider contacting a local university to see if their relevant ethical committee would look at your research with an 'ethical eye'.

The ESRC's 'Research Ethics Framework' states that:

> although it is expected that a research organisation will establish its own REC (Research Ethics Committee) or RECs to review research, smaller institutions or those that do not conduct a substantial number of studies involving human participants may make arrangements to secure ethical review in another institution. (ESRC, 2005)

Less formally, you could make contact with individual researchers in your field, either from universities or other organisations, to see if they would run their eye over your project. Of course, if you do not seek official ethical approval, it is still good practice to conduct your project in an ethical and professional manner.

Box 4.4 presents a list of questions that should give you a flavour of the sorts of issues you need to consider when completing your ethical approval form. These questions are a useful starting point for ensuring that ethics are woven into the design of your research project and will be helpful even if you do not need to officially apply for ethical approval.

Box 4.4   Questions to consider for ethical approval

General issues

- What is the main research question?
- What methods are you adopting?
- How will you report and disseminate the findings?
- Who will benefit from the research? In what ways?
- Are there likely to be any conflicts of interest as a result of you conducting this research?
- Are there any risks to the researchers themselves? (You may be required to carry out a risk assessment.)

Research participants

- How will you sample or recruit your participants?
- How will you brief them and gain their informed consent both at the outset of the project and as the research progresses or develops? This should include copies of any documents that they will receive and written consent forms.
- Are there any possible negative consequences of participation in the research? What are these possible negative consequences and how will you limit this?

(Continued)

(Continued)

- For how long will each participant be asked to take part in the research?
- Will the participants benefit from taking part in the research? If yes, in what ways?
- How will the participants be made aware that their participation is voluntary?
- How will the participants be made aware that they can withdraw from the research at any time?
- Does your research involve sensitive issues? If so, how will you ensure that participants are not harmed by the research?
- Does your research involve participants who are prisoners or young offenders?
- Does your research involve work with children or other vulnerable members of society, who are unable to give informed consent?
- If yes, have you undergone Criminal Records Bureau screening?
- What are the arrangements for debriefing the participants? Will you inform participants of the findings?

Anonymity

- How will you ensure participant anonymity?
- Does the research involve the cooperation of a gatekeeper for initial access to research participants? How will you ensure that participant anonymity is respected with regard to the involvement of this gatekeeper?
- Will the research data be available outside of the research team?
- How will you store the research data? What procedures will you use to ensure security?
- Will the data be anonymised?
- For how long will you store the data?

Obtaining ethical approval is not always straightforward and you may be turned down when your first apply. Although this might seem like a frustrating delay, it is something that you will need to accommodate if you wish to proceed with your research. Often the board will suggest changes for you to make that can be quite easily worked into the project. If this is the case, you can quickly make the changes to your research design and resubmit your ethics approval form. On other occasions, the board will require that you make more substantial changes in order to meet the standards required. Then it is possible that you will need to rethink your whole approach to the research.

Of course, ethics committees are not infallible or necessarily always right. If you believe that the committee has made a mistake then you may wish to appeal and persevere with your original approach. Other researchers before you have successfully disputed the rulings of ethics committees and been able to conduct their research in the way that they had originally proposed. For example, Cummins' (2006) proposed research revolved around one-to-one interviews with children and the ethics board, in its concern to protect the children involved, requested that she had a neutral third party present during her interviews. This was problematic for Cummins as she did not know who this third person could be and whether they would respect the anonymity of the research participants. Cummins appealed and argued that the original make-up of the ethics board had been inappropriate as it did not include a sociologist, and therefore, she argued, no one on the committee fully understood what she was proposing. Her appeal was successful and she was given permission to conduct the research as she had originally intended, although the whole process had taken a year from start to finish.

Conclusion

This chapter has introduced research ethics and research governance to the reader and should have equipped you with the knowledge to place ethics at the centre of your practitioner-research project. Specifically, you should now have a detailed understanding of how informed consent and anonymity need to be built into your project at the design and proposal stage. You should also appreciate how ethics are integral to the professional standards that are expected of the practitioner-researcher and how to avoid some of the ethical problems that can arise as you try to maintain professional integrity. This chapter has also supplied guidance on obtaining ethical permission for your project and given details about which authorities you will need to approach for different types of project, including advice on how to apply, the sorts of questions you will be asked and where to find further information.

Acknowledgement

The author would like to thank Dr Peter Allmark for his advice on research governance.

Further Reading

British Sociological Association (2002) *Statement of Ethical Practice for the British Sociological Association.* Available at: http://www.britsoc.co.uk/equality/Statement+Ethical+Practice.htm (accessed 2 December 2009)
Although an old publication, it still contains very useful information, but does have a particular slant towards the Sociological Association.

(Continued)

(Continued)

Campbell, A. and Groundwater-Smith, S. (2007) *An Ethical Approach to Practitioner Research*. London: Routledge.
This is an international collection of essays on the ethics of practitioner-researcher. It is not a 'how to' guide, but interesting and thought-provoking nonetheless.

The Data Protection Act 1998
This document contains everything you need to know about the Act, but is not easy going. More accessible information can be found by searching the Internet for university websites that have information pages about the Act that are very specific to research.

Department of Health (2005) *Research Governance Framework for Health and Social Care*, 2nd edn. London: Department of Health.
The research framework document has a very helpful section on ethics as well as the other areas covered by research governance guidelines. It is also useful in terms of deciphering the layers of responsibility involved in a health and social care research project. Again, you may find it helpful to look at university websites, many of which have very clear information about research governance. In particular, those universities with a strong tradition of medical research are particularly good at providing information.

Economic and Social Research Council (2005) *Research Ethics Framework*. Available at: http://www.esrc.ac.uk/ESRCInfoCentre/Images/ESRC_Re_Ethics_Frame_tcm6-11291.pdf (accessed 2 December 2009).
This is an accessible and all round guide to research ethics that is useful to the practitioner-researcher. The document is periodically reviewed after consultation with stakeholders; for the latest Framework readers are recommended to check the ESRC website (http://www.esrc.ac.uk).

FIVE

Writing a Research Proposal or Brief

Colin McCaig and Lena Dahlberg

By the end of this chapter you should be able to:

- identify the main types of funding opportunity;
- identify the main sources of research funding for the subject area;
- understand the bidding process;
- understand the importance of political and legal context of funders;
- express the aims and objectives of the research;
- identify a set of answerable research questions;
- present a methodology that answers those research questions;
- accurately cost the proposed research methodology;
- develop a realistic timetable for the research;
- write a research brief calling on practitioner-researchers to tender.

Introduction

This chapter outlines how practitioner-researchers can develop proposals for research that are both reactive and proactive. Most research and evaluation proposals are developed in response to specific *expressions of interest* and *invitations to tender* by funding bodies and will be referred to herein as reactive proposals. This chapter will also look at proactive proposals, developed by the practitioner-researcher relating to specific social policy issues, and submitted to research funding bodies issuing *open calls* for research projects. The characteristics of a good proposal (of either type) will be discussed from both a researcher and commissioner point of view. For those practitioners who find themselves commissioning research or evaluations, this chapter will provide a useful framework to ensure that your responses are more readily comparable. Commissioners (and practitioners thinking of developing proactive proposals) will be well advised to allow sufficient time to develop the brief/proposal and discuss their brief/proposal with colleagues.

Types of Funding Opportunity

The most common type of research funding opportunity that is likely to be available to practitioner-researchers are those that are commissioned by funding bodies to answer a specific question or set of related questions. From the funders' perspective these are often referred to generically as 'the brief', an outline of what they want doing. In practice, briefs usually appear in the form of calls for researchers to submit expressions of interest (EoIs) after which researchers receive invitations to tender (ITTs), though the first stage may sometimes be bypassed and ITTs issued generally.

Expressions of Interest

Funding bodies sometimes issue calls for EoI, and as a commissioner of research you may be in the position to develop such calls. Such calls are usually only a few pages long and for the potential researcher little is required except for a brief explanation of why you/your organisation would be suitable (knowledge of field, experience of similar work and so on). Sometimes the funding body also asks for financial and legal information to find out whether you are based at a credible organisation. Often this information is provided via a questionnaire (sometimes known as a pre-qualification questionnaire or PQQ) or *pro forma* prepared by the funding body.

Calls for EoIs may appear in the professional/practitioner press, on websites or be passed around the research community by mail, email or by JISCmail distribution lists (subscriber distribution lists organised around subject areas, see the Glossary) and thus are heavily slanted at organisations that are practitioners or who have a track record of research in the field. From the researcher's perspective EoIs allow you to think about the feasibility of tendering or any potential partner organisations you may think necessary or desirable, without having to delve deep into the subject area or think too closely about specific methods and costings.

Some funding bodies ask potential researchers to enter framework agreements. These are conceptually similar to EoI in that they ask for research teams proven capabilities in the field, though they are not tied to specific pieces of research but are a way of creating a list of 'preferred suppliers' for any contracts that may be issued over a set period (usually several years). Once such agreements are made, research opportunities are only offered to the preferred list.

Invitations to Tender

For those wishing to commission research, the ITT is where you have the opportunity to specify what you want the research to entail. It is essential to present clear aims and objectives so that the research will focus on the most relevant issues. Commissioners should also be clear about any preferences relating to how the research should be carried out, in what way(s) findings should reported, time schedule and so forth in the ITT.

ITTs usually invite researchers to send for or download fairly long ITT documents (usually in more than one part) consisting of the following elements:

- An outline of the general policy background and the funding body's role in the field usually followed by a section on the specifics of the problem identified or issue that needs more exploration and a section on the research aims and objectives (sometimes including suggested research methods).
- A section about the submission conditions for the tender document, for example, how many copies are required and in what format, when and where it is to be submitted, the dates on which any interviews will take place for short-listed research teams, the date by which decisions will be made, the date by which contractors will be expected to start the research (often these are indicative or approximate only and subject to slippage at the funders prerogative).
- A section outlining timings for the actual research, for example the dates by which interim reports, final reports or other dissemination events will be due for delivery as outcomes of the research.
- Some ITTs also specify the order of the tender document, how long it should be, the format of CVs, references from previous research and evidence of your policies on such issues as data protection, quality assurance, or health and safety.
- There may also be a final section or appendix that can take the form of a draft contract with basic terms and conditions.

From the point of view of the commissioner a well written brief should be unambiguous about the application and assessment process and the nature of the issue that needs to be researched, but at the same time invite those tendering to demonstrate knowledge of the political context and methodological range in their application.

Open calls for funding will be discussed in the section on proactive proposals. Now the basic concepts have been outlined, the remainder of this chapter provides detailed guidance for developing research proposals, beginning with reactive proposals.

Invitation to Tender: What the Funder Wants

Once the practitioner-researcher has possession of an ITT, (s)he will be in a position to investigate the research problem identified by the funders. Potential researchers should at this stage have some idea about the funding organisation, including how it operates in relation to the political context (see also Robson, 2002). Knowledge of what kinds of research such bodies have funded in the past and what other partner organisations are involved in the same policy arena can usually be gleaned though a few hours of desk research.

For example, information on how the tendering body is funded may have an effect on whether the work you propose to carry out will be subject to VAT, or when and in how many stages the work will be paid for. If this level of financial detail is not fond found within the ITT document, researchers should not hesitate to contact the funders. On some occasions (usually where the research specification is technical in nature), funders collate frequently asked questions and provide the responses to all those invited to tender to maintain a level playing field (see Box 5.1)

Box 5.1   Checklist – what does the funder want?

- Why do they want to know what they want to know?
- Where do they fit in the policy environment?
- How are they funded? Voluntary sector or statutory body?
- What sort of research do they usually fund?

Policy Environment or Broader Context: What We Already Know

From the researchers point of view there are two aspects to this part of the tender document or proposal. One is to demonstrate understanding of the policy context; the other is to demonstrate suitability for the research contract, and this can be a matter of capacity to undertake a large piece of research. From the commissioner's point of view, the tender – potentially together with interviews and/or presentations – will allow you to identify which organisations would be most suitable for the work you are commissioning.

A typical ITT asks respondents to demonstrate their experience of the field and this invites potential researchers to show a sophisticated understanding of the problems identified and the nature of political context: of the subjects of the research (for example, an understanding of the socio-economic and cultural circumstances of young offenders in former mining communities) or the impact of a government agenda on behaviour (for example, how successful have efforts to widen participation to higher education been among the Bangladeshi community). If the research proposal is close to the practitioner-researcher's area of work then they will probably be aware of the legal framework, but even so it is worthwhile spending a few days on desk researching the most recent legislative activity, including all reforms proposed by lobbying organisations, pressure groups and political parties.

The tender or proposal has to both demonstrate that you have experience of carrying out research on that subject and that you have a genuine understanding of the political environment (Robson, 2002). If you do not have any research experience, it may be useful to enter into a sub-contracting or consortium arrangement with another research organisation. This does not have to be as complex as it sounds; for example, if the ITT calls for a survey, but your expertise is qualitative, it makes sense to seek out an organisation that carries out surveys and to find out whether they have the capacity and what they charge for their services. Funding bodies usually prefer one organisation as a point of everyday contact and for invoicing purposes, so the usual arrangement is for the practitioner-researcher to be the budget holder and sub-contract the other party at a fixed cost for survey (or other) services.

If such an arrangement can be suitably agreed, your proposal can then extol the virtues of a team that merges complimentary skills (in this case your policy and issue knowledge with their track-record of running surveys). Alternatively you could work in partnership with practitioner colleagues who have research skills that you do not have (in data analysis for example) and a shared general interest in the issue.

The overriding importance is coverage of the requirements of the ITT. For example, if the brief calls for sensitively handled face-to-face interviews with vulnerable clients in their homes, there is no point proposing to use a market-research company that specialises in street surveys. However, the potential of working with partner organisations has many advantages: it allows you to expand your capacity, and to broaden the skills base and experience of the team, if the right kind of partner is chosen. Often a highly experienced and well-known researcher named on a proposal as a consultant for just a few days work reviewing your methods and contributing to report writing can make the difference. Many research skills are generic and can be carried out by anyone with the requisite competence and experience, but thorough subject knowledge and insight into what might be an arcane or obscure political context can give your tender (and subsequent analysis) a competitive advantage (see Box 5.2).

Box 5.2   Checklist – what we already know

- Show that you know the issues and the context.
- Show that you can handle the job.
- Show what you are good at.
- Show what other people you can include if necessary.

Focus of the Research: Aims and Objectives

ITTs usually outline the main aims and objectives of the research and those wishing to tender for the work should use these as a starting point for their desk research reading (see above), enabling the tender document to cite a broader and deeper set of questions to be addressed. The aims and objectives section of any tender is where you can demonstrate knowledge of the specific issue that the funding body wish to research or the specific programme they wish to evaluate the impact of. Broadly speaking, the *aims* of the research are higher-order questions that outline aspects of the problem at hand, while the *objectives* are specific questions the research intends answer in order to shed light on the higher-order aim/question. For example, if the *aim* of the research is to explore the impact of government investment in improved disability support services for higher education students then the *objectives* may include establishing or exploring:

- how and in what ways disability support policies have changed over the period of the investment;
- how information on disability is gathered and used by higher education institutions (HEIs);
- how support is organised and how disability fits into the institutional systems of equality governance;
- the impact government funding policies have had on the recruitment and satisfaction of disabled students and staff;
- the extent that such policies have altered the culture and management of HEIs.

How the Research Is to Be Carried Out: Methodology

The methodology section can be seen as a natural extension of the aims and objectives and should go into more detail about how and when the various research objectives will be carried out. Any given research topic can be studied in a number of ways. If the preferred method is not specified in the ITT, it is important that you make a strong argument for the methods that you suggest (see also the section 'Justifying Your Research Methods' later in this chapter). More guidance on how to choose methods and design a piece of research or an evaluation is given in Chapter 3, which also discusses the advantages and disadvantages of various methodologies.

For the purposes of this chapter, the key point is that the methodology section of the tender has to be developed in close conjunction with other aspects of the ITT, such as the timescale identified for the research and the costs (if a limit is identified, see below).

How Long the Research Will Take to Carry Out: Timescale

You should bear in mind the timescale required for individual elements of the research. For example, if you are considering a survey you need to build-in time to:

- develop the questionnaire (ideally including a pilot);
- create or acquire a database of those you wish to survey;
- sample from the database if that is required (see Chapter 12);
- issue survey, including reminders, and receive responses;
- register the data;
- clean the data;
- analyse the results (see Chapter 13).

Depending on the length of the questionnaire and the number of respondents, it can be expected that this process will take about eight weeks (it is normal practice to allow respondents at least a month to complete the survey to maximise response rates). At the end of the survey process you need to allow time for additional analysis (see Chapter 13) before writing up.

Qualitative research methods can take as much if not more time to organise. If you propose a case study approach, you must build-in time to arrange contact with key people in your potential case study. Even a simple plan to carry out 10 telephone interviews can take several weeks to organise and may involve writing letters and emails to encourage individuals to take part. When planning timescales a sensible approach is to work backwards from the date you have to submit the final report, so for example you should want to have at least two weeks clear between finishing your data collection and analysis and the draft final report submission date (more if you do not have a lot of experience of writing reports) and so on right back to the first stage. To express the research proposal chronologically it is worth including a tabular timeline, even if the ITT does not specifically request one (for an example see Figure 5.1).

Task	Feb		March		April		May		June	
Literature review	▓	▓								
Survey design (questionnaire design, sampling, etc.)		▓								
Survey			▓	▓						
Registration of responses					▓					
Survey analysis					▓					
Interview design (selection of case studies, topic guide design, etc.)						▓				
Case study interviews							▓			
Case study analysis							▓	▓		
Draft final report									▓	
Final report										▓

Figure 5.1   Timeline by task – an example

As a commissioner of research, you will find timelines in tenders useful. Here, you will be able to judge whether the planned project seems realistic and feasible within the time limit. You do not want to find yourself in a situation where the deadline is not met, as this could have knock-on effects on your policy development, implementation of findings and so on.

How Much the Research Will Cost to Carry Out: Budget

Cost issues are harder to calculate than time. Only a minority of ITT documents indicate the budget for the research; more often they contain statements such as 'there is a limited amount of money available for research of this nature' or 'tenderers are advised that there is a limited budget available to fund this evaluation, which reflects its short duration'. Some ITTs actually specify the number of researcher days they anticipate the work will take. The latter formulation is a reminder that, when it comes to tenders, cost equates mainly to researcher daily rates (see Box 5.3). Therefore if the work you are proposing to carry out takes 10 days of researcher time, the funder will only expect to pay 10 times the daily rate. A funder that asks for proposals for a piece of work that involves some desk research (often a literature review, see Chapter 6) and 10–15 interviews with a final report due two months after the start date will work on the calculation that at 20 working days per month the maximum labour costs will be 40 times the daily rate, plus non-staff costs. Unless there is a justifiable need for more than one researcher on a project on any one day, the number of days indicated in the ITT plus non-staff costs will be the effective ceiling that the funder has in mind for the research.

Box 5.3 Daily rates – notes for self-employed or freelance researchers

For individual researchers who are either self-employed or offering research services on a freelance basis, the calculation of daily rates is very important. Researchers have to build into their daily rate certain overhead costs to cover their inevitable outlay on such items as power, light, heating, stationary, telephone, Internet connection, rent and a host of other items over and above what you may consider a reasonable wage as an employee. Researchers employed by universities or private sector consultancies charge at daily rates from between approximately £250 and £800 depending on seniority (far more than they actually earn) to take overhead costs into account. It is important to be realistic about the daily rate because you will not be able to sustain research activity, whether as a one-off or on an ongoing self-employed or freelance basis, if you do not cover all your costs.

Non-staff costs are fixed cost items such as survey costs (based on number of questionnaires printed, postal costs, booking in the responses and so on) and travel, accommodation and subsistence for research field trips and to attend meetings with the funders, all of which have to be calculated in the tender (Robson, 2002). Given that many non-staff costs are fixed once you have decided, for example, how many people to interview or the size of the survey sample, researcher days are the only variable factor. Assuming you do not want to lower your daily rate then you may be tempted to squeeze the days available for analysis and report writing. You are well advised not to do that, but other people tendering for the same piece of research may well come up with lower overall costs. This may be because they have lower non-staff costs or lower daily rates, but more likely because they propose to use methodologies that are cheaper (for example, telephone interviews are cheaper than face-to-face interviews, and electronic surveys are cheaper than paper surveys, see Chapters 8 and 11).

It is also important to keep in mind that cost is rarely the deciding factor for funding bodies considering multiple research tenders. In practice daily rates and survey costs do not vary much. The methodological rationale for choosing a paper-based survey and face-to-face interviews over electronic surveys and telephone interviews are likely to be decisive, because they clearly affect both the integrity and outcomes of the research process.

Many ITTs stipulate that costs be outlined in tabular format. Costs may be expressed in two ways, the first of which shows the total number of days by task and by individual researcher (see Table 5.1).

Table 5.1   Researcher days by task and researcher

Task	Jane	Sean	Sangita	Tom	Andrew (consultant)
Desk research including literature review	5		5		
Survey sampling	2	1			
Survey analysis			5	5	
Selection of case studies	1	1	1	1	
Case study interviews	10	10	10		
Analysis of case studies	2	2	2		1
Attendance at meetings/steering group	1				3
Final report writing	1	1	1		2
Total	22	15	24	6	6

Second, costs can be presented in a format that provides a link between daily rates and the total cost of the research, as illustrated in Table 5.2.

Table 5.2　Researcher by day rate

Research team	Day rate (£)	Number of days	Total cost (£)
Andrew (consultant)	800	6	4,800
Jane	350	22	7,700
Sean	300	15	4,500
Sangita	300	24	7,200
Tom	300	6	1,800
Total staff costs			26,000
Total non-staff costs (including survey and travel, accommodation)			3,450
Total project cost (including non-staff costs)			29,450

In addition to detailed methodologies and costs, many ITTs require a risk assessment. This can take the form of a paragraph in the methodology section but it may also be useful to tabulate the main areas of risk and potential solutions. There are various formats and levels of detail that can be employed; the main point to keep in mind is that this section can be used to further demonstrate understanding and promote your own professionalism to the funding body (for an example, see Table 5.3).

Table 5.3　Sample risk assessment

Nature of risk	Likelihood	Countermeasures
Difficulties in arranging to see busy staff at case study institutions	Medium	Difficulties acknowledged by allowing considerable time for this activity. Use of specialist and sensitive interview staff who are particularly effective in this area.
Difficulties in pulling together all elements of such a large-scale project	Low	Strong project management. Good administrative systems and regular team meetings. External expert consultant to oversee our monitoring/ quality processes.

One final note when preparing reactive research tenders or proposals is that in many cases the successful proposal is just the beginning of a negotiation process. If the funding body is impressed by a proposal to use a methodological approach they had not considered they may invite the team to discuss this at a research interview. Funding bodies genuinely want an issue researched or a policy evaluated, and while they may have preconceived ideas about what methods are appropriate, they are not professional researchers themselves and will usually put their trust in their preferred contractor to deliver the contract in their own way once convinced of their capabilities and capacity. What is finally agreed between the funding body and the research team will then be formalised in a contract, usually outlining the milestones and outcomes expected as well as financial and legal details.

Box 5.4   Checklist – aims, objectives, methodology, costs and time

- Have you demonstrated an understanding of the aims?
- Can you add to the objectives specified in the ITT?
- Can you justify the methods?
- Is the study realistically costed?
- Do your daily rates cover all costs?
- Are the timescales realistic?
- Have you discussed potential risks?

Proactive Proposals

Proactive proposals share many of the same characteristics and content as reactive proposals. Indeed you should refer to the examples in the previous section (Figure 5.1 and Tables 5.1–5.3) as useful ways of presenting data for your own purposes. However, the funding council or body may well have its own requirements; usually they will require actual salaries of staff rather than daily rates, for example. Whatever the format, the proposal serves four functions: to make a case for the importance of the study; to let funders know that you can clearly espouse what has to be done and that you can do the task required; to present a workplan for action should you succeed; and to form the basis of a contract on which you have to deliver (Locke et al., 2000: 16–17).

In the absence of an ITT (see above) or any detailed prescription of how the bid should be laid out, the potential practitioner-researcher should develop a checklist in the form of a skeleton or structure (similar to an essay plan), as in the example from Onwuegbuzie (1997) presented in Box 5.5.

Box 5.5   Checklist for proactive proposals

- Title
- Introduction to the issue
- Summary of the proposal
- Review of related literature

(Continued)

(Continued)

- Aims and objectives
- Methodology
- Analysis
- Ethical considerations
- Timetable
- Costings
- Risk analysis
- Strengths of research team
- CVs of key members of research team
- Bibliography

Many of the items on this checklist will be the same as those you would need to put into a reactive proposal, however the development of a proactive proposal has to be deeper and more persuasive at each level, especially the sections relating to background/rationale for the proposed research, the aims and objectives of the research, the methodology adopted and the plans for analysis (often these sections are collectively known as the 'Case for Support'). Perhaps the most important point to note is that any potential bidder should spend sufficient time becoming familiar with the rules of the funding body, which may be found in a guidance document or in other documents issued by the funding body. For researchers or students based at a university there are faculty rules and institutional procedures to be considered and inevitable constraints on timescales, but the principles of developing proposals remain broadly the same.

In return for all this additional work, however, those choosing to make proactive proposals for research funding will find they have much more leeway in terms of theoretical and methodological approaches. Whereas government departments and agencies may be deterred by, for example, radical feminist or critical theory when considering tenders, research funding councils and other bodies will understand that researchers' own interests and values inevitably influences research (Kelly, 1998) and may take a more open-minded attitude to the idea of research as subjective empowerment for researchers from some perspectives (Denscombe, 2002). In this sense proactive proposals to funding councils and voluntary sector bodies may resemble those developed by research students.

Study Potential Funding Sources

Proactive proposals can be developed by practitioner-researchers if they have a particular social policy issue they wish to explore, or a specific hypothesis they wish to test in a specific set of circumstances or context. Once the problem or issue is identified, researchers need to be aware of the various funding opportunities in their field. In the UK context the best place to start is government research funding councils such as the Economic and Social Research Council (ESRC), the Medical Research Council (MRC) or the Arts and Humanities Research Council (AHRC). For proposals likely to cross the social science boundary, there are also research councils covering biotechnology and biological sciences, the natural environment, engineering and physical sciences and science and technology facilities. There is a central site for UK research councils (http://www.rcuk.ac.uk/default.htm).

There are also myriad charitable trusts and other voluntary sector bodies that may welcome research proposals such as the Leverhulme Trust, the Joseph Rowntree Foundation, the Nuffield Foundation or the Big Lottery fund. The European Union (EU) and other international funding organisations, such as UNESCO or the World Health Organisation (WHO) also call for proactive research proposals, though generally of a comparative nature involving participants from more than one country.

Open Calls

These take the form of announcements by funding bodies (including those mentioned above) requesting proposals for research across a given theme (for example, the link between poverty and health) but welcoming proposals from within various disciplines (such as sociology, criminology, health) and using a variety of methodologies. Some grants are available with no theme attached, for example the ESRC Research Grant and Small Research Grant schemes.

Open calls from these bodies may be less suitable for small-scale practitioner research, mainly because of the amount of time required for proposal development. To be successful, proposals have to be based on a deeper understanding of the research environment, though they involve many of the same organisational and research skills, methods and competencies as reactive research proposals. Because of higher expectations of the funding body, you would have a greater chance to be awarded a research council grant if you have a PhD, are employed by a university, and have a research and publication track record in the field of enquiry, though the rules are often more relaxed for charitable trusts.

Open calls, like ITTs, may be distributed via the JISCmail or other mailing lists, advertised on websites or other electronic systems and in the professional press. You may also find literature referring to such calls at academic or research conferences and they usually have a much longer lead time than ITTs, or even allow you to submit the proposal at any point in the year (for example, the ESRC Research Grant and Small Research Grant schemes). Applicants are expected to make far more investment in time and effort in developing their thinking, and thus have more time to read around the subject to make the proposal as precise as possible and to seek out suitable partners.

Open calls from the funders usually come within a framework of a fixed total amount of funding and size ranges for proposals and bids. For example, some of the funds may be earmarked for up to 10 small projects costed between £40,000 and £150,000, with another tranche for up to five proposals costed between £150,000 and £1,000,000. The first task is to work out what you can realistically propose to do within these parameters. Individual practitioner-researchers may have more luck applying for a relatively small amount from a funding call like this than responding to an ITT from a government department or agency that may already have a fixed idea of the kind of research organisation it wishes to contract (usually one with a track record of successful research in the field) though they often value practitioner knowledge.

Once a funding body has been identified it is important to thoroughly read and understand the guidance notes, submission processes (which may be web-based) and timescales. Preparing a proactive proposal is usually a highly bureaucratic process, especially when submitting a proposal to an international funding organisation such as the European Commission (EC).

Box 5.6 Notes on full Economic Costing (fEC): for practitioner-researchers based in universities

Many large funding bodies, including the UK Government research councils (such as the ESRC), the EC and some large charities, fund research on the basis full Economic Costing (fEC), which is defined as 'the full cost of a project/activity, incorporating all direct and indirect costs, including cost adjustments required to fulfil the project/activity'. fEC is seen as a method to make UK higher education institutions sustainable in the future. The definition of sustainability in terms of fEC is: 'An institution is being managed on a sustainable basis, if taking one year with another, it is recovering its full economic costs across its activities as a whole, and is investing in its infrastructure (physical, human and intellectual) at a rate adequate to maintain its future productive capacity appropriate to the needs of its strategic plan and students, sponsors and other customer requirements' (University of Edinburgh, 2008).

Developing a proactive proposal, including following all the rules for submission, can take up a substantial amount of labour time, for the main applicant (or principal investigator in funding-council speak) who has to bring all the information together in the required format. Even proposals for relatively small amounts of funding may require a significant time commitment. There are two main reasons for this: first, the range of proposed research questions, aims and methods is so wide that comparison between proposals is only feasible when the elements are broken down into fine detail; second, every element of the proposed research has to be accurately costed and that includes thinking deeply about how much equipment and travel costs you might incur, how much time you will spend on each stage of the research, the names and salary details of any other investigators that you may wish to include in the proposal and a host of other variables. Proposals without that level of detail may be dismissed out of hand so it is not something that should be rushed. If necessary (and possible) researchers should consider delaying submission until the proposal is as good as it can be (assuming a call with several or no fixed submission dates) and take advice from as many people with experience of this kind of application as you can find before submission.

The voluntary and community sector (VCS, also called Third Sector) offers less formalised sources of funding for potential researchers. Most geographical areas will have a VCS infrastructure that is managed by informal voluntary management committee and small teams of paid staff. Regional voluntary action groups are affiliated to a national infrastructure of voluntary action groups. VCS organisations' funding sources are usually issued on CD-ROM or websites and the support on offer can range from research grants to free access to software and books. It is worth noting that funding bodies sometimes have money they need to allocate towards the end of their financial year and this may be distributed to researchers without recourse to the usual tendering and selection processes. A quick and limited research proposal, successfully carried out, can establish researchers' name and reputation to the funders, which will be of particular value if the initial work can be used as a pilot for a larger more detailed application in the future.

Justifying Your Research Methods

In contrast to reactive proposals, which are, as we have seen, often hidebound by the needs of the funder, in the case of proactive proposals the methods employed are likely to be key to the selection process. Anyone considering proactive research proposals would be well advised to read the relevant sections of this and other volumes (see Chapter 3 on research design, Chapter 4 on ethical considerations, Chapter 8 and 9 on qualitative methods, Chapters 11 and 12 on quantitative methods, and the recommended reading list at the end of this chapter).

Your desk research should involve 'immersion' in the policy community if possible; this implies a close reading of the relevant literature, becoming an active member of forum discussions and JISCmail distribution lists and attendance at sector conferences, none of which can be achieved quickly if you are not already involved at this level. At the very least you should be aware of all the contemporary debates and theories relating to research and evaluative methods in the field.

You should use the literature review section to illustrate gaps in the knowledge, and thus provide the rationale for your research. The literature review is important as it is here that you can demonstrate knowledge of what research is currently being carried out as well as what has already been published (see Chapter 6). It needs to demonstrate understanding, not just of the wider policy context (usually sufficient for a reactive proposal), but more specifically it should review only that literature relevant to the specific proposal:

> The writer's task is to employ the literature artfully to support and explain the choices made *for this study*, not to educated the reader on general developments in the subject area. (Locke et al., 2000: 59; original emphasis)

Feasibility: The Whole Picture

As mentioned above, ITTs tell the researcher what to do, by when and (obliquely at least) for what cost, and they often steer researchers towards particular methodologies. In such cases, demonstrating feasibility is merely a matter of track-record and risk-assessment. By contrast, proactive proposals have to have feasibility built into every element of the research design, from the research aims and objectives, methods, the availability of the team, the timelines and costs, the plan for analysis and report writing, ethical considerations right through to the dissemination plan.

Overall your proposal should demonstrate that 'general decisions about resources and design are made in parallel and are major criteria for the do-ability of the study' and this applies regardless of the size of the proposal (Marshall and Rossman, 2006: 178) The benefit, should you receive the funding, is that you then have framework to keep the work on track.

Conclusion

This chapter has attempted to explain the practicalities of developing research proposals in a variety of circumstances and from the various perspectives of practitioner-researchers and those who are involved in developing research briefs. The issues covered herein are some of the more prosaic aspects of the research process, but they are as important to successful social science research as the research design and the methods chosen.

The reader should now be confident that they can identify and understand the needs of a variety of funding bodies and how and where these bodies advertise their research needs. Hopefully, also, readers will have an understanding of the importance of understanding the political and legal framework in which social science research takes place in their specific field. Furthermore, readers should be confident of being able to develop costed proposals based on appropriate methodologies that answer feasible research questions of interest to themselves and their funders.

For those commissioning research it is important at all times for the ITT or brief to clearly espouse the aims and objectives of the proposed research; the avoidance of ambiguity will save time and prevent wasted effort on all sides during the tendering process, and bear fruit in the outcomes of the research you fund.

Further Reading

Robson, C. (2002) *Real World Research. A Resource for Social Scientists and Practitioner-Researchers*, 2nd edn. Oxford: Blackwell.
This is an exhaustive research methods volume that contains an excellent appendix on writing a project proposal and another on the roles of practitioner-researchers in the context of 'real world research'.

Punch, K.F. (2006) *Developing Effective Research Proposals*. London: Sage.
Punch offers one of the few methods books that restricts itself to the process of writing research proposals and as such covers some of the same issues as this chapter. However, there is comparatively little from the perspective of the practitioner-researcher with the main focus being on graduate students.

SIX

Literature Reviews

Tamsin Bowers-Brown and Anna Stevens

By the end of this chapter you should be able to:

- understand the purpose of a literature review;
- set parameters for literature searches;
- differentiate between different types of literature;
- identify key sources for literature searching;
- undertake critical reading and synthesise the literature;
- understand how the literature review informs the methodological approach;
- reference sources.

Introduction

A literature review is the starting point for a research enquiry. It is where the practitioner-researcher will gather information to gain a greater and more thorough understanding of the area that is the focus of the research. It offers the opportunity to analyse what has already been researched, to identify whether there are any gaps in the knowledge that require further exploration and to examine different theoretical positions that have been used to interpret the results. This chapter will provide a guide to conducting an effective literature search using both paper-based and electronic resources. It will outline the purpose and process of conducting a literature review, including setting appropriate parameters for the search based on a thorough understanding of the research question. It will discuss the importance of an effective and analytical literature search, including previous systematic reviews of the field as well as 'grey' literature.

The chapter will explore how a literature review can improve a research proposal and the research itself, enabling researchers to provide a critical analysis of published research that not only demonstrates understanding of the field but establishes the context for their own research hypotheses and design. For those developing research proposals it is sensible, if time allows, to begin the process of searching for relevant literature that can be built on during the research process itself.

The process will then be explored through identification of appropriate existing subject-related databases and how to use them, and the use of electronic search techniques such as the use of search terms, use of Boolean operators, and combining different data sources. Practitioner-researchers', sometimes limited, access to databases and journals will be taken into consideration. The chapter will also cover critical review and appraisal of publications.

Rationale for Conducting a Literature Review

The literature review is the first step in a research project and it forms the 'foundation for the research proper' (Hart, 1998: 26). Conducting a literature review allows the researcher to assess the 'current state of play', in other words, what is already known. It will enable the practitioner-researcher to explore whether the research question has already been addressed and if so what type and depth of evidence has been gathered, and whether it is an area that is under-researched, or if there are omissions in the evidence that need further exploration for example. The review enables a much more focused approach to the research that is being undertaken. Barron sees the literature review as fundamental to ensuring that primary research is viable:

> Failure to undertake a literature review prior to carrying out social research may have serious repercussions as the research progresses because the literature review serves to establish the originality of a chosen research project. (2006: 163)

The literature review can also be useful in identifying research methods that have been employed to answer particular research questions. Research that warrants repetition or updating can be identified and a judgement can be made about whether the same technique could be used in your own data collection. From the outset some challenging questions should be asked; if planned and carried out correctly the literature review can help define the purpose of the research, identify the type of information to be sought, and be assessed against any expected outcomes. Be honest about whether the literature review is a way of supporting your existing viewpoint, or whether it is being used to establish a new perspective through the synthesis of different standpoints which will be critically evaluated before arriving at and justifying your own position.

A literature review can also be a way of summarising research in a specific area. For example, Gorard and Smith (HEFCE, 2006) used a literature review to locate and synthesise research in the field of widening participation in higher education on behalf of the Higher Education Funding Council for England. The authors used

JISCmail (a network of university based researchers) to put out a call to researchers working in the field; this gave them access to 'grey' and institutional research to augment published documents that could be found from other sources (for example, accessing electronic databases of journals and education resources and online educational libraries).

Planning a Search

Know How to Set Parameters for Literature Collection

In the case of research that is funded by policymakers (for example, government departments or agencies) or voluntary sector organisations the requirements of the literature review or desk research are likely to be very specific. In conducting research for your own interests a broader enquiry can be undertaken. However, there will almost always be an enormous amount of literature to be found: published and unpublished, paper-based and electronic. Many sources that were traditionally paper-based, such as journal articles, policy documents and newspaper articles can now be located electronically (accessing Internet-based sources is discussed towards the end of the chapter). As it will generally be impossible to review every piece of literature that has ever been written about a given subject, the first step is to outline the scope of the research and to set parameters that reflect this. The scope will be determined by the size of the research budget and the time available.

Prioritise in whichever way you think is most relevant to your research question, but do not limit the search to one type of literature. Any limitations should be by content rather than the type of source (unless your review is of specific documents, for example, education policy documents since 1944). It is essential that limitations are defined and rationalised. Search parameters that are sensible include gathering literature written before, after or between certain dates, with the search restricted to certain agreed search terms. It may be that you wish to take a selection from each of these areas and more, but the key thing to remember is that there must be a point when you decide to stop searching.

In some instances there will be very little literature published that meets the research criteria, in which case it will be necessary to use what Punch refers to as 'levels of abstraction' (2006: 39). So, although there may be very little literature that answers the research question directly, at a more abstract level there could be vast amounts of relevant information. An example may be research into the nature of childhood obesity. It could be that you want to focus on childhood obesity among five-year-old children from white British families. Although there may be little literature that goes to such a micro-level of analysis, if the search parameters are expanded to 'childhood obesity in England', this will provide an overarching starting point, which will contextualise the research and provide ideas for honing the research questions in your own research.

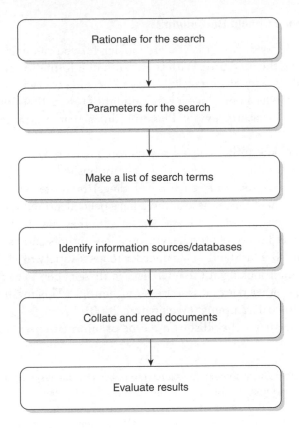

Figure 6.1   Planning a literature review

Overall, the aim of a literature review is to position the research in context, to help the reader to understand why the issue being investigated is of importance and to help establish the methodology that will best answer the research question. In the Gorard and Smith example (above) the authors wished to explore the evidence that supported the notion that widening participation *policy* actually succeeded in widening participation in the higher education sector (HEFCE, 2006). The literature that is chosen must add to the evidence, and it is necessary to critically evaluate each document and justify its inclusion. It is not sufficient to list every article that has been read without explicitly identifying the contribution the piece of work makes to the argument. In reviewing literature, the aim is to pick out the key arguments or areas that you believe are pertinent to the research and assess this information against your preconceived notions, for example, whether you agree or disagree with the arguments, whether you think the argument is valid and why, and whether it is supported by other evidence. It may be helpful to develop a visual structure that will help you keep your literature review 'on track', such as that shown in Figure 6.1.

What Evidence Should Be Sought?

Once you have decided what it is you are looking for you can begin to construct a plan for searching the literature. With the wealth of information that is now available from a wide variety of sources it is easy to become overwhelmed with material. An online search can produce a vast amount of results that may not be useful or relevant to a literature review. Planning out a search strategy will help to overcome this.

Often there are key authors on a research topic who will emerge during an initial search. Key authors are those who have published widely in the field (in journal articles, books or conference proceedings) or those who have been frequently cited by others. Once these authors have been identified it is useful to carry out a search on them in order to identify what else they may have published. It is important however not to rely too heavily on a few authors and to include authors who come from different standpoints in order to get a variety of views. Once these have been identified, looking at the references in these papers is a valuable exercise in order to locate other relevant resources on the topic. This method of searching can be called 'snowball sampling' (Wellington, 2000).

Try putting together a checklist of the type of information you are seeking, for example:

- Issues that set the political context, for example a policy document(s) that show how the issue has developed and how it is being considered at a strategic level.
- Evidence that supports or rejects a theoretical position.
- Level of applicability in practice, for example, evidence of interventions, suggested implementation criteria.
- Triangulation, that is, mixed method approaches or different research studies using various methods to assess the same research question.
- Looking at who the research has been published for, such as government bodies, lobbying organisations.
- Try to assess the validity of the evidence: is the source a peer-reviewed article or an Internet chat room and to which would you give more credence? It may be dependent on the research question.
- Interest – look for what captures your imagination and merits further investigation.

Before beginning a literature search, the practitioner-researcher needs to consider which search terms will be used, how search phrases will be constructed and which sources or databases are appropriate for the topic area. This will help to achieve an effective search. The more the practitioner-researcher knows about the research area the easier it will be to conduct a search since prior knowledge of the topic will mean familiarity with commonly used terms, key authors and sources. In any case before beginning a search it is useful to make a list of all the search terms you are planning to use.

Prior to searching for literature on the specific research question it may help to consider the broader subject area. For example, a specific research question might be 'Are obese children and adolescents more at risk of developing psychological health problems?' Here the broader research area would be 'obesity in children and adolescents'. It may be useful to initially search for literature on this broader area and investigate the general context of the research area before narrowing down the search. This should help to identify common terms used in the research area to add to the list of search terms. The initial list would include terms in the research area but also any synonyms or alternative words authors may use. The list of key words for the above research question may be something like those presented in Box 6.1.

Box 6.1   Search key words – an example

- psychological
- mental
- emotional
- health
- well-being
- obese
- obesity
- overweight
- children
- childhood
- adolescents
- young people
- teens

Once the search is underway other useful or commonly used terms on the topic should become apparent. You should systematically keep a record of search terms used and sources consulted in order to identify what has been most useful in retrieving results. The use of electronic databases and the myriad Web-based sources (including search engines) will be covered in the final section of this chapter along with referencing techniques.

Differentiate between Different Types of Literature

Once the practitioner-research has established what information is to be sought, it is important to consider the different types of literature available. There are a number of literature sources that can be used to establish the arguments within your field of research. Each has its own value and none should be avoided because it does not seem academic or authoritative enough. Grey literature that incorporates unpublished institutional or organisational data is often just as revealing as a published text-book, government report or journal article. The monitoring of how often your subject is referred to in popular publications such as newsletters, newspapers and transcripts from radio or television broadcasts can help you to gauge the level of importance the issue occupies within the public domain. Using a number of types of literature can strengthen your knowledge base and the overall justification for the research. Consider using the following types of literature:

- books;
- journal articles;
- conference papers;
- government (or agency) research reports (grey literature);
- government (or agency) policy documents (grey literature);
- PhD theses;
- organisational newsletters;
- websites;
- popular publications.

Systematic Reviews

In the realms of a small research project it is unlikely that you will want to conduct a systematic review. However it is useful to begin your literature trawl with a search for systematic reviews to see if an extensive literature search has already been carried out in your field (Box 6.2). For systematic reviews of medical research the Cochrane library is a useful place to start (http://www.cochrane.org).

Box 6.2 Systematic reviews

Systematic reviews are generally used in health and social care research, although they can be used to evaluate any research that has used a replicable, controlled and transparent approach (Glanville and Sowden, 2001). The primary concern of the systematic review is to collate the research findings that have answered a clear question in order to evaluate the effectiveness of an intervention or procedure. It will outline and identify success rates through a summary of the findings, effect sizes and conclusions.

The systematic review, unlike the literature review, attempts to remain value neutral in so far as it is not attempting to prove a certain outcome. Although the reviewer may believe that a certain intervention has a greater effect than another, the evidence gathered will not be collated on this basis. This is not to say that the results of a systematic review are necessarily a true reflection of effectiveness, as research where a significant finding was identified is much more likely to have been published than those where effect sizes were found to be insignificant (Field, 2003). This means that an intervention may appear to be of greater importance than is the case, and that data may be unrepresentative from the outset. This can be avoided in part through access to unpublished, or grey literature, which can in itself be problematic in terms of verification of quality.

Critical Review and Appraisal of Publications

Organising the Data Collected

The methods used in analysing and evaluating an argument need to be 'clear, consistent and systematic' for it is 'these qualities which give coherence and intelligibility to analysis and evaluation' (Hart, 1998: 87). It is useful then not only to identify a structure for conducting a critical review, which will result in a coherent argument, but also to enable better management of data. An organisational framework is a useful tool for outlining the key parts of the document. An example of a possible structure is given in Box 6.3.

Box 6.3   Organising your data

Introduction

This section should include the method undertaken to collect the literature: the parameters of the review, the search terms and the reason for undertaking the search.

Background information

The background section is a useful way to set out the context of the research, for example, the policy developments surrounding the issue in question and any recent developments that have bought the issue into the political/public arena.

The debate and research findings

This is where presentation of the hypotheses, arguments and methodologies that were used in the different pieces of literature are presented. They should be interwoven with your own reflections and perspectives on the findings. Remember that this is where the argument is presented; it offers the opportunity to convince people reading your research that this is an issue worth pursuing. Therefore it is important that this is critical rather than a mere acceptance of what has been published. If you agree wholeheartedly or passionately disagree with the views of an author this would entail outlining the reasons why, what the strengths and/or weaknesses of the argument are and how effective the method used in data collection was in gathering the information. The literature should be synthesised. This does not mean producing a list of all the publications and a summary of their content, rather it implies taking the significant elements from across the literature and presenting them within your own framework. Your own argument should be based on the evidence that you have gathered from the literature.

Conclusions

The concluding part of the literature review should be a summary of the key findings of the search. It is useful at this stage to reiterate how this evidence fits into your research project as well as informing further primary research.

Constructing the Debate: Identify Theoretical Positions

There are some key elements that should be sought when critically analysing literature. You will of course be searching for evidence that supports or negates your own hypothesis but there are some key areas that you may wish to explore. Try to identify the different perspectives and theories that explain the issue under investigation. Is there a prevalence of key theorists (for example, Marx, Weber, Durkheim in sociology, Bourdieu, Bernstein, Halsey in education)? Evaluate whether you agree with the way the research has been aligned with theory; consider whether it is a good fit; whether there are other theories that would better explain the findings or that would support or reject the conclusions. Think about how these theoretical arguments fit with your own assumptions and expectations and whether you will use or adapt them for your own research.

Appraising the Literature

In conducting a literature review it is unlikely that all the sources retrieved will be utilised in the overall analysis. Therefore it is necessary to work to criteria that enable clear distinction between high quality publications and those that have rather more dubious credentials. Creating a checklist will enable you to make this evaluation in a straightforward manner (see Box 6.4)

Box 6.4   Appraising the literature – a checklist

- What is your literature source – is it a peer reviewed article or a leaflet published by an action group?
- Are claims that the author makes supported by evidence or research?
- Is the research question clearly identified?
- Are the research methods well described?
- Are the methods appropriate to the research question?
- Did the research engage the most appropriate sample (size, demographic)?
- How clear are the findings? For example, has the mode of analysis been described?
- Is the conclusion supported by the findings?

Assess the Methods Used in Research Studies

It is necessary to explore the different methods and approaches that researchers have chosen. It may be that you are more familiar with certain methods than others, indeed you may already have a preference. Try to be open-minded when looking through the literature so that interesting findings are not overlooked; this especially relevant given the increasing amount of grey literature that is not officially 'published' and yet is easily available and citeable from institutions' or organisations' websites. Compare research findings that have employed different methods or used different sample population. Assess whether the information contains similarities and explore the differences in outcomes and conclusions and see whether the method employed could have caused them.

Understand How the Literature Review Informs the Methodological Approach

In assessing the methodologies in the literature review sample, a decision can be made about which method will: (1) best suit the research participants; (2) achieve the level of data required (for example, quantitative or qualitative, breadth or depth); and (3) produce the most fruitful data. In most research articles the authors will outline the methodologies employed and critically evaluate their effectiveness.

In evaluating the literature it is important that the following questions are kept in mind:

- What were the strengths/weaknesses of the research?
- How could the research have been done differently?
- Are there methods that seemed more appropriate than others to the research participants? (In this instance you may have to read between the lines in assessing the quality of the data that was gathered.)
- Although a method may have been extremely successful in achieving a great depth of understanding of the issue in question, it may be difficult to replicate if budget and time constraints are an issue. These factors will also need to be considered.

Electronic Sources of Data

There are a variety of different types of electronic sources available for those conducting a literature review, including: academic subject-based databases that offer a gateway to peer-reviewed resources and journals; Web-based search engines that provide access to general websites and newspaper articles; and governmental websites that provide access to government papers. It is generally good practice to use a combination of these when conducting a literature review, as retrieving information from a wider variety of sources will allow for a more diverse understanding of the material that is available.

Academic Databases

There are many academic subject-based databases available online, though some will require a subscription for access to full text articles (but anyone can access abstracts). If your employer is a large public sector organisation (such as in health or education) or a large private firm it may be a subscriber.

If you face difficulty accessing the full text of articles, it may be worth contacting the author of an article if possible since they may be willing to send the full text version of their article without payment. It is also useful to try searching the Web for the title of the article as the full text may be available on the authors' own webpage or elsewhere.

There are several publicly available online databases that provide access to a vast range of peer-reviewed quality resources. These databases cover a wide range of subject areas in social science disciplines and physical science disciplines. The following is a non-exhaustive list of current online databases:

- http://scholar.google.co.uk – a freely available tool for finding published journal articles (requires publisher subscription for full text articles).
- http://www.intute.ac.uk – a free online service providing access to Web resources for education and research that have been evaluated by subject specialists.
- http://www.base-search.net – provides access to scholarly Internet resources.
- http://www.proquest.com – contains large digital newspaper archive, periodical databases, dissertation collections and other scholarly collections.
- http://www.sciencedirect.com – a collection of science, technology and medicine full text and bibliographic information (requires subscription for full text articles).
- http://www.eep.ac.uk – Educational Evidence Portal provides access to UK education resources.

If you have collaborating partners based at a university your options will be greater as universities usually subscribe to a number of academic databases such as Web of Science, and to many online journals. Often, there are links directly from the databases to the online journal article.

The type of databases that will be most useful to the literature search evidently depends on the topic area. In our childhood obesity example the subject is health related therefore it would be useful to identify a list of health-related databases to use. The following databases are all publicly available and require no subscription.

- http://www.dh.gov.uk – UK Department of Health (DoH) website providing access to government reports.
- http://www.cochrane.org – an international independent organisation producing and disseminating systematic reviews of healthcare interventions.
- http://www.library.nhs.uk – national library of guidelines for the UK National Health Service (NHS) based on systematic reviews of evidence.
- http://www.nlm.nih.gov/medlineplus – brings together information from the UK National Library of Medicine and the National Institutes of Health. Gives access to medical journal articles and latest health news.
- http://www.embase.com – provides access to pharmacological and biomedical literature.

Web Resources

Though people tend to use the terms 'Internet' and 'Web' interchangeably, in technical terms they are two different things. The Internet is an electronic communications network, while the World Wide Web allows the sharing of information via a collection of hyperlinked addresses which are accessed via the Internet (Boswell, 2004). Search engines are used to retrieve information from the Web, working by storing and indexing information about Web pages (Sullivan, 2007).

While the Web can be a valuable source of information it is sensible to approach it with some caution since it is an open environment where anyone can publish material. Researchers have expressed concern about the reliability of information on the Internet and advise to carefully evaluate resources before using them (Chowdhury, 1999; Fink, 2005).

The vast number of results that can be retrieved on the Web can be time-consuming to sort through, although the way in which search engines work usually ensures that large governmental bodies and reputable sources of information are found near the top of any list. For example, typing 'health' into Google (http://www.google.co.uk) will produce links to the National Health Service (NHS) and the Department of Health's main websites in the top 10 places (along with BBC and other media sites devoted to health). Typing 'obese children' into Google produces mostly media stories on the first page but also links to health pressure groups such as the National Obesity Forum and the British Medical Association.

Advanced Search Techniques

To attempt to filter through the extensive amount of material available on the Web search engines use sophisticated techniques to rank results in order of relevancy. Search engines may look for search terms in the title of a webpage, or look at how frequently search terms occur on the page. Most search engines use 'link analysis' to determine the relevancy of a website. This involves the analysis of how pages link to one another, which allows the search engine to determine whether a page is significant (Sullivan, 2007).

While search engines are effective at retrieving relevant results it is important to be aware of search techniques that will further refine a search. The majority of search engines and online databases will have an advanced search option, which can be a valuable tool when conducting a search. For example the Google advanced search (http://www.google.com/advanced_search) allows for various filtering options such as language and region and even by domain name, so entering '.ac.uk' would retrieve results from UK academic or educational organisations only. In addition Google allows the user to search by document type. Restricting a search to retrieve only '.pdf' documents for example may help in finding articles or government reports and papers.

The majority of online databases and Web search engines will also allow Boolean operators to be used. These are illustrated in Figure 6.2. Boolean operators can help refine or broaden searches by using the commands 'AND', 'OR' or 'NOT'. For instance using the phrase 'obesity AND children AND health AND problems' will only retrieve documents which contain *all* of these words. Furthermore if you wanted to exclude *adults* from the search results for example a 'NOT' operand can be used. Your search phrase would then be 'obesity AND children AND health AND problems NOT adults'. The 'NOT' operand should be used with some caution however since you may be excluding relevant literature. For example, by searching for 'NOT adults' you would exclude all papers containing the word 'adult', even if they say that adults were not studied. Quotation marks can also be used to refine searches. This allows results to be retrieved which only contain certain phrases. For example entering "childhood obesity" will retrieve results that contain only that precise phrase.

Whereas refining searches is a useful process it is important not to be too restrictive. Using the operand 'OR' can broaden the search and attempt to account for any variation in language. For example, using the phrase 'psychological OR emotional' would retrieve results containing either of these words. Another way to broaden a search is by using a symbol at the end of a word stem which allows for all alternatives of the word. For instance, using child* will retrieve the words 'children and childhood'.

While it is useful to be aware of how Boolean operators and other truncations work in a search phrase, most advanced search options will now allow for this and will construct a search phrase for you in this way. For example Google will find resources that contain all the words in your search phrase (so it uses the 'AND' operator by default). The advanced options allow for:

- 'this exact wording or phrase' (so using quotation marks around the search phrase);
- 'one or more of these words' (so using the 'OR' operator);
- 'any of these unwanted words' (the equivalent of the 'NOT' operator).

Databases usually allow for field searching in the advanced options such as searching by author, title or year published. This is useful if you find a key author on the topic or want to restrict the search to recent years. Once a key paper has been found it is useful to look at other sources cited by the author(s). Google Scholar will show how many other papers have cited the paper and will retrieve all the papers which have cited that article via a link. It also enables the retrieval of 'related articles'.

Evaluating Web-based Sources

Not all sources found on the Web will be of equal provenance of course. While Intute, Sciencedirect, Web of Science and others referred to above will only

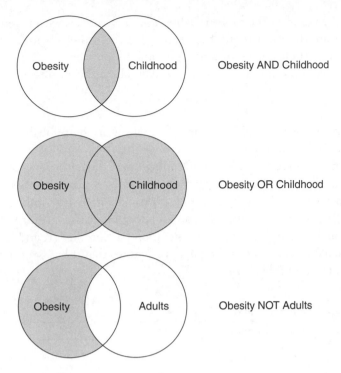

Figure 6.2   How Boolean operators work

retrieve peer-reviewed research journal articles, and policy-oriented sites will offer governmental research reports, White Papers, consultations, legitimate media reports and so on, there are thousands of other websites containing documents of variable value to serious practitioner-researchers. If you choose to use such sources then the next stage in the process is to evaluate it for usefulness or relevancy. It is necessary to carefully evaluate Web resources for quality since it is an uncontrolled environment. There are four general criteria that can be used to evaluate websites: accuracy; authority; objectivity; and currency.

Accuracy

Prior knowledge of the subject area makes it easier to determine the accuracy of a website. First, consider the remit of the website and the audience it is aimed at. Generally speaking, if the website content is concurrent with other literature in the field it is more likely to be accurate; if the content stands out it is probably less accurate (see objectivity, below). This may be because the site is sponsored by a commercial organisation with a remit to sell a service or product, or by a political party or pressure group with a particular agenda. That does not mean the information is inaccurate, however, so the second level of accuracy checking should be to consider any references (or links) the website contains to other research in the field. Generally the more references it has to research that can be found via other sources the more reliable it is likely be. However, general advice would be to use the most reputable source that cited the research (that is published research articles; governmental documents or websites; reputable media outlets) and avoid the murkier side of the Web altogether if possible.

Authority

Any reputable website should contain information on the publisher, that is, legal information about the operators of the website. Carrying out a search on the author's name can be a helpful way of finding out if the author has published any other work in this area, and if they have been cited by other authors in the field. The domain name of the website can also provide an insight into the source of the website, for example, a domain name ending in .ac.uk or .edu indicates that is has been published by an academic institution (within the UK and USA, respectively) while a domain name ending in .gov denotes that it has been published by a government body (Table 6.2).

Table 6.2   Domain names

Suffix	Types of website
.ac.uk	Academic institutions
.edu	
.gov	Government websites
.gov.uk	
.co.uk	Commercial websites
.com	
.uk	Identifies country location of websites (American sites rarely have one)
.au	
.fr	

Objectivity

As we have noted, certain websites may have an agenda and this may or may not affect the accuracy of its content. Objectivity is a different issue. The author of any Web-published documents may well be using the site to express an opinion and therefore not intending to present a balanced viewpoint. The issue is whether the author is publishing here because the research did not stand up to the required level of scrutiny for publishing in more legitimate sources, or whether the research referred to is sound but is considered 'beyond the pale' by fellow researchers (which is usually the case with radical research: much research-informed literature about global warming may have started out this way if the Web had been available in the 1960s).

To determine objectivity, the practitioner-researcher needs to look at whether the site is affiliated to any lobbying group, political party or corporate organisation. Another indication of whether a website or author has an agenda is to see whether other established researchers refer to it; if they do, the website is less likely to be heavily biased towards a certain opinion or agenda. If an agenda is explicit then judgements have to be made about whether or not information from the source can be utilised within the review. Value-laden research or information does not make it invalid, in fact very little research is non-partisan, it just requires recognition when citing the findings.

Currency

Consideration should be give to the currency of a literature source, in other words how current the source is. Although it is viable to use some older literature it is important to ensure factual information is up to date. Reputable websites should contain a date when they were created and last updated. Another useful way to determine currency is to check if any external links on the website still work.

Referencing

Referencing literature is important as it enables the reader to judge the value of any arguments that have been identified. To this purpose sourcing the data using a recognised referencing system is required. There are three main systems for presenting references: the Oxford, the Harvard and the Vancouver systems:

- The Oxford system uses footnotes and a bibliography. Footnotes are number referenced and all citation details for that page are included on the same page. A bibliography includes all the texts you have consulted rather than just those that have been referenced within the text and may include 'annotation' to provide the reader with additional information about the text.
- The Harvard system uses the author and the date of the work in the main body of the text, and an alphabetical reference list at the end of the text.
- The Vancouver system is most frequently used in medical journals; it uses a numerical reference system in which reference numbers are assigned in the order in which they appear in the text. References are not listed alphabetically or by date, but are numbered consecutively at the end of the text.

It should be noted that although academic journals tend to follow one of these systems, there are slight variations across journals. If you intend to submit your paper to an academic journal, you will find this information in the journal's author guidelines.

As the Harvard system is commonly used in social science, we will present this in further detail. Referencing involves citing all the authors whose work is referred to within the body of the text; all the reference should then be ordered alphabetically by author name at the end of the text. Within the body of the text arguments that have been taken from a source should be referenced with the author's name and the year of publication; where a quote has been used directly the reference should also include the page number, for example (Bowers-Brown and Stevens, 2009: 35). In the references section the full bibliographic details are given, for instance of a book: author name(s), date of publication, full title of the publication, location of publishers and publisher name. Below are some examples of how to reference from different sources.

Books
Author, Initial(s) (Year) *Title of Book*, Edition. Place of publication: Publisher.

Example:

Aveyard, H. (2007) *Doing a Literature Review in Health and Social Care*, 2nd edn. Buckingham: Open University Press.

Books (chapter in edited volume)
Author, Initial(s) (Year) 'Title of chapter', Editor (ed.), *Title of Book*, Edition. Place of publication: Publisher. Page range.

Example:

Aveyard, H. (2007) 'Designing a literature review', in A Smith (ed.), *Doing a Literature Review in Health and Social Care*, 2nd edn. Buckingham: Open University Press. pp. 100–24.

Journal articles
Author, Initial(s) (Year) 'Title of article', *Full Title of Journal*, Volume number (Issue/Part number): Page numbers.

Example:

Saelens, B.E., Sallis, J.F., Wilfley, D.E., Patrick. K., Cella, J.A. and Buchta, R. (2002) 'Behavioural weight control for overweight adolescents initiated in primary care', *Obesity Research*, 10: 22–32.

Journal articles from an electronic source
Author, Initial(s) (Year) 'Title of article', *Full Title of Journal*, Volume number (Issue/Part number). Website Address (Accessed date).

Example:

Viner, R. and Cole, T. (2005) 'Adult socioeconomic, educational, social, and psychological outcomes of childhood obesity: a national birth cohort study', *BMJ*, 330. Available at: http://www.bmj.com/ (accessed 15 July 2008).

Newspaper articles with named reporter
Author, Initial(s) (Year) 'Title of article', *Full Title of Newspaper*, Date: Page numbers.

Example:

Carvel, J. (2006) 'Childhood obesity has doubled in a decade', *Guardian*, 22 April: 1.

Newspaper articles without named reporter

Full Title of Newspaper (Year) 'Title of article', Date: Page numbers.

Example:

Guardian (2006) 'Childhood obesity has doubled in a decade', 22 April: 1.

Websites

Author, Initial(s) (Year) 'Title of document or page'. Website Address Locating details (Accessed date).

Example:

University of Bristol (2002) 'Issues and action in childhood obesity'. Available at: http://www.bristol.ac.uk/news/2002/obesity.htm (accessed 15 July 2008).

All website addresses (URLs) should be systematically recorded in the same way as any other published source. As resources on the Web change and move frequently you should include an accessed date. Software packages such as Endnote can be useful for storing notes about what you have read and for keeping a bibliography. Without access to this type of software package an electronic bibliography document can be created, in a word processing package if necessary. The recording document could be arranged as illustrated in Table 6.3.

Table 6.3   Recording sources

Record: 001	
Where document was found (for example, URL, Library ref no.)	www.madeupstatistics.com
Author(s)	Smith, J. and Wesson, D.
Date	2002
Name of publication	Debunking the myth of childhood obesity
Type of document (policy, book, journal article, grey literature, popular publication)	Book
Publisher details	London: Angular Books
To be included in review	Yes
Research method(s) employed	
Key findings	
Key arguments	

Conclusion

The key functions of a literature review are to set the context for your research. It should involve a synthesis of the arguments, methodologies and outcomes of research findings and current debate and policy placed within your own critical evaluation. The review forms the basis of the primary research and helps avoid unnecessary duplication, identify where replication would be useful and highlight omissions that require further investigation. The search should be systematic in so far as you have a framework for searching, collecting, collating and synthesising the literature in order to provide a coherent argument, which links previous research to your current (or proposed) research.

There are a number of resources that can be exploited to achieve a comprehensive review; the Internet serves as a good starting point. Ensure that search terms are recorded in order to revisit searches later in the research process. All the literature that has been analysed should be referenced both within the text and as a reference list at the end of the document. Once the literature review is complete you should be ready to commence with your primary research study. However, you will find that you will refer back to the literature throughout the research design process, in analysing your data and in your reporting. To this purpose it is paramount that the information you have gathered is organised in an easily accessible format.

Further Reading

Hart, C. (1998) *Doing a Literature Review*. London: Sage.
Hart offers a comprehensive guide to the literature review process. It breaks down the stages of the review, including how to gather information; structure the argument, evaluate the content and synthesise the findings. This is a core text for a number of social science courses.

Fink, A. (2005) *Conducting Research Literature Reviews: From the Internet to Paper*. London: Sage.
Fink's text is useful for its comprehensive review of undertaking literature searches using traditional methods as well as the Internet. Fink explores the use of key word search terms, Boolean operators as well as the wider questions of reliability and validating sources.

SEVEN

Action Research

Scott Fernie and Karen Smith

By the end of this chapter you should be able to:

- describe the distinctive nature of action research;
- understand the basic assumptions the underpin action research;
- make informed judgements about employing different forms of action research;
- know how to develop action research projects;
- understand how to incorporate appropriate research methods into action research;
- describe the context(s) within which action research can be applied.

Introduction

This chapter sets out to explore the content and forms of action research and provide a basic introductory guide to its practice. Due to its concerns with both action and research, *action research* is a widely used research methodology in many academic and vocational disciplines. Its emphasis on collaboration between practitioners and researchers on context-specific problems makes it a particularly attractive as a problem-solving approach and can be particularly suited to practitioner-researchers.

In order to frame action research, the chapter begins by briefly outlining and discussing the background to, and history of, action research. A section exploring and answering the question 'what is action research?' follows. This section explains the basic assumptions that underpin most action research approaches and makes clear the distinctive nature and benefits to be drawn from carrying out action research projects. The third section provides a detailed account of the different forms/types of action research and their connection to research methods. The fourth section discusses, through the use of examples, how to structure a basic action research project. Finally, the chapter concludes by providing a general discussion on the use of action research and various associated concepts and activities.

Historical Background

The historical background to action research is not entirely clear. The following draws heavily on a selective account given by Huxham and Eden (2008), McNiff and Whitehead (2002, 2006), Coghlan and Brannick (2005) and Reason (2006). The story of action research approaches begins in the 1940s. The social scientist Kurt Lewin is argued to be the first to coin the phrase 'action research' and to use the approach. His work remains heavily influential and a pivotal touchstone for many researchers interested in action research. Early adoption of action research was, however, challenged on the basis that it was not 'real' research, was open to interpretation regarding its application and lacked rigor (Smith, 2007).

The work of the Tavistock Institute in connecting the exploration of socio-technical systems with action research in the late 1960s and early 1970s helped bring about a resurgence of interest in action research. Similarly, the development of action research as an integral part of teacher education in the 1970s to form educational action research provided a significant platform for further development (McNiff and Whitehead, 2002). The use of action research began to spread throughout the 1970s and the 1980s within different academic and practitioner communities including social science, organisation studies, teaching and nursing. How action research projects play out in these disciplines differs in many respects but they do all form part of an action research movement. There is, therefore, a significant body of research and application to support the use of action research especially within public and private organisations. The shift to a service based economy that is heavily supported by professional practitioners has also served to emphasise the importance of research focused on practitioners' practice.

It is worth noting that in the last 20–30 years, action research has been interpreted very differently by different groups of people. These interpretations have led to various challenges and debates such as: the values that form and inform action research projects (for example, democracy, equality, respect and freedom); the importance of data collection; methodological assumptions; academic rigour and validity; and the legitimate 'subject' of action research projects (social, technical or socio-technical). Drawing on such debates, there is unfortunately no universally defined, widely agreed upon or 'pure' form of action research. The contextually rooted nature of the problems resists any attempt to develop a singular universally accepted form of action research.

This has not prevented the significant use of action research. Its growing importance as an approach that focused upon specific problems and social phenomena (Greenwood and Levin, 2008) of interest and relevance to professional practitioners looks set to continue. The approach, therefore, has much to offer practitioner-researchers looking to solve their perceived contextually rooted problems and to improve the relevance of academic research to practice. Action research is now undoubtedly a well-established research approach particularly noted for its emphasis on practitioners, practice, action and reflection but, what is it exactly?

What Is Action Research?

There are many definitions of action research provided in the literature. Together with Costello (2003), Greenwood and Levin (2007), Reason and Bradbury (2008) and other contributors, the following list gives a number of useful characteristics of action research for practitioners to consider such as:

(1) Action research is meant to be practical and accessible.
(2) It can be done by anyone.
(3) It may or may not involve more than one person.
(4) Reflection, research and action form its basis.
(5) Action research aims to change practice.
(6) The research is problem driven.
(7) It involves participation and is cyclical.

These aspects are further considered below to understand their central place in any action research project. Judging from the list given above, however, it should be clear that action research is quite different from many other research approaches that frequently appear to be inaccessible to everyday practitioners. We can all intervene to take action in a situation and see whether that intervention has improved practice. Research is not necessarily the sole domain of academia and professional research institutes – practitioners are also legitimate researchers.

'Action' in Action Research

First and foremost, as a practitioner interested in carrying out an action research project, it is useful to focus upon the 'action' aspect of action research. This is arguably its greatest asset. Connecting ideas with action presents opportunities to intentionally strive for specific radical or incremental change. Action research is thus a form of social research that is concerned with changing social practice for the better (Alasuutari, 1998). This occurs within social contexts, such as taking action to change, for example:

(1) production practices to affect productivity improvements within a manufacturing organisation;
(2) trade union practices to improve the working conditions of members across an industry sector;
(3) nursing practices to improve patient care within a hospital or;
(4) teaching practices to better engage students in a classroom.

The scope for conducting action research is significant. The emphasis on making substantive and sustainable changes to social practices and/or contexts must be borne in mind by those considering its use.

Who Does Action Research?

Action research is primarily concerned with 'people taking action to improve their personal and social situations' (McNiff and Whitehead, 2002: 12). The use of 'people' is a deliberate choice of language in the context of action research because it frees action research from the domain of professional academic researchers (otherwise known as 'official researchers') (McNiff and Whitehead, 2002). This means that anyone can do it. 'People' doing action research also act to liberate research (as something that official researchers do) from the sometimes complex and confusing language of professional researchers and places it closer to practice – where it is much needed. The language used by 'people' rather than professional researchers in action research makes action research much more accessible to practitioners (Stringer, 2007). There are also fewer pressures placed upon action researchers to publish their findings in traditional academic domains. They may choose to do this but it is not entirely necessary since action research is not primarily concerned with seeking generalisable explanations that would be interesting to the wider academic community.

Action research is principally concerned with explanations related to solving practical problems which are experienced in specific contexts by particular people (Stringer 2007). Drawing upon Kemmis, 'action research is research into one's own practice' and as such 'it follows that only practitioners and groups of practitioners can carry out action research' (2007: 176). Fundamental to these practitioners is the formation of 'communicative space' (Kemmis, 2007) or 'arena's for dialogue' (Greenwood and Levin, 2007) within action research projects. Within such space, fundamental aspects of action research inquiry such as democracy and participation evolve. Such spaces may also be coupled with problems and issues for practitioners to consider such as power, politics, time and tensions related to the facilitation of groups (Reason, 2006). How such space is developed and managed is therefore fundamental to the success of action research. The following four characteristics sum up an action research process of inquiry that shapes the communicative space:

> democratic, enabling the participation of people … equitable, acknowledging people's equality of worth … liberating, providing freedom from oppressive, dehabilitating conditions and … life enhancing, enabling the expression of people's full human potential. (Stringer, 2007: 11)

Undoubtedly, the ability to understand and change social practice should lie predominantly with those who practise practice – the practitioners. In the main, practitioners do lead action research projects to address the problems that concern them – not (solely) academic researchers. In explaining the rise in popularity of action research in the last 30 years it is this practitioner friendly, practitioner oriented and focused aspect of research that makes it attractive and useful to practitioners.

Action research is thus dominantly practitioner-led and highly responsive to their interpretations of dynamic and changing social problems and phenomena. It can change shape, form and focus over the course of a project and the emergent nature of questions and answers provides an ongoing cycle of reflection and research. In action research, practitioners are the researchers and can be referred to as 'insider researchers' who are part of the situation they are investigating (McNiff and Whitehead, 2006). Ethnography aside, few other forms of social research provide research with the opportunity to get so close to practice. Most other forms of social research use an 'outsider researcher' who observes rather than acts to change social practice: they are spectators. An 'outsider researcher' tries to develop and/or explore theory whereas an insider researcher in action research attempts to challenge taken-for-granted assumptions and change embedded institutionalised routines.

The persuasive nature of knowledge created by insider researchers that are close to practice means that practitioner-led action research will have a significant impact on everyday lives. Such research need not only involve a single practitioner though. Action research could involve numerous practitioners working collaboratively on one action research project. While the practitioner(s) in some action research projects are researchers, in other forms of action research, the practitioner may work collaboratively with a professional action researcher (Greenwood and Levin, 2007). Collaborative action research, such as this, is commonplace within organisation studies and has a dual focus that is concerned with changing social practice *and* exploring and developing academic theory. Such research will ask both 'official researcher' and 'practitioner as researcher' questions. For example, drawing on McNiff and Whitehead's (2006) distinction between social science questions and action research questions, the following Table 7.1 demonstrates the differences and similarities between such questions in collaborative action research.

Table 7.1   Collaborative action research questions

'Official researcher' questions	'Practitioner as researcher' questions
What is the relationship between teacher motivation and teacher retention?	How do I influence the quality of teachers' experiences in school, so that they decide to stay?
Does management style influence worker productivity?	How do I improve my management style to encourage productivity?
Will a different seating arrangement increase audience participation?	How do I encourage greater audience participation through trying out different seating arrangements?

Collaborative action research involves both an insider and outsider researcher. The real value of such collaboration is in the way in which the connection between theory and practice is explored and contextually rooted. Notably, both practitioner and 'official researcher' become the researchers in action research and indeed, practitioners. They bring different perspectives to the social research problem and provide a richness to research that cannot typically be achieved outside of such collaboration. Both practitioner and 'official researcher' benefit greatly from such collaboration. Collaborative action research, therefore, requires negotiation between practitioner and 'official researcher' to determine the problem, aims and objectives of the research. Typically such research will attempt to address both 'practice', theory and their connection as a way to satisfy the concerns and interests of all project participants. Action research cannot however be solely considered to be concerned with just solving specific problems, it must also, as Reason (2006) puts it, be about articulating the subtle ways in which the inquiry is affecting our world. In this sense, action research projects frequently have unintended consequences that are just as significant and fascinating as any solution to the original problem set out in the project. It is therefore necessary to be sensitive to these consequences arising through the process as distinct from the original intended outcomes.

In summary, action research may involve people doing research in isolation on their own practice, or in collaboration with others that may include other practitioners or professional researchers. What binds these people together is a concern to understand, change and learn about practice, and to address problems of immediate and apparent relevance. The question surrounding who to involve in action research projects will largely depend upon: who is motivated and empowered to make change happen; the problem situation, available resources and networks. Who to involve and the roles they play within the research can therefore differ considerably across action research projects.

Different Types of Action Research

Many different approaches or types of action research exist, reflecting differences in purpose. Despite being somewhat dated, Carr and Kemmis' (1986) contribution provides a helpful typology for those new to action research, which includes technical, practical and critical perspectives. These perspectives are useful to begin to comprehend some of the disparities between action research approaches and also to highlight what Kemmis (2007) describes as their 'teleoaffective structure' (see Schatzki, 2002), that is, their overall structure and purpose as 'projects' for the people involved.

In technical action research projects, the main outcome is clear, unambiguous and undisputed. For example, the outcome of a technical action research project may be to improve the performance of athletes as a consequence of working with a dietician. The means of achieving this outcome, the practitioners practice, forms the focus of such research. Such research is aligned with the concerns of the practitioner, described by Kemmis (2007) as practitioner-researchers or as described previously – insider researcher. There is less concern with 'others' involved in the research such as other practitioners or 'official researchers'. Decision making, data collection, analysis and interpretation are under the control of the practitioner regardless of who else is involved in the research process. Indeed, there need not necessarily be anyone else directly involved in the research. Practical action research, in contrast, shifts slightly away from the overly dominant position of the practitioner to a process of research where the practitioner is concerned with the effect of any action taken on others and indeed their view on the process of decision making, data collection, analysis and interpretation. As such, both the means and ends (outcomes) of practical action research become more open to debate but, importantly, still lie within the control of the practitioner.

Take, for example, an athlete, his dietician and coach between whom active participation would be likely. In this scenario, action taken to alter the practice of the dietician would be to some extent negotiated with the athlete and coach and possibly evaluated more broadly to include the effect of the action on each other's practice. The dominance however would still be on the dietician's practice and the athlete's performance. Critical action research shifts this dominance still further away from the practitioner to a position where full consensus regarding decision making, data collection, analysis and interpretation is sought among numerous practitioners. Critical action research is argued to involve participants who are actively seeking to 'change their social world collectively, by thinking about it differently, acting differently, and relating to one another differently' (Kemmis, 2007: 10). Significant discussion, dialogue and debate would ensue between the active participants with maybe even more participants being included in the group. The outcome, actions taken and process of research and evaluation would have to be determined through consensus and agreement.

Carr and Kemmis' (1986) typology also resonates with a similar typology used by Reason and Bradbury (2008) whereby first-, second- and third-person research/practice labels are used describe action research practices. Both typologies, however, concede to the notion that critical or third-person action research is more rigorous for being grounded in prior technical/practical and first-/second-person action research respectively. It is perhaps wise to think about where you might intend to begin your action research project and to be sure that you can explain and provide a rational for the limitations for your adopted approach. This should at least allow new action researchers an ability to set out some form of scope for their inquiries and to assess to what extent goals and objectives are achievable.

In the typology above, the emphasis on practitioners does not necessarily exclude professional academic researchers being considered as just another practitioner in an action research project. Indeed, it is common practice for action research projects to involve academic researchers in the capacity of professional action researchers. For the purposes of this chapter, an emphasis has been placed upon action research that typically involves researchers and practitioners. It is described by some as participatory action research (PAR) (see McIntyre, 2008) in that the research predominantly revolves around central themes of participation and collaboration. We have also used the term collaborative action research in this chapter to mean the same thing. Notably, others view PAR as associated with a distinctive branch of action research that is not necessarily connected to organisation studies (see Coghlan and Brannick, 2005). We will briefly return to this debate later but, for practitioners looking to get involved in action research and to initiate their own studies, it is more important at this point to become familiar and comfortable with the basic tenets of action research set out below.

'Research' in Action Research

The main purpose of action research is clearly to make change happen and to learn from experience. The ability to actively take action and make change happen lies with practitioners' interpretations of a problem and their motivations to do research and enquire into their own practice. Similar to research in general, action research is characterised by the existence of a problem or issue that is perceived to exist; an adherence to some form of inquiry process to provide rigor and validity; and a search for explanations (Stringer, 2007). Constantly drawing upon these basic characteristics of research is an extremely useful way for practitioners to think about research.

It is perhaps useful to think of action research as a research process largely mirroring the experimental research methods used in the physical sciences – as a quasi-experimental research approach if you like. For example, a scientist puts a small piece of sodium into a beaker of water and then observes how the sodium bounces and fizzes over the surface of the water as it reacts, giving off energy until it disappears. This experiment could be compared with a larger-scale one where a bigger piece of sodium is used resulting a more violent reaction or even an explosion. In the same way that variables are altered within a controlled experiment to test their effect, specific changes to social practice/context are implemented through action research projects as ways to address specific social phenomena or problems. For example, a librarian working in a local library may take action to change specific aspects of how (s)he works with borrowers in response to poor scores in a customer satisfaction survey. These changes would then be assessed to see whether customer satisfaction had improved. Or alternatively, a manager may take action to change current processes and practices of communication within an organisation to address issues of recurrent internal conflict and observe the subsequent changes in how people interact with each other. Thus, action researchers share activities such as searching for variables, making changes and recording the effect in much the same way as experimental researchers – the white lab coat is optional.

While it is useful to initially think of action research as quasi-experimentation it must be understood to be fundamentally different in specific ways. Notably, it is concerned with actively changing social practice within messy and complicated contexts in which people live and, in exploring the specific dynamics of such change in flight, change that has been provoked through the action taken by the practitioner (Alasuutari, 1998). You should also bear in mind that while taking specific action to change practice is similarly unpredictable in its outcome to experiments, the consequences and changes emerging from actions within an action research project can carry certain risks. Indeed, changes may be unwanted, irreversible and/or irrelevant. Once actions have changed social practice, it is difficult, if not impossible, to reset such practice back to its previous position in time and space. It is therefore crucial to fully consider the ethical issues inherent in taking action, to ask the ethics questions raised in Chapter 4, and to pay careful attention to the anticipated consequences arising from such action.

Action research is also value laden in that, as an insider researcher, practitioners (including professional researchers) in action research projects bring their values to the way research is framed and conducted. It is argued by some that insider researchers contaminate research and give it a specific bias. Action research projects, however, embrace the values and bias that practitioners bring to research as something that provides guiding principles for the study. These values are important in shaping and framing action research questions that matter to practitioners and in determining those actions that will achieve specific value laden change in specific circumstances. You should, however, recognise that you bring these biases into your research and remember that certain values held by individuals may be considered less ethically or morally responsible in contemporary societies such as racism or discrimination. Insider research can also be perceived to be subversive and the results potentially threatening for some people (Coghlan and Brannick, 2005). You will need to be politically astute as to how you deal with the different groups of people within your organisation because you will have to carry on working with them after the project has finished. Again ethical considerations must be carefully considered within action research projects. Closely related to ethical issues are power and politics. Simply put action research projects are conducted within organisations that have associated values, culture, power dynamics and politics. These will all have an effect on the implementation of any course of action and therefore must be thought through carefully.

Basic Models and Processes of Action Research

One of the most famous and enduring model of action research is that offered by Kurt Lewin in the 1940s. It is a very basic model that others since have used, adapted and extended. The model is represented in Figure 7.1.

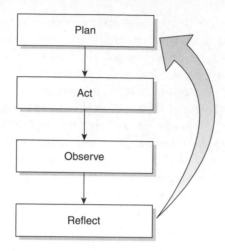

Figure 7.1   A basic action research model
Source: Adapted from Costello (2003: 7).

The cyclic nature of action research is apparent from this model and helps to frame the following basic action research process (Table 7.2).

Table 7.2   Cyclical action research

PLAN	A practitioner or practitioners (if a group of practitioners are involved) possibly in conjunction with an 'official researcher' (if it is collaborative) thinks about, discusses and negotiates the concerns and issues of a particular situation or problem.
ACT	The action research team then develops actions (changes to practice) intended to address and improve the situation/problem and then plans how such changes should be implemented, monitored and observed. These plans would then be put into action.
OBSERVE	Using different methods, data is collected to evaluate the success of the actions.
REFLECT	The results of these observations are reflected on critically and further plans explored to address the problem if required and therefore beginning the action research cycle once more. Indeed the process may throw up a variety of new, unexpected and complex research questions demanding an entirely new action research project.

Many other models and processes exist (see Costello, 2003; Stringer, 2007) but, they all seem to be informed by Lewin. The appeal of Lewin's basic model is its simplicity and the fact that it can be adopted very easily by practitioners in the workplace as a way to develop their professional practice. The model and process do not necessarily require professional level research skills as a prerequisite for carrying out this style of research. This does not, however, indicate that action research projects and practitioners' concerns and interests would not benefit from 'official researchers'' expertise. It does indicate however that action research can continue in the absence of such expertise.

For practitioners new to action research, the model and process above provides a useful starting point. It is inevitable that as experience with using this model develops, practitioners or research teams will begin to develop their own specific model and process. The point is that it is easy to get started with action research and that the process of reflection needs to be directed at both the content of the action research study and the process in the early stages of adoption. Action research in use can be an evolving approach that is highly reactive to emergent findings. This flexibility provides significant benefits to professional practitioners keen to explore and develop their everyday practice in relation to their perceived everyday problems

While Kemmis' (2007) typology was used earlier to broadly frame action research approaches with respect to purpose, Coghlan and Brannick (2005) talk of action research approaches as either having developed from sociology where the emphasis is on social change within the community (social exclusion, power, politics, control) or behavioural science where the emphasis is on social change within organisations. This is mirrored by Huxham and Eden's (2008) two schools; social action and organisational research. While the former addresses social issues regarding emancipation, empowerment, social inequalities and injustice, it is to the latter that this chapter is focused as the emphasis is on practitioners within organisational contexts seeking to transform their practice. As explained earlier, we also view the focus of the chapter to be loosely based around participatory action research. This does not, however, discount the bewildering array of alternative approaches, associated concepts and terminology used to describe action research such as critical participatory action research, feminist participatory action research, participative inquiry, action inquiry, action science, traditional action research, action learning, developmental action inquiry, cooperative inquiry, collaborative action research and insider action research.

The focus here is to get you started and familiar with the basics of action research. Remember, it need not be consumed by academic language, aims, objectives and values. It is to some extent about breaking down the barriers and perceived separation between theory and practice, academics and practitioners, and the subject and object of research. Theory is *not* solely the domain of academics and, we all practise some form of practice.

Action Research and Research Methods

Research methods are largely designed to collect specific data relating to the nature of the problem under investigation. As an approach, action research does not favour one research method over another. Indeed, the flexibility inherent in action research and its cyclic nature mean that over time various research methods may be employed as findings emerge from the study. In other words, as a better understanding of the problem emerges from action research, so too will the research method used to collect data relevant to the problem(s).

Action research may, therefore, employ any number of research methods considered by the participants to be relevant to the problem under study such as: interviews, focus groups, observations, reflective journals, questionnaires and surveys. The dominant method used in action research, however, is interviews. The main advantage of using semi-structured or unstructured interviews is in the way in which they allow an opportunity for those being interviewed to describe the problem and situation in their own terms. This allows a much richer understanding of the problem and potential relevant solutions to emerge. How to conduct such interviews and avoid various pitfalls, such as leading questions, is covered in Chapter 9.

Reflection in Action Research

Reflection is the key activity that brings together the action and the research in action research (Coghlan and Brannick, 2005: 37). It is through the process of reflection that you will be able to plan for future action based on your concrete experience and your observations around those experiences. Reflective processes challenge you to stand back from your experiences and to ask questions about what was happening, why, and what you are going to do the next time. It is, as Gordon notes: 'identifying the gap between what I claim and what I know' (2001: 247). This inquiry might lead you to question your original beliefs and understandings and then to use these new understandings to plan new actions (Martin, 2001: 168). You can develop your reflective practices through the maintenance of a research diary. In this diary you note your observations and your experiences and your way of understanding them (see Chapter 10). By being critically reflective of your research, you will learn more about the question you are pursuing and yourself.

Action Research in Action: Some Examples

An action research example, drawn from our own experience of collaborating on an action research project within the context of higher education, is presented in Table 7.3. Scott, a lecturer in construction management, was positioned in the practitioner role and Karen, as a higher education researcher, the 'official researcher'. However, as with any action research project of course, both of us were actually the researchers in this project.

Action research can also involve different configurations of researchers. In a study aiming to improve the health and work environment for 3500 bus drivers in Denmark, the research team included externally funded researchers, two bus drivers, two managers and an employee from Copenhagen Traffic. During the project, more than 200 interventions were made and their impact on health and the work environment were evaluated through the scrutiny data

Table 7.3 An action research example

PLAN	As a practitioner (lecturer), Scott experienced difficulty getting his students to become more involved in his lectures. His class were overly quiet and students were reluctant to enter into debate and answer questions asked of them. The lectures were not fun for either Scott or the students and on this basis alone – unsustainable. This lack of involvement and fun coupled with the style of lecture was considered by Scott to be highly influential with respect to students' overall performance on assessments. In discussions with Karen, an educational developer and the 'official researcher' in this example, the problem was considered to be all about the wider concept of student engagement. The problem also extended to incorporate issues surrounding how education developers (Karen) relate to and help lecturers (such as poor old Scott) improve teaching quality and continuously reflect on their practice.

Note, however, that Scott need not have involved an 'official researcher'. In the circumstances, Scott and Karen felt that collectively they would benefit more from collaborative action research than working on their concerns and interests in isolation. If you do not have ready access to an 'official researcher' or, do not see the value of involving one, this is perfectly acceptable. Indeed, it may be preferable and more likely to succeed without such involvement.

Through discussion, both practitioner and 'official researcher' conceptualisations of the problem were negotiated between Scott and Karen. Notably, the interests of both Scott and Karen are represented and form the basis for developing questions and action. The questions that emerged from early discussions included the following:

- Will activity/problem-based approaches help improve the experience and performance of students?
- How do activity/problem-based approaches relate to engagement?
- Is action research a suitable model for education development?

The emphasis on action is, however, heavily influenced by practitioner concerns and interests as the whole point is to take action that improves the experience and performance of Scott's students. The nature of the action taken is also heavily influenced by an understanding of the context within which the action will take place – that is, number of students, type of classroom, level of students, what other lecturers do with the students and the form of assessment.

ACT	In negotiation and over many meetings, Scott and Karen devised a plan of action that was designed to answer the questions, address the problems and change practice. The main action was to be taken by Scott in shifting his dominant teaching approach towards more problem/activity-based classes. This heavily influenced Scott's teaching practice and the ways in which he previously attempted to engage the students. It involved weekly research by the students; debates in class among students and with Scott; games, student presentations and a much looser structure over how the class would run on the day. Relinquishing control in this sense would therefore not have been suitable for all lecturers or indeed in any situation. The action was designed to specifically suit Scott and the context within which his problem was rooted.

The risks were also weighed up by both Scott and Karen regarding what could go wrong, how the action would affect the students and their studies and indeed whether such action would lead to poorer student engagement and performance – and if so, how would that be addressed. There was also a plan devised between Scott and Karen regarding how the changes to Scott's practice would be implemented. The plan included details of the kinds of alternative activities that would be deployed to support the changes to practice. It also included details surrounding what data would be collected, who would collect the data and how it would be collected and analysed. This provides the basis of observation that was to follow.

(Continued)

Table 7.3	(Continued)
OBSERVE	A number of methods were used to observe and monitor. First, Karen regularly observed Scott in class taking action towards adopting a new teaching approach and all the changes to practice that required. These were fed back to Scott regularly as the basis of making small changes to practice to improve performance. Second, Karen set up a number of focus groups with the students to explore their collective experience of the shift in teaching approach. These were recorded for analysis. Similarly, Karen interviewed five of the students on an individual basis to record views, opinions and interpretations. These were also collected in class through feedback mechanisms. Lastly, the performance of students completing the assessment were analysed and compared to previous years.

In other words, there was significant data collected that could either be analysed very simply and/or in-depth to provide a basis for determining whether the changes to practice had effectively changed (improved) practice. Less data could have been collected but the purpose in this action research project was to answer both 'official researcher' and practitioner questions. |
| REFLECT | The process of reflection in this action research project was very intensive and involved both Karen and Scott meeting on a regular basis to explore the results from the data analysis as it emerged. These meetings formed a similar framework to that of the diary approach mentioned earlier in this chapter. They framed the process of critical reflection on the research and allowed us to learn more about the questions we were pursuing and why they were relevant. They were also continuously in the process of writing up the research for a number of audiences that took the form of reports, papers and presentations. These similarly acted as reflective acts and framed and gave purpose to our reflections on the research.

Notably, the changes to practice were instrumental in improving engagement and performance of the students. The reflection threw up a number of significant issues of interest to both Karen and Scott. This action research project therefore continues. It has, however, dramatically changed scope based on such reflection. New and unexpected questions have arisen that now require more attention. Of course, this need not have been the case but it frequently is with action research. |

from multiple sources. The interventions were found to have decreased stress levels and body pain, increased job satisfaction and improved the drivers' cabins (Poulsen et al., 2007).

Fine and Torre (2006) describe a participatory action research project that was designed to evaluate a college-in-prison programme for women in a maximum security prison. Here the research team included prison-based and university-based women. Their study continued for four years and included archival research, focus groups and interviews. The findings from the research project have been disseminated with the aim of highlighting the importance of education in prisons and some progress has been made in this area in the USA where the research was carried out.

These examples are not meant to be overly prescriptive but to give you a flavour of what action research looks like in practice. Read them with a view to understanding how anyone can engage in such research. Think of a problem or issue you are experiencing and try to imagine how the following examples could form the basis of helping you address and improve these problems or issues.

Conclusion: Recommendations for Your Consideration

This chapter has attempted to introduce action research to the keen and uninitiated in a way that will engage you. The intention is to help and encourage you to view research not as something that others do but as something that anyone can do. It is fortunate that action research lends itself easily to this task and indeed, there are few other research approaches that can effectively bridge the gap or level the playing field between academics and practitioners in quite the same way. Before finishing this chapter we would like to offer a number of 'tips' for future action research practitioners to help guide the way and also to keep it simple:

- Focus on an issue that is of interest and importance to all involved in the research team. A lack of interest leads to problems of procrastination, tension and conflict.
- Be aware that it takes time to do this sort of work and be prepared to commit adequate resources.
- If it is a collaborative action research approach involving practitioners and 'official researchers' you should play to each other's strengths.
- Take every opportunity to talk to people outside the research team about your work – such as seminars, internal conferences, dissemination events, team meetings. The more you are forced to talk about the research the more you reflect upon your findings and their potential for change.
- Identify mutually beneficial joint aims for all in the research team at the start of the project – you need these to get full commitment.
- Be curious enough to go beyond data collection – it is with the analysis that the fun really starts.

Further Reading

Costello, P.J.M. (2003) *Action Research*. London: Continuum.
Coghlan, D. and Brannick, T. (2005) *Doing Action Research in Your Own Organization*. London: Sage.
Stringer, E.T. (2007) *Action Research*. Thousand Oaks, CA: Sage.
There is no shortage of books on action research, but the most useful and accessible for practitioners new to research are probably Costello, Coghlan and Brannick, and Stringer. These offer good entry level texts to a readership other than academics and provide a good level of detail for practitioners to initiate and complete an action research project.

Reason, P. and Bradbury, H. (2008) 'Introduction', in P. Reason and H. Bradbury (eds), *The Sage Handbook of Action Research*. London: Sage. pp. 1–10.
There are also a number of other highly influential books that provide significant expert advice for action researchers seeking to develop their research approach. These include Reason and Bradbury's *Handbook of Action Research*, which has significant

(Continued)

(Continued)

detail about methodological trends, traits and arguments within the field coupled with explanations regarding the challenges and skills required to execute action research. The handbook also provides numerous case studies of action research used throughout the world within areas ranging from poetry to power, leadership to stress and health to policy.

Greenwood, D.J. and Levin, M. (2007) *Introduction to Action Research*. Thousand Oaks, CA: Sage.

Greenwood and Levin offer an introduction to action research for those seeking to gain some perspective on action research. While their work focuses particularly on higher education institutes it does nonetheless provide an insight into the origins and generic characteristics of action research. Coghlan and Brannick's (2005) book also provides guidance and experience to those looking to research their own organisation through action research and provides a good set of checklists and tips for readers to follow.

McNiff, J. (2002) 'Action research for professional development: concise advice for new action researchers'. Available at: http://www.jeanmcniff.com/booklet1.html (accessed 30 November 2009).

McNiff, J. and Whitehead, J. (2006) *All You Need to Know About Action Research*. London: Sage.

McNiff and Whitehead (2006), coupled with McNiff's useful website, is also extremely useful for those new yet keen to use action research.

Reason, P. (2006) 'Choice and quality in action research practice', *Journal of Management Inquiry*, 15 (2): 187–203.

For those looking to explore in greater detail some of the issues that action researchers need to address and a framework of dimensions to help evaluate quality in action research, a reading of Reason's article would prove very useful.

Dick, B., Stringer, E.T. and Huxham, C. (2009) 'Theory in action research', *Action Research*, 7 (1): 5–12.

Finally, for those keen to develop a high level of understanding concerning action research theory, the journal *Action Research* and, in particular, a recent special issue in this journal on 'theory in action research' (see Dick et al., 2006) will provide the necessary food for thought.

EIGHT

Different Kinds of Qualitative Data Collection Methods

Maria Smith and Tamsin Bowers-Brown

By the end of this chapter you should be able to:

- understand the meaning of qualitative research;
- understand the kinds of questions that can be addressed with qualitative research;
- identify different qualitative techniques;
- know which qualitative methods are appropriate for your research project.

Introduction

This chapter offers an introduction to qualitative research. There is guidance on the advantages to the researcher-practitioner taking a qualitative approach to a research study, the kinds of questions qualitative research can answer and the ways that it can complement other methodological approaches.

There is an array of qualitative methods that can be used when conducting research, some of which are more applicable to certain types of questions than others. Unfortunately, there are no hard and fast rules and it is up to you to weigh up advantages and disadvantages, and to adopt the method or methods that seem to fit with your aims and questions. Therefore to help the practitioner-researcher decide which method(s) are the most appropriate for their particular project, this chapter discusses some of the most commonly used qualitative methods and explores how these methods are likely to play out in the field (although there is much greater detail on the process and analysis of qualitative research in Chapters 9 and 10). The main focus will be on semi-structured interviewing and focus groups, two of the most common methods that are likely to be used by practitioner-researchers. However, the chapter also discusses the uses of unstructured interviewing, observation, diaries and documentary analysis.

Furthermore, the chapter considers the more practical elements of conducting qualitative research, such as access to participants, sensitivity of approach and cost implications. The aim of this chapter is to provide an understanding and 'feel' for qualitative research.

Understanding Qualitative Research

Chapter 2 has already suggested ways of distinguishing between qualitative and quantitative research and warned that much of the discussion about the differences between qualitative and quantitative approaches is over-simplistic and describes two diametrically opposed methodologies and accompanying theoretical positions. In reality, there are many researchers who use both approaches and are aware of the uses and advantages of both methods.

Qualitative research is about looking at the depth information involved in an issue; Flick expresses qualitative research as seeking 'to contribute to a better understanding of social realities and to draw attention to processes, meaning, patterns and structural features' (2009: 1). Qualitative research attempts to interpret meanings, emotions, behaviours and/or perceptions by 'analysing concrete cases in their temporal and local particularity and starting from people's expressions and activities in their local contexts' (Flick, 2009: 30). Practitioner-researchers are therefore well placed to conduct qualitative research as they often have ready access to research participants in their local contexts.

Qualitative research produces data that informs us about the nature or the 'quality' of people's lives, circumstances or situations. As a rule, if your research question includes the words 'how' or 'why' or you wish to explore ideas and experiences with your participants, then qualitative research is likely to be the approach that you want to use. For example, if you are conducting research about a school cohort that has participated in widening participation events at a higher education institution you may want to use an interview or focus group method. Either of these methods will help you to understand how pupils' viewed certain aspects of the activities; using an interview would garner individual responses about personal preferences or dislikes while a focus group would help you to understand the range of experiences and perhaps a collective group experience.

There is no single accepted way of undertaking qualitative research. Rather, it depends on the researcher's beliefs about the social world and what they think can be discovered about it (Snape and Spencer, 2003). As these beliefs vary considerably, so too do the beliefs about how data can be interpreted. One of the defining features of qualitative research is that it is broadly associated with what is referred to as the interpretivist sociological tradition, an approach that begins from the premise that society itself is a human construct in a continuous process of revision and rebuilding (Becker and Bryman, 2004). Qualitative research looks at the world in depth and aims to uncover reality, as seen from the eyes of the research participants themselves or, in other words, by examining life worlds 'from the inside out' (Flick, 2009). The core aim of qualitative research is to make sense of the social world through interpretation, thus qualitative research penetrates beneath everyday life to reveal the reality that lies underneath (Woods, 1988).

Many qualitative researchers are therefore interested in the life history of their research participants. Bolton argues that our nature as humans is 'storied', and that we are brought up surrounded by stories which tell 'us who we are and where we belong, what is right and what is wrong' (2006: 205). As a practitioner-researcher you may find that exploring the life stories of your participants can be a valuable tool. For example if you are researching transitions to higher education then it will be important to understand the educational life history, along with other influencing factors such as family background, peer group or childhood experiences of your research participant in order to understand how this has impacted upon the choices they have made.

Another defining feature of qualitative research is that it is generally seen to be 'inductive' that is, ideas, concepts and theories tend to grow and develop from the data as opposed to being fixed and in place before the data is collected (Becker and Bryman, 2004: 248). Qualitative research is also advantageous because it can be adapted organically. Looking again at our research into widening participation events at higher education institutions, you may begin to think that it is important to know what young people think of the university campus but discover that in fact they actually report fears about making new friendship groups once they get to university. Therefore, what facilities are available within the institution or pupils' opinions of them is relatively unimportant. Thus, the qualitative researcher allows the research findings to lead 'from the ground up, rather than handed down entirely from a theory or from the perspectives of the enquirer' (Creswell, 2007: 19). However as Strauss and Corbin (1990) argue, within an effective piece of research, data should be explored through a combination of induction, deduction, and verification and that all parts are absolutely essential (see also Chapter 2 in this volume).

When conducting qualitative research, it is important that you consider your own moral, ethical, political or emotional position about the research question. This is rather clumsily called your 'positionality', and essentially means recognising and acknowledging where you stand on an issue. Very often, the reason for pursuing an area of research is intrinsically intertwined with a researcher's own values or experiences (Carspecken, 1996). It is important to remember that holding up a pretence of value neutrality is not always helpful and it can lead to the research being misread. It is important to be honest about the reasons for investigating an issue but it is equally necessary to conduct research without pursuing a desired outcome. Without an open mind, evidence may be lost, or important issues neglected. This is not to say 'anything goes' but as May makes clear 'procedures through which we understand and interpret our social world are now necessary conditions for us to undertake research' (2001: 15). Therefore a balance is needed in both acknowledging your 'positionality' and maintaining professional practice (see Chapter 4).

Given the importance of acknowledging one's own 'positionality', some qualitative researchers prefer to write in the first person because they accept that the argument is theirs and a different outcome would be likely if someone else had conducted the research. Humphreys bemoans the writing of research in the third person as such:

> This world is inhabited by scholars who teach, research, publish, and often conceal their presence within third-person research accounts. (2005: 843)

Furthermore, Becker concurs that use of the passive voice 'conceals any traces of the ordinary human activity which produces results' (1987: 36) and therefore removes any personal attachment or responsibility for the findings or statement that is being made. In some instances you may feel that your research will only be accepted by your practitioner community if it has been written in a way that appears 'neutral', that is, in the third person. Therefore, you will need to consider which method is more effective for your research purpose.

The boundaries of qualitative research are set to achieve an understanding of the issues involved within a subject rather than being able to quantify the extent to which the findings are applicable across the population. Therefore, you can make claims about the findings based on the specific location of the research, but it does not mean that a general claim can be made about the likelihood of the same results being found across wider groups. Qualitative research tends to be small scale and to have small sample sizes primarily because in having a small sample size the researcher is able to concentrate on producing in-depth data that gets at the real experiences, thoughts and feelings of participants. Silverman refers to this as a 'sacrifice of scope for detail' (2006: 229). A small sample size is something that is often criticised by the quantitative research community and findings drawn from small sample sizes may have limited acceptability in the broader research community (Crouch and McKenzie, 2006). However, qualitative researchers such as Ball argue the case for 'working small', he values the 'events and specifics and locations, in contingencies, concatenations and contexts, in the odd as much as the typical' (2006: 4). This emphasises the point that qualitative research is seeking factors of interest that may be found in only a single case rather than trying to find widespread evidence that can be generalised.

Qualitative research will be particularly useful for practitioner-researchers who are likely to have immediate access to some research participants, for example user groups such as patients in a hospital or tenants in a housing complex. However, it is important to think about the research you could undertake by consulting non-users as well as those who engage with your services, this might include, for example, whether measures should be implemented to engage people who feel marginalised and that they are not catered for. Qualitative research can be useful for evaluating projects through investigating people's experiences of that project, for consultations on proposed policy implementations as well as in the development of new strategies or policies. It is useful to look at some of the advantages of using a qualitative approach in order to decide whether it will help you to address your research questions.

Advantages of Qualitative Research

There are a number of advantages in conducting qualitative social research. These are highlighted in Table 8.1 and discussed further below.

Table 8.1   Advantages of qualitative research

Advantage	Detail
Exploration	If research is done an under-researched area we may not know which questions to ask straight away and therefore qualitative research would be much more appropriate than quantitative research. It helps the researcher to explore the area in an open manner before developing a more nuanced approach (if so desired).
Detail	You may require a detailed explanation to understand an issue.
Access	It is easier to reach 'hard to reach' groups using qualitative methods, for example, homeless people, youth groups, or individuals with literacy problems.
Sensitivity	When something is taboo, delicate or intimate then people may need an approach which builds trust and confidence before responding to such issues.
In the development of quantitative methods	Asking open-ended questions through a focus group or interview can help you to develop a more nuanced structured questionnaire through which you would attempt to find out how widespread the issue is.
Cost	The cost is in 'time resource', that is, practitioner researcher time rather than in equipment costs.

Exploration

Within qualitative research there is the opportunity for the practitioner-researcher to explore new issues as they are uncovered in the fieldwork stage. Thus, the researcher is not bound and tied by a pre-determined set of questions or assumptions and can pursue areas of interest as they arise. Often interviews can meander off what was initially thought of as the main point and this can reveal some of the underlying assumptions of the interviewee, greatly adding to the data you can gather. For example, you may be conducting interviews with residents on an estate with outdated housing stock with the aim of discovering how the condition or size/layout of the physical buildings affects day-to-day life. However, in the first few interviews, it becomes apparent that it is not the housing that is perceived as problematic but the lack of public transport to the area and the poor local facilities that cause concern. Thus, the researcher is free to explore these issues at depth and will learn more than if he or she had simply continued with the line of questioning about the physical buildings. Exploration allows the researcher to understand in more detail the issues that concern the research participants, it gives them a 'voice' and minimises the risk of imposing the researchers own agenda.

Detail

Qualitative research allows the practitioner-researcher to explore issues at a great depth. If a research participant becomes comfortable with the researcher, they are more likely to provide a deeper level of response than if they had been asked a one-off structured 'closed' question. The researcher can concentrate on one response and probe further in order to illuminate both the explanations and emotions associated with the topic. It is also useful within the context of face-to-face qualitative research to record non-verbal factors, such as facial expressions and body language which can often reveal what the 'plain text' cannot.

Access

Qualitative methods are the most effective way of reaching people who are classified as 'hard to reach' groups. Hard to reach groups will be different depending on the sector in which you work. However, homeless people, disaffected youth groups, and people with mental health problems are some of the groups that have been identified as hard to reach.

It will often take an innovative approach to recruit and conduct research with these groups and therefore qualitative methods are most appropriate. For example, to gather the views of disaffected youths, it may be necessary to go and find out where they congregate and get to know them before they will consider participating in the research. In this instance a practitioner-researcher could be a youth worker who may be the only person likely to have the opportunity to get to know the young people. Youth workers may also act as a gatekeeper for other people attempting to conduct research with young people; this could result in the same group of youths being consulted on a number of issues. There are gatekeepers who represent many hard to reach groups but it is problematic to always rely on them as you then run the risk of hearing only those who are most visible or active in that community and who may not be representative of the entire community. Some gatekeepers may have an agenda (the 'local vocal') that they are seeking to promote and therefore only allow access to those participants who will 'tow the party line'; practitioner-researchers should be wary of this when selecting their research sample.

Sensitivity

Some issues in social research are regarded as 'sensitive' and include asking questions beyond those that a participant would normally answer to a stranger. Sensitive issues may even concern a subject area that is normally considered taboo. Examples would include questions about sex and sexuality, terminal illness or mental health. In these cases, it is likely that participants will respond more openly in a trusted environment, where they are able to expand on their answers. This entails building confidence in the participant to enable them to give this information. Qualitative research over a period of time can allow the researcher to build a rapport and ultimately, can enable participants the confidence to talk about sensitive issues. For example, if you are researching a very sensitive subject, such as bereavement, you may need to spend time asking preliminary questions, possibly, focusing on happy memories, which will enable you to gain the trust of your participant before you ask difficult or upsetting questions about loss and grief; building confidence in the participant, until they feel comfortable enough to discuss the issues in depth.

Development of Quantitative Methods

Qualitative and quantitative research can often complement each other and can be used for triangulation, that is, checking the reliability of the data either before or after the quantitative research has been conducted (see Chapter 3). By using qualitative research before a quantitative measure (for example, a survey) you can uncover the issues that appear relevant to that group, assess the terminology that they use and develop questionnaire schedules that are more appropriate to the sample group of participants. The survey will then quantify how widespread the issues that were identified in the qualitative research appear to be. Qualitative research can also be used after a survey to explore the issue in more depth and thus address 'how' and 'why' questions. Using both approaches in your research also allows you to draw on the advantages of both methods and to minimise criticism that you may receive about sample sizes, applicability across the general population or depth of responses.

Costs

There is a myth surrounding qualitative research that suggests that because sample sizes are smaller, the research will be more cost-effective. In some instances this may be true, however in the majority of circumstances qualitative research will produce such a vast quantity of data that the time spent in analysing the findings contributes heavily to the overall cost. Wellington warns of the danger of falling into the trap of over-collecting and under-analysing, and reflects that many novice researchers 'tend to collect far too many data, for fear that they won't have enough, and then either run out of time, words or energy when it comes to analysing, interpreting, discussing, or locating the data' (2000: 133). It is important to consider the amount of data you are likely to collect in only a few interviews, and assess whether you will be able to conduct, analyse and reflect on the total sample data within the timeframe for which you have budgeted.

Transcription is very expensive in terms of labour time. If you decide you want full transcripts of interviews and focus groups it may be worth considering outsourcing this part of the research to a professional transcription service. If you are not experienced in transcription it can take a lot longer than you might expect (it can typically take a beginner up to four hours to fully transcribe one hour of interview). The cost of a transcription service is often a wise investment in comparison with the cost of practitioner-researcher time. If you do decide to have the interviews transcribed, ensure that you listen through the recording with the transcript in front of you to check for accuracy and to add any notes that you took relating to non-verbal data. Alternatives to transcription include note taking or summarising the discussion noting the key points that were discussed. It is sometimes useful to return the summary to the interviewee to check that they are happy with your précis.

Types of Qualitative Research

Qualitative research encompasses a number of methods, a selection of those which may be most relevant to practitioner-researchers are highlighted in Table 8.2.

Table 8.2   Qualitative methods: an overview

Method	Detail
Semi-structured interviews	Interviews that follow a question guide but have scope to deviate from the script.
Focus groups	Small group discussion on a specific issue.
Unstructured interviews	Like a conversation with loose ideas about what should be included.
Participant observation/observation	Recording incidents that are observed and looking for certain actions.
Diaries	Notes made by participants relating to the issue in question.
Documentary analysis	Intensive analysis of either 'official' or personal documents.

Semi-structured Interviews

The semi-structured interview is a popular qualitative method that typically uses a list of questions set by the researcher, usually known as a topic guide or interview schedule. All participants are asked the same questions, usually in roughly the same order. However, there is flexibility in this approach and the researcher can change the order and wording of the questions in order to achieve a more natural style of conversation. Thus semi-structured interviewing requires more skill than structured quantitative interviewing because the interviewer must recognise moments in the interview that have potential for further questioning and be able to formulate questions 'off the cuff'. Consequently, if someone only partially answers the question or alludes to an area that is of interest to the researcher, the interviewer can ask further questions. Although much of the data the researcher collects will essentially be comparable, due to the flexible nature, each individual interview will be unique and adapted to the circumstances of each participant. Additionally, since semi-structured interviews are usually (although not definitively) of a one-to-one nature, participants will be more likely to provide information which they might not wish to divulge in a group setting.

To illustrate, semi-structured interviewing would be a good approach to adopt if you are researching the work experiences of black or minority ethnic employees in a large organisation. The structure of the interview would enable you to explain, at the recruitment stage, what the interview will cover. However, the flexibility within the actual interview, would allow you to tailor your approach and questions as appropriate. Additional questions asked of an employee who has had a very positive experience of working for the organisation would be very different from those asked of an employee who has experienced racism.

The semi-structured approach would also allow you to 'probe' for further information.

The example below shows how a discussion on employment led the respondent to talk about experiences of racism; this is taken up and pursued further by the researcher.

Researcher: Could you tell me your experiences in this job?

Participant: Well, I wasn't happy with certain people in the office from the start, with their attitudes to me.

Researcher: In what way weren't you happy? What was it about their attitudes?

Participant: Well to be blunt, I thought they were racist.

Researcher: Could you give me any examples of things that were done or said?

Participant: Yes, of course. I must have been there only a week when … (tells anecdote).

Being an effective semi-structured interviewer takes a degree of skill and expertise in knowing when to 'probe' for further information either at the time, or else by 'storing' the information and returning to the issue later in the interviewer. If you are new to research, giving the participant your full attention throughout the interview will maximise the chances of not letting these opportunities slip through the net. However, you should be wary of questioning your participant too much; Wellington advises that the interview's purpose is to 'probe a respondent's views, perspectives or life history, that is, the exchange should be far more in one direction than another' (2000: 73). If you feel you are doing more questioning or talking than the research participant, you need to readdress the balance and ensure it is the participant's voice you are hearing.

Focus Groups

A focus group is a discussion usually involving 6–10 people lasting for one or two hours. This discussion is facilitated by a researcher who asks the group to discuss experiences and attitudes to a particular issue or to respond to specific questions. Focus groups are not simply a method of group interviewing as participants are encouraged to discuss and engage with each other rather than just with the researcher. As with other qualitative methods, focus groups are limited in terms of their ability to generalise findings to a whole population, mainly because of the small numbers of people participating and the likelihood that the participants will not be a representative sample (Gibbs, 1997).

Focus groups can be used for exploratory work at the beginning of a research project, as a method in their own right or as a complimentary approach to other methods (Gibbs, 1997). For example, you may wish to use a focus group to expand your knowledge and understanding of an issue, the findings would then inform the development of quantitative research tools, concepts for questionnaires or interview guides (Gibbs, 1997; Wellington, 2000). They may also be used to explore or generate hypotheses (Powell and Single, 1996).

Focus groups can be used to target specific sectors of society and participants may be selected because of certain characteristics, for example, living on a particular estate or being a member of a political party. In addition, focus groups are very useful for gaining insight into a group's shared understanding; as Cohen, Manion and Morrison note, within a focus group discussion 'It is from the interaction of the group that the data emerge' (2000: 288). Indeed, it is the conversations between participants that provide the most interesting data.

The advantages of focus groups are best illustrated by an example of researching the opinions of Bangladeshi women about local midwifery provision. Women from an area with a large proportion of Bangladeshi residents could be approached, the event could be held locally and benefit from the fact that it might be easier to recruit to an event where the women know they will be in company of their peers and as such, will not personally feel 'put on the spot' or under pressure. Additionally, if held in a 'neutral' environment it might also provide a 'safe' setting where women are away from the potentially inhibiting presence of health providers or other family members.

When conducting a focus group, the researcher has to avoid interrupting too often with further questions as this can interfere with the flow of the discussion.

Bryman believes that 'because the moderator has to relinquish a certain amount of control to the participants, the issues that concern them [the participants] can surface' (2008: 475). This relinquishing of power, allows the group to introduce ideas that may not have been considered by the researcher. Once individuals find that other people have had a similar experience then this can precipitate a lively discussion. Indeed, focus groups 'capitalise on communication between research participants' (Kitzinger, 1995: 299). Thus, in our focus group of Bangladeshi women discussing midwifery provision, it is likely that if one woman relates her experience, it will inspire confidence in others to do so. Participants may even disagree strongly about an issue and a debate will follow 'this process of arguing means that the researcher may end up with a more realistic account of what people think, because they are forced to think about and possibly revise their views' (Bryman, 2008: 475). Wellington concurs with this, noting that 'members of the group, brought together in a suitable conducive environment, can stimulate or "spark each other off" (2000: 125).

Of course, there are disadvantages to this approach and in some instances it will be necessary for the researcher to mediate between the different members of the group and to ensure that one or two people do not dominate the discussion while encouraging more reticent members to have an input (Flick, 2009). In this way, the researcher is then able to ensure that the views of the group are not submerged by the opinions of one or two vocal participants (see Chapter 9, for a discussion of engagement techniques). Conversely, the researcher must not intervene so often that the discussion becomes a question and answer session between the researcher and individual participants.

Another disadvantage of focus groups relates to disclosure of information. For example, participants in the focus group of Bangladeshi women might be inhibited because the individuals all come from a minority community where the women know each other. Consequently, some participants might feel reluctant to talk about sensitive issues in front of neighbours or other family members. If this is the case, private semi-structured or unstructured interviews might be more appropriate. In other cases, familiarity can improve the discussion; Cappuccini et al. (2005) found this to be the case when conducting focus groups with international students at higher education institutions to discuss their experience of the careers service.

Unstructured Interviews

Unstructured qualitative interviews do not rely on a list of questions that are set by the researcher; instead interviewees are free to tell their story in their own way and order, although possibly with guidance from the researcher. The interviewer may have a rough schedule of issues to be covered, but the interviewee has greater freedom and agency than with semi-structured interviews. The main advantage of the unstructured interview is that the researcher can gather information that (s)he had not thought of asking originally. Therefore, unstructured interviews are suited to exploring subjects with your participants when there is an initial lack of clarity about the type of information you are likely to find or exactly which questions are most appropriate. As such, these sorts of interviews are especially useful for life history or (auto) biographical accounts. Conversely, although there is scope for the researcher to gather information that (s)he had not hitherto thought of asking there is, similarly, the possibility of gathering a larger amount of irrelevant material (Arksey, 2004).

The unstructured interview is particularly valuable in ethnographic research (where you are exploring an issue in the research participant's lived environment, for example, their home, community or workplace). Conversations are likely to arise naturally, but the content may be pertinent to the overall research question and therefore the researcher will want to develop the line of enquiry further. This type of interview requires the practitioner-researcher and the research participant to develop a rapport that enables discussion to flow easily and naturally (see Chapter 9, for more on rapport and engagement).

Participant Observation/Observation

Sometimes a researcher will wish to study a group or culture by immersing himself or herself in the day-to-day activities of the group. Known as participant observation, this can be open (discussed below) or covert. For example, James Patrick gained entry to a violent Glasgow gang and studied their behaviour by participating in the gang activities, which included drug taking and carrying weapons (Patrick, 1973). Covert research can raise many ethical issues, such as whether the researcher should become involved in criminal activities in order to continue the research and not risk 'blowing his/her cover' (Pearson, 2009: 245). There is also the impact the researcher has on the group if (s)he is seen as an additional member, conducting activities that become accepted due to the agreement of another willing participant. Tedlock (2000: 465) describes participant observation as an 'oxymoron' arguing against the idea that the simultaneous emotional involvement and objective detachment it implies is somehow feasible (for a fuller discussion of the 'researcher effect', see Chapter 9.) In addition, there are ethical issues around the deceit involved in this type of research as well as the influence the researcher, by virtue of their involvement in the group, has on the research participants (for further discussion on ethical issues, see Chapter 4).

Open observation is a more common approach, which can involve the researcher becoming directly involved in activities. For example, a researcher may choose to act as a carer in a nursing home, even though it is known to everybody that (s)he does this as research rather than as a practitioner, the researcher gets accepted and can gather information. Open observation could also rely purely on observing events in a detached and independent manner, for example, doctor and patient consultations whereby events are systematically recorded.

Open observation is regularly used by action researchers within school settings, where children's actions or behaviours are analysed. Observations can be quantitative (observing the number of times something occurs), as well as qualitative (looking at the detail such as temporal and spatial influences in what is happening). The researcher does not get involved in activities but remains unobtrusive:

> Direct observation as a research method is most appropriate to open, public settings where anyone has a right to be or congregate. Conducting direct observation in private or closed settings without the knowledge or consent of members is more likely to raise ethical concern. (Childcare Research Organization, 2009)

Diaries

The diary is a data gathering method that can be used to record people's lives and patterns of behaviour. It is a participant-led research method that requires subjects to record certain experiences or activities in their own words or by answering structured questions. The diary can make use of a variety of technologies, such as pen and paper, audio or visual recordings and online questionnaires.

Diaries can be used in many research fields and are relatively common way of recording dietary and other behaviour patterns in contexts where research needs to capture the incidence of repetitive events. For example, diaries can be used to record and analyse the way in which subjects spend their time (how many hours watching television; how many individuals spoken to per day); to record their usage and experiences of public transport systems; or to identify associations between diet and, for example, the incidence of migraine attacks. Usually, diaries are content analysed and are sometimes used to triangulate other research findings. However, on their own research diaries completed by unsupervised participants cannot represent the whole context of the participants' experience.

Practitioner-researchers themselves may choose to keep another kind of diary, that records their own field notes, events or discussions that have occurred during the research process or that otherwise contribute to the topic of investigation. Although this kind of diary is a tool to facilitate qualitative research by recording thoughts and events that might otherwise be overlooked during the research process, it should not be seen as a data collection method (see Chapter 10, for more on researcher diaries).

The private diary or journal differs from the diaries outlined above as it is unsolicited and not written for the purpose of participation in research (Jones, 2000). Diaries of this nature deal with a multitude of everyday events, activities as well as personal thoughts and perceptions. As such, they provide fascinating, invaluable and unique accounts. For example, Jokinen studied the diaries of three women, one writing in the 1960s, one in the 1980s and one in the 1990s to examine how concepts of motherhood and mothering change over time (Jokinen, 2004). Examining documents such as these can be invaluable when contextualising an issue socially and politically.

Documentary Analysis

Documentary analysis is the systematic scrutiny of the content of documents to identify patterns of change or development on specific issues; content can be the language, tone or terminology used, and also non-textual issues such as layout styles and use of graphics. Such analysis, though largely a qualitative exercise, has a quantitative element. For example, by taking a series of party political manifesto statements over a time series (such as five general elections) and tracing the changing use of language and rhetoric, researchers can come to certain conclusions, for example, about how seriously the issue of teaching standards are being taken by various parties. Quantifying the content analysis, by counting the incidence of certain key words, measuring the length of statements (by word count) and recording the relative position of the section relating to teaching standards in manifestos offers another level of analysis.

Analysis of less directly comparable documents can also be useful in certain contexts, for example, noting the incidence of certain key terms in a variety of media can demonstrate a changing social context that may be important in specific cases. For example, if your research involves the changing perceptions of young people, analysis of how the mass media report on anti-social behaviour may in fact reveal that perceptions have changed since the media began to use the term 'ASBO' (to mean those under anti-social behaviour orders) as a convenient shorthand for any 'problem kids'. In this case content analysis can aid your understanding of the context of young people's lives. Chapter 10, on qualitative data analysis, offers a discussion of various software tools that can enable the analysis of large amounts of textual data.

Conclusion

Qualitative research is an interpretivist methodology that provides an excellent way of identifying in-depth information about a subject, especially concerning under-researched areas, sensitive topics or groups that are hard to reach. Although it can be cost-effective in terms of the cost of equipment, there can be huge costs in the form of people 'resources', especially with regard to transcription and data analysis.

Which qualitative method you choose not only depends on access, cost and time but should also consider the nature of the data required and the research questions you wish to answer (see Chapter 3). This chapter has covered the main qualitative techniques that will be of interest to the practitioner-researcher with the aim of providing a succinct overview of these approaches, how they can be used and their advantages and shortcomings. Chapters 9 and 10 will now provide you with further information about these methods, in particular how to undertake them in the field and how to analyse the data that they produce.

Further Reading

Cresswell, J.W. (2007) *Qualitative Inquiry and Research Design: Choosing Among Five Approaches*. London: Sage.
Cresswell offers a useful introductory, yet informative, text which looks at narrative research, phenomenology, grounded theory, ethnography and case study.

Flick, U. (2009) *An Introduction to Qualitative Research*, 4th edn. London: Sage.
This is a thorough introduction to the theory and practice of qualitative research, including design, fieldwork and analysis.

NINE

Preparation and Process
of Qualitative Interviews
and Focus Groups

Joanne Davies

By the end of this chapter you should be able to:

- select and sample participants for interviews and focus groups;
- understand different ways of recruiting participants;
- design interview/focus group schedules and topic guides;
- understand how to engage participants effectively when conducting and interview/focus group;
- undertake and understand the benefits of carrying out a pilot study;
- understand the benefits of note taking and recording;
- understand the importance of obtaining the participants' consent via a consent form.

Introduction

In the previous chapter different kinds of qualitative methods were explored. This chapter continues with the theme of qualitative research, but here we deal with the preparation and process in particular how to organise and plan for the carrying out of qualitative interviews and focus groups (also known as group interviews). This chapter covers these two methods primarily because they are the most commonly used in qualitative research. The chapter will initially cover preparatory issues such as selection and recruitment of participants and the drawing up and piloting of research tools in the form of interview schedules and topic guides. The second half of the chapter will address the process of conducting interviews and focus groups, including how to engage effectively with respondents to best elicit useful information, obtaining participant consent and capture the data through note taking/recording.

Preparation

Selection of Participants

As with any type of social research, a sample of participants must be selected whether the research is qualitative or quantitative (see Chapter 11, for more on sampling in quantitative research). When selecting participants for interviews and focus groups certain decisions need to be made about how your selected group can best represent the wider cohort (such as all the auxiliary nurses in a hospital or Year 10 pupils in a school). This is perhaps even more important in a small research project when only interviewing a few people with a small sample size, the researcher will need to make certain decisions about who to include in the project as cannot include everyone. Box 9.1 outlines some of the most common sampling techniques within qualitative research. Consider these approaches when selecting participants for the research project.

Box 9.1 Different approaches to qualitative sampling

Convenience/opportunistic

It is common for qualitative researchers to adopt these sampling techniques. Opportunistic sampling involves the researcher taking advantage of certain situations throughout the research as it develops (Richie and Lewis, 2006). Convenience sampling can be done in various different ways, for example, utilising existing contacts for ease of access or when a particular organisation or group are involved in a project as part of the research they select the sample for the researcher (Bryman, 2004).

Snowball

This approach recruits participants for the research while undertaking fieldwork with existing participants. For example, the researcher may recruit another participant for the project while interviewing another from their existing contacts.

Theoretical

Also known as 'handy' sampling. This approach is an iterative one, moving between sampling and theoretical reflection. This approach can be viewed as a technique of triangulation, which involves interviewing until you achieve theoretical saturation and selecting new interviewees on the emerging focus (Bryman, 2004).

Purposive

This approach uses specific criteria. Participants for the research are chosen because of particular features or characteristics that can relate to behaviours, roles and characteristics. This approach has two aims, first, to ensure that the participants are relevant to the research subject, and, second, to ensure some diversity is included (Richie and Lewis, 2006).

How Many?

Once a decision has been made on how to select participants for the research project, the sample size also needs to be considered. Generally, the number of participants involved in qualitative research tends to be a lot smaller than quantitative research. Richie and Lewis (2006) outline three main reasons for this:

- Increasing the sample size in qualitative research does not necessarily create new evidence.
- Unlike quantitative research, there is no need to have a large sample to provide significant statistics or estimates.
- The nature of qualitative research results in detailed data, therefore the sample size needs to be relatively small for analysis.

The actual number of participants included in a sample will depend on the nature of the research project, budget and time. When deciding on a sample size it is important that the sample covers all variables relevant to the research. For example, if age group is one variable the sample must cover the range of age categories. It is important to ensure that the sample is not too big or too small; a qualitative sample of over 50 for one-to-one interviews will be difficult to manage (Richie and Lewis, 2006).

Focus group samples need separate consideration. If conducting focus groups, the practitioner-researcher will need to consider how many groups and the number of participants within each group. A sample of around 90 focus group attendees (assuming 12–14 focus groups of between six and eight people) is probably the largest you would want to manage. It is very unlikely that one focus group will be sufficient to cover the range of variables, and you will almost certainly want to draw comparisons between focus groups with different characteristics. Practical and theoretical considerations need to be made when deciding on the number of focus groups to undertake (see Table 9.1). The nature and the issues covered in the research project may influence the actual numbers within each group. For example, Bryman (2008) recommends that if the researcher believes that a particular group will have a lot to say on a specific issue or subject then

Table 9.1   Focus Group considerations

Practical considerations	Theoretical considerations
• Time • Resources • Recruiting participants • Analysis – the larger the groups and the more that are conducted the harder the analysis in terms of pulling the data together and time	• Researchers sometimes reach a point where the data is saturated, therefore do not need to conduct any more • Numbers might be increased if the researcher is taking into account socio-demographic factors, e.g. age, gender. The project may require a range of participants and larger or more groups may need to be conducted to reflect this

Source: Bryman (2004).

numbers should be kept small (to enable the accurate recording of detailed, perhaps critical comments about, for example, a health or educational programme respondents have been subject to). However, if the researcher wants to obtain lots of different views on a more general set of questions (such as, what is it like living on this estate as opposed to where they lived before) then larger groups (and/or more groups) maybe more appropriate as they will likely offer a broader range of responses.

Gaining Access

Gaining access to a 'field' (institution, family, group of people, organisation and so forth) can be a difficult task especially when trying to secure participants for a particular research project (Flick, 2009). How easily access can be organised will depend on the nature of the research project. In some instances the participants may be pre-selected by the person or organisation commissioning the research and thus access will be less of an issue. For example, a practitioner-researcher conducting research in a healthcare setting may be an employee of the organisation and therefore will have ready access to both the management for consent and the subjects of the research. However, in other cases researchers need to gain access to the population being studied which may involve negotiating with, often reluctant, managers and other gatekeepers, as well as with the subjects of the research, which can prove very time-consuming.

If a research project requires access to a particular institution, for example, school, university or counselling services there are several points to consider when trying to negotiate access, including:

- the researcher will need authorisation from the person responsible for the institution/ organisation; and
- the researcher will need authorisation from the individuals within the institution/organisation that they are willing to take part in the research and invest their time. (Flick, 2009)

Gaining access to individuals within an organisation/group/institution can also be a challenge, even though the researcher may have gained access to the group. There are ways in which a researcher can promote a research project encouraging potential participants to come forward. For example, strategies can be put in place to recruit participants via marketing material such as posters and flyers in and around a particular area and the media via announcements and local press as well as using existing contacts such as word of mouth or the cascading information down from a managerial level. Once access has been gained to a small number of individuals the researcher may be able to 'snowball' from one participant to another through contacts and friends within the organisation (Flick, 2009).

Another useful way of recruiting participants is the use of incentives. The amount and type of incentive a particular researcher offers will very much depend on the subjects of the research, timing and budget. For example, students may be incentivised by £10 whereas professionals, such as teachers or healthcare staff, will not. There are also issues to do with accepting cash that are against some individuals' principles, in which case vouchers may be an acceptable alternative. Incentives can vary and can be financial or non-financial, beneficial to an individual or a group of people. In a research project focusing on teaching staff in primary schools, incentives that benefited the whole teaching staff (such as catering packs of coffee and biscuits or larger sums such as £150 to be spent collectively) have been shown to incentivise participation. It is important to get the views of (in this case) senior teaching staff as they are most likely to know what type of incentive will work best in each circumstance. Box 9.2 provides some examples of incentives used and where they might be appropriate.

Box 9.2   Example incentives

Vouchers – one voucher could be given to a group of people at a particular organisation or to individuals, for example, book vouchers, retail vouchers.

Gifts – these could be one off gifts as a token gesture for taking part in a particular project, for example, chocolates or biscuits for a staff room.

Cash – one-off cash payments might be a suitable option if several members of an organisation are taking time out of their normal duties that require cover such as a school teacher.

Recognition – depending on the nature of the research, recognition for taking part maybe an attractive option especially if the project has a high profile. An organisation could receive recognition for taking part by receiving a plaque or certificate or have their name publicised on project material such as a website or report.

Equipment – if doing a piece of research for an organisation or institution, it might be beneficial to offer equipment they could use and benefit from such as stationary or school equipment.

Interview Schedules

As part of the research design, preliminary research questions will have been outlined (see Chapter 3). These preliminary questions need to be adapted into themes, topics and questions to be asked when undertaking the fieldwork stages of the project. In qualitative research, interview schedules can be either semi-structured or unstructured. An interview schedule can be in the form of an interview guide (also called topic guide), which covers a range of issues with prompts and open questions rather than a list of structured questions (more common in quantitative research).

Introduction

(Purpose of study, what interview or focus group going to cover, issues around confidentiality, methods of recording the information)

Beginning of interview/focus group

(Opening questions, background information, easy to answer questions, straightforward information and details)

Main body of interviews/focus group

(In-depth questions and discussions, very specific information, probing for further information)

Finishing the interview/focus group

(Winding down the discussion, closing remarks, suggestions for the future, any additional information that maybe relevant)

Figure 9.1   Stages of design
Source: Richie and Lewis (2006).

Semi-structured interviews follow a general order and more often than not the interviewer will have a series of questions and or themes that are flexible in nature and need not follow a fixed linear path. Unstructured interview schedules can be even more flexible with a list of issues rather than questions; here the interviewing style can be very informal with the questions being asking varying from one interview to the next (Legard et al., 2003).

When designing an interview schedule, thought needs to be given to the introduction and the order in which the researcher wants the themes and issues to be discussed. Figure 9.1 outlines the process of designing an interview schedule.

Designing an interview schedule is a process that needs careful consideration. The flexibility and length of the guide will depend on the nature of the project, however in all cases the guide needs to be straightforward and easy to understand using comprehensive language that will not confuse the participant and the researcher undertaking the fieldwork. A qualitative interview schedule 'should be seen as a mechanism for steering the discussion in an interview or focus group but not as an exact prescription of coverage' (Richie and Lewis, 2006: 115). The schedule may need re-drafting several times and, depending on the nature of the research project, it may need agreement from other members of the team and sometimes the funding body who may wish to 'sign them off'. When planning a project, it is good practice to allow for additional time for review and amendments.

Box 9.3 illustrates an example interview schedule exploring recruitment and retention in a local authority via interviews with HR staff. The guide is divided up into key themes and sections, which makes it easier to follow and, rather than having lots of specific questions, key themes and issues are listed under bullet points. The schedule also uses prompts, instructions and other notes throughout to remind the person undertaking the fieldwork of any important issues to cover.

Box 9.3   Example interview schedule

Local Authority Recruitment and Retention

Interviews with local residents

Introduction

Offer the participant some information about who we are, our funders, and our project's aim and objectives and benefits to the participants Explain the information provided will be confidential and anonymised, not revealed to anybody outside the research team and it will not be possible to identify individuals in any reports. Also check if the participant would like to see the notes made of their interview and if they have any questions.

Obtain permission to record the interview (or take notes, if participant does not wish to be recorded). Get participant to sign a consent form and provide them with a sheet outlining details of the project. Explain that the interview should not take longer than 30 minutes and discuss incentives is appropriate.

General background

Local authority information:

- key characteristics of local authority;
- size;
- challenges;
- priorities.

Human resources (HR) information:

- length of time in current role;
- description of current role and responsibilities;
- current HR recruitment and retention policies (prompt – Who manages it? Who is responsible? How is the policy determined?).

Overall recruitment and retention

Staff profile and numbers:

- Staff numbers (prompt – How many employed in different staff groups? Have numbers changed in the last 3 years? Why?).

- Trends in recruitment and retention (prompt – What have been the overall trends? Do you anticipate things changing? In what staff groups?).
- Staff profile (prompt – Age/experience/gender/ethnicity? Is it the kind of profile the LA would like?).
- Difficulties (prompt – Has any recruitment or retention issues reduced the LAs effectiveness or achievement of its aims?).

Recruitment
(Note: some of the questions in the next two sections may have already been covered above)

Current recruitment position:

- Current situation (prompt – Please describe current recruitment situation within the LA? Are you able to recruit the number and quality you need for different roles and departments? Difficulties? Why?).
- Categories of staff (prompt – Are there any difficulties in recruiting particular categories of staff? Which posts? Why? How does the LA overcome these difficulties?).

Retention

Current position and turnover:

- Turnover within LA (prompt – How much in the last 3 years? Which staff groups? Has turnover affected any particular category of staff disproportionately?).
- Reasons for turnover (prompt – Why staff leave LA? Which groups? Natural wastage? Other reasons?).
- Current retention position (prompt – Please describe current retention position. Difficult? average? Compared with other LAs?).

Recruitment and retention strategies

Strategies and processes:

- Approaches for recruitment and retention (prompt – Does the LA adopt specific recruitment procedures and retention procedures? Does this vary for different categories of staff? How effective are they? Are they in line with other LA procedures?).
- External support (prompt – Does the LA call on any outside help from external agencies with recruitment and retention? Who? Why?).

Closing comments/additional information

- Additional information.
- Any changes that may help in the future.
- What could and should be done.

Thank the participant for taking part

Once the interview of focus group interview schedule has been designed, it is important that the researcher and any other people who may be involved with the fieldwork become familiar with it, feeding back any changes or amendments. Before starting the fieldwork it is important to pilot or test the schedule. In practice, interviews that are conducted as part of the piloting process maybe or may not be included depending on the sample. Once schedules have been piloted, changes maybe required as a result for example, order of questions, omitting questions or adding specific issues or themes.

When designing an interview and/or focus group schedule it is useful to include a list of themes in a specific order to allow for flow, flexible enough to allow for change during the interview or focus group due to the openness of the discussion. You should also use straightforward easy-to-understand language appropriate to the respondent's characteristics and avoid leading questions, such as 'So, how bad is the crime round here?'. It is also important to record the participants demographic information, such as name, gender, age, ethnicity (if relevant), as this enables the researcher to contextualise the participants' responses when analysing the data (Bryman, 2008).

Process

Obtaining Participant Consent

Before embarking on an interview or focus group, the researcher must obtain informed consent from the participants that they agree to take part in the research. Before they can give their informed consent they must be fully informed about what is involved and what is required of them (see Chapter 4, for more information). Informed consent:

> involves ensuring that potential participants have a clear understanding of the purpose of the study, the funder, the organisation or individual conducting it, how the data will be used, and what participation will mean for them. (Richie and Lewis, 2006: 76)

Informed consent can be obtained verbally or, preferably, in writing using a consent form including some information about the research that participants can sign if they are happy to do so. Depending on the research it maybe appropriate to have two copies of the consent form, one for the participant to keep and one for the researcher (see Figure 9.2 for an example consent form). If conducting a focus group with several participants, informed consent must be obtained from each member of the group by giving each a form to read and sign. If written informed consent is not possible, the researcher must get consent verbally. For example, if conducting a qualitative interview over the telephone consent could be obtained prior to the telephone call in writing or verbally at the time of the interview. If using a tape/digital recorder the researcher can obtain informed consent verbally while recording the information. One point to note is not too scare the participants too much by bombarding them with information. By giving informed consent, participants are giving consent voluntarily, agreeing to the information given by the researcher either verbally or in writing and are agreeing to go ahead and have their comments included in research outputs (albeit anonymously) (Flick, 2009). Box 9.4 provides a checklist of what should be included when designing a consent form.

Box 9.4 Checklist of key points to consider when obtaining informed consent

- Inform all participants about the purpose/nature of the research project.
- Explain who is funding the research and why it is being carried out.
- Make participants aware of how much time is required.
- Give full contact details.
- Brief participants on the themes and issues that are going to be discussed.
- Inform participants on how the data is going to be recorded, e.g. note-taking or audio recording.
- Explain what will happen to the information after the interview or focus group.
- Assure of anonymity and/or confidentiality.
- If more than one researcher is present explain why, for example, in a focus group situation, and make sure that the participant is comfortable with having two researchers present.
- Make participants aware that they can stop at anytime or refuse to answer a particular question if they wish to do so.
- If sensitive issues are going to be covered, make sure that participants are aware of this in advance and are happy to proceed.
- If the information is to be used elsewhere for example published on a website or another type of publication, make sure to obtain consent for this via the consent form.

Depending on the nature of the research, informed consent might need to be obtained from more than one person. For example, if a practitioner-researcher conducts qualitative interviews in a large voluntary organisation with 20 members of staff on an issue internal to the organisation, such as their new employee initiative, (s)he would need to obtain consent from the managerial board to undertake the interviews and use the information provided and from the individuals taking part in the interviews. If conducting interviews or focus groups with children or young people, informed consent must be obtained via the parent/guardian and, depending on the nature of the research, the school or local authority as well. Where participants are young people and children it may be necessary to either create space on consent form for a parent/guardian to sign or create a separate form. Figure 9.2 offers an example consent form.

Participant Consent Form

Title of Project:

Name of Researcher:

Name of Organisation: _____

	Yes	No
1. I have understood the information sheet provided	O	O
2. I agree to the interview being audio-recorded	O	O
3. I would like to receive a copy of the transcribed interview	O	O
4. I understand I can withdraw from interview at any time without explanation	O	O
5. I agree to take part in the research outlined in the information sheet	O	O
6. I agree that the information can be used in the following ways:	O	O
➤ Identified in any publications/web publications	O	O
➤ I do not agree to being identified in any report or publications, where data is used my name and details must be removed and comments made unattributable	O	O

Name of Participant   Date   Signature

_____   _____   _____

Name of person taking consent   Date   Signature

_____   _____   _____

If you would like any further information about the research please contact [name of researcher] on [telephone number].

Copies: One copy for the participant and one copy for the researchers.

Figure 9.2   Example consent form

The researcher must keep a copy of the consent form for each individual participant as they may need to refer back to this when disseminating the research findings. When conducting any type of research it is good practice to retain research data including consent forms for up to five years. This is because some participants might be willing to attribute their details and quotations on reports, publications and project websites, while others may not and keeping all the consent forms will make the checking process much simpler.

Engaging Participants

Engaging participants while conducting interviews and focus groups is imperative to any research project. There are several factors that can affect participant engagement which in turn can affect the quality of the information gathered, for example, the setting, the 'interviewer effect', building up a rapport, the topic and types of questions used. We will now look at these factors in turn.

Setting

The setting in which an interview or focus group takes place can have an effect on the information gathered and on participant engagement. For example, if participants are in surroundings that are familiar they may feel more at ease, for example, in their own home, and this may result in more in-depth lengthy information being gathered. If an interview or focus group is taking place in a more formal setting such as their place of work, the participants are more likely to behave in a professional manner as they would at work. When deciding on an appropriate location, the researcher needs to consider the nature of the research, travel time, what will make the surroundings more comfortable and, if conducting fieldwork in the workplace or school situation, will need to be aware of timing and room booking requirements. Researchers should bear in mind the following when arranging a suitable location and setting:

- Offer privacy, for example, meeting to ensure no one else can hear what the participants are discussing.
- If a private space is not available, offer a space that is reasonably quiet.
- Arrange seating to allow for easy interaction, for example, for a one-to-one interview make sure both parties can maintain eye contact, and for a focus group arrange a circle so everyone in the group and see and hear each other.
- Allow sufficient time.
- Make sure the room is comfortable, that is, not too hot/cold. (Denscombe, 2007)

If conducting a telephone interview, the setting is not an issue although it is important to ensure that any equipment used is working properly and both the interviewer and participant can allow for the conversation to flow without any interruptions or background noise.

It is also important to be aware of participants' individual needs when deciding on a particular location and setting. For example, some respondents may need disabled access, child care provision, a translator or have particular religious beliefs that effect where and in what conditions the respondent will feel comfortable.

Interviewer Effect

When conducting interviews and focus groups all researchers should be reflective and think about their own effects on the situation and the data gathered. Participants may not act or speak as they would in a normal situation; being interviewed or participating in a focus group as the situation is likely to be new to them and they may feel outside their 'comfort zone'. When interviewing or holding focus groups with young people it is common for them to be reticent and uncommunicative at first (as they may be with a new teacher, for example), and before they 'open up' they may need to understand why you want to talk to them and be reassured that their comments will not be fed back to those in authority.

The personal identity of a researcher can effect the quality of the data, for example, factors such as the age, sex, ethnic origin, educational background, social status and business expertise of the interviewer can all influence the amount of information participants are willing to disclose (Denscombe, 2007). If researching a sensitive issue, for example, sexual health or religion, it is possible that the researcher will have an effect on the information gathered. There are several ways in which a researcher can minimise the interviewer effect (see Box 9.5). Interviewer effect is also issue when conducting telephone interviews, where gender, accent, voice and tone may affect interviewees' responses.

Box 9.5   Reducing the effect of the interviewer

- Consider the participants' characteristics/situation in advance of the fieldwork.
- Think about your appearance – it may be appropriate to ensure that appropriate clothing is worn.
- Throughout the interview/focus group make sure that you try to remain objective, that is, by not agreeing or disagreeing with any statements made (see Chapter 8, for more information on positionality).
- Always be polite – think about your manners, be courteous.

Rapport

Establishing a good rapport with participants in focus groups and interviews is essential and means that the researcher must build up a good relationship in a short space of time which will encourage the participants to proceed and feel comfortable disclosing information about a particular subject (Bryman, 2008). From the outset a good working relationship needs to be built up with an individual or group who may be from a range of different backgrounds, some maybe in difficult circumstances and others in a position of power (Richie and Lewis, 2006). Box 9.6 contains some useful tips for establishing rapport.

Box 9.6   Establishing rapport

- Think about facial expressions, for example, eye contact and smile when appropriate.
- Maintain a good posture, for example, leaning forward can appear as showing an interest.
- Mirror the participants body language where appropriate.
- Think about any habits you have, for example, fidgeting and fiddling may distract participants.
- Light humour may lighten the situation, if appropriate.
- Think about the pace and tone of your voice.

Engaging Participants: Focus Groups

Engaging participants during focus groups follows the same principles as interviews, however, as there is more than one person involved in the discussion the level of moderator involvement and controlling the group discussion needs careful consideration to ensure that all participants are engaged in the discussion. It is common for a few more confident individuals to initially dominate the group discussion, so researches should ensure that all attempts are made to 'tease out' the views of the quieter ones. Researchers conducting focus groups need to get the balance right between allowing the group discussion to flow and refocusing/controlling the discussion. The aim of a focus group discussion is to allow participants to interact with each other, speaking freely on a particular issue, therefore it is important that the moderator allows this as well as intervening if necessary (Cohen et al., 2000; Bryman, 2008). This is particularly important if you start to get the impression that pre-existing power relationships in the group are preventing the free expression of views. For example, this can occur in situations where there are a small number of, for example, minority ethnic or disabled individuals, a large gender imbalance in the group or with young people (Wellington, 2000). The level of moderator involvement will depend on the nature of the group and the research topic and the role of the moderator is crucial to the success of the group (Richie and Lewis, 2006). Focus groups are discussed in more depth in Chapter 8.

Probing and Prompting for a Fuller Response

When trying to engage participants in and interview or focus group key skills and techniques need to be adopted to encourage a fuller response. As we have noted, probing and prompting participants throughout an interview or focus group can encourage participants to give further information (Table 9.2). Prompting may be necessary if the participant is struggling to answer a specific question and needs

Table 9.2   How to prompt and probe during interview

Prompting	Probing
Allow silences	Ask for clarification
Repeat the question	Ask for further details
Offer examples	Ask for an examples

Source: Denscombe (2001).

help recalling the information. Probing may be necessary if the interviewer requires more in-depth information on a particular issue before moving onto the next question (Flick, 2009). When prompting and probing is it important not to demand information but to subtly engage the participants for a fuller response (Denscombe, 2007).

Interviewer Safety

When conducting any type of research interviewer safety must always be considered. In some instances, depending on the nature of the research project, interviews and focus groups maybe conducted in respondents' own homes, with vulnerable or difficult groups, and with young children in different settings for example, schools. In some instances, interviewers may also need consider travel arrangements and if they are carrying any cash or items of monetary value to give to respondents as an incentive for taking part. Box 9.7 gives some key hints and tips on interviewer safety to consider when conducting fieldwork.

Box 9.7   Interviewer safety – hints and tips

Location – make sure the fieldwork location is accessible by public transport. Also consider if there are any local tensions within the area, such as cultural or religious beliefs.

Respondents – some respondents may pose a greater possibility of risk than others. If any particular characteristics are known in advance, the interviewer should understand the precautions and implement necessary action, that is, taking another person along.

Awareness – if possible obtain information about the respondents and the setting in which the fieldwork will take place. Upon arrival, make sure you are aware of emergency exits and have access to a telephone or mobile phone. Always make sure that someone knows where you are and when you are expected to return, and keep mobile phone switched on (on silent).

Out of hours – if working out of hours make sure that members of your team are aware of where you are and what you are doing.

Cash – if carrying cash and/or vouchers as incentives for respondents keep them in individual envelopes. Also make sure that personal money and valuables are kept out of sight.

Travelling – plan travel arrangements in advance and take relevant maps and information. Leave mobile phone switched on and take care if walking alone at night. If accommodation is needed, book this in advance.

In homes – if interviewing in a respondents' own home do not enter if you feel it is unsafe. Always assess the quickest way out and sit near a door. If there are any pets in the house it is not unreasonable to ask the respondent to put the pet in another room.

Methods of Recording

When conducting interviews (face-to-face or by telephone) and focus groups, methods of recording the information need to be considered prior to starting the fieldwork. Although researchers can rely on their memory as a way of recalling information, this may prove to be unreliable and lead to partial recall as well as error and bias (Denscombe, 2007). The method of recording the information will depend on the nature of the research project and the methods chosen. There are several ways of recording information gathered while conducting an interview or focus group, for example, note-taking, audio-recording (tape or digital), and field notes (to record context, environment and atmosphere).

Note-taking and audio-recording are the most commonly used when conducting qualitative research. The method a researcher chooses will depend on a number of factors such as research topic, budget, experience, time and participant consent. In many cases researchers may decide to both audio-record and take notes throughout. The advantages and disadvantages of both techniques are outlined in Tables 9.3 and 9.4.

Audio-recording has become the standard method of gathering interview and focus group data (Denscombe, 2007) though many researchers choose to record information using a mixture of both audio-recording and note-taking in interviews and focus groups. This combination not only enables the researcher to obtain an accurate record of what is discussed verbally but also to note down important points and the context of the situation (Richie and Lewis, 2006). In some instances a researcher may decide to audio record a discussion, noting down key words, issues and points throughout as a prompt for further note-taking immediately after the interview/focus group. Taking notes immediately after an interview or

Table 9.3   Advantages and disadvantages of audio recording

Advantages	Disadvantages
By using an audio-recorder the researcher is obtaining a permanent record of the discussion that can be referred back to at a later date if necessary (with the participants consent).	Although audio-recording may in some ways create a setting where conversation can flow, some participants might be alarmed at the thought of their voices being recorded and this could have an effect on the flow of the conversation and the content of the discussion.
If more than one person is involved in the research project, other researchers can refer to, check and analyse the data gathered as and when required.	Audio-recording creates a massive amount of verbal data that will need analysing and possibly transcribing. One hour of interview can take up to four hours to transcribe, so this may affect the number of interviews/focus groups conducted (depending on the timescale and budget of the research project).
Using an audio-recording can help in engaging the participants as discreet, recorders tend to be small and conversation can flow without interruption by a researcher taking notes.	All verbal interaction is captured by the recorder. However, audio recording does not pick up contextual factors such as body language, the setting, facial expressions and so on.
A full verbal record of what is being discussed is obtained.	Technical failure of recording equipment prior, during or after the interview or focus group.
Specialist equipment designed for recording a telephone interview eases the conversation.	

Table 9.4   Advantages and disadvantages of note-taking

Advantages	Disadvantages
Less time consuming at the analysis and report writing stage.	May create a less natural setting, thus interrupting the flow of the conversation such as pauses and silences while researcher takes notes.
No technology involved, therefore less likely that anything will go wrong.	Note-taking relies on the researcher's own interpretation of the discussion and recollection.
Participants maybe less nervous as not being recorded 'word for word'.	Cannot record all of the information that is discussed, therefore only partially recorded.
Note taking could be more appropriate when researching sensitive issues.	If conducting a qualitative telephone interview it maybe very difficult to have a telephone conversation while taking notes.
Note taking could include not only the conversation but also the wider context, including non-verbal communication.	
Less time-consuming and expensive.	

focus group is a good way of recording any non-verbal contextual information while it is still fresh in the researchers mind.

Recording information gathered via a focus group is less straightforward, as there are more voices and comments to note and it can be difficult to attribute comments to individuals (Bryman, 2008). Therefore, audio-recording might be more appropriate. It is generally good practice (though obviously more expensive) to have two people at a focus group, one to conduct and moderate the discussion and the other to ensure the recording device is set up and to take written notes (see Box 9.8).

Box 9.8 Recording information – key points

- Use good quality equipment.
- Check recorder prior to interview or focus group.
- Make sure recorder has sufficient memory/tape.
- Buy extra batteries and spare tapes.
- Take sufficient note-paper and pens.
- Obtain consent that the participant is willing to take part in the research and the chosen method of recording the information (verbally or in writing).
- Check recording immediately afterwards.
- Make any further notes immediately afterwards.
- Write up notes.
- Consider whether the data gathered needs to be transcribed word-by-word or key points, this will have an impact on expenses and time.

Conclusion

This chapter has aimed to give you an overview of the preparation and processes of qualitative interviews and focus groups. Whatever approach you choose, you should be clear about what you are doing and how why. Specifically, you should now have a detailed understanding of the different approaches selecting participants for focus groups and interviews and different approaches to sampling including how many participants to include, gaining access, the use of incentives and designing interview schedules. Additionally, you should be able to understand the process of obtaining participant consent including informed consent and the use of consent forms. Finally, this chapter has supplied guidance on making sure that you engage participants when undertaking interviews and focus groups getting the best possible information from the participants and appropriate methods of recording the information gathered.

Further Reading

Bryman, A. (2008) *Social Research Methods*, 3rd end. Oxford: Oxford University Press. Bryman's book covers the practical aspects of qualitative research including processes, design and analysis of interviews and focus group data.

Flick, U. (2009) *An Introduction to Qualitative Research*, 4th edn. London: Sage. Flick provides an overall introduction to qualitative research including research design, sampling and undertaking fieldwork in a variety of environments and circumstances.

TEN

Qualitative Data Analysis

Karen Smith and Joanne Davies

By the end of this chapter you should be able to:

- manage your qualitative data;
- understand the different kinds of transcription;
- choose from a range of approaches to qualitative data analysis;
- start the process of coding;
- make informed decisions about whether to analyse manually or with the support of software;
- move beyond description of data to analysis and interpretation;
- know how to present the data.

Introduction

Over the previous two chapters, different kinds of qualitative methods and the process of using these methods to generate data have been explored. This chapter takes qualitative research further by looking more closely at how the data that you collect can be analysed. Qualitative data collection processes frequently result in large quantities of rich textual data and it can be difficult to know where to start the analysis. It is both an advantage and a disadvantage that there are no hard and fast rules about the best way to go about analysing your data. The disadvantage is that it can be difficult to know where to start when you do not have a recipe to follow; the advantage is that data analysis can be the most creative and rewarding part of your research. In this chapter, we aim to make the qualitative data analysis process a little clearer.

The first section of this chapter will discuss how to manage qualitative data (keeping track of interviews, keeping data safe and so forth) and how recorded interviews can be transcribed. Next, the process of studying, reducing and analysing text will be discussed. The first steps in this process are familiarisation with the data and identification of key concepts in relation to the aim of the study. This is followed by the emergence of profiles and themes – which could also be presented as models – and coding of data. The various tools and the use of appropriate data analysis software will be discussed. At the final stage of the data analysis process, the researcher needs to interpret the findings and reveal their primary essence and key meaning.

Managing Your Data

You are likely to have collected a lot of data during the data collection period. That data could include: transcripts of interviews, field notes, official documents, newspaper articles, memos, pictures and so on (see Rapley, 2007). For example, in a study of the work environment of bus drivers, Poulsen et al. (2007) drew on qualitative data from interviews, focus groups, observations, activity plans, log books, diaries, newspapers and journals.

The volume and variety of qualitative data that you could potentially collect mean that you have to be systematic and organised in how you deal with that data. In this section, we will suggest techniques for keeping track of your data and also look at ways of securely storing what you have collected.

Research Diaries

One of the simplest ways of keeping a hold on your data (and your research more generally) is to keep a research diary (also referred to as a research notebook or journal). A research diary is the place where you can note all the activities relating to your research project: when interviews took place or the reference for a particularly useful article, for example. It is also the place where you can record more subjective responses to your research: observations on the data you have collected and the process of capturing that data, ideas that come out of your prior reading and the reading of your own data. Newbury (2001) describes the research diary as 'a melting pot' where you can capture the 'interplay of elements' in your research project. So, not only is the diary a useful tool for keeping track of data, it is also a good starting point for your data analysis. It should be noted that a research diary is not the same as a diaries used as a data collection methodology (discussed in Chapter 8).

Data Management

In the same way as Chapter 6 (Literature Reviews) advised you to keep a track of the references for the sources that you read, it is important that you carefully log the data that you collect. There is nothing worse than trying to locate data that you know you have collected but that you cannot find. If you are collecting interview data, make sure that you clearly label the tape or name the audio file. Chapter 4 on Ethics and Research Governance outlined the importance of anonymity and confidentiality; so do not name your file: 'interview with Karen Smith', for example.

You may choose to record some metadata on your sources; for example, where and when the data was collected and a brief summary of the key points. This metadata will help you to find the information that you need at a later date.

Your field notes should also be dated. Any documents need to be clearly labelled and organised. For paper copies, this might be in a simple ring binder in alphabetical or date order; for electronic resources, clear file structures will keep the data organised. If you go on to transcribe your data (see below), you also need to keep your transcriptions organised. The key to good data management is to be clear and systematic about how you record and organise your data from the very start of your project. Your data is the most valuable aspect of your research project, so you should treat it with care.

Data Storage

Given the importance of your data to the research, your data needs to be protected. This is important not only to you as a researcher, but also to your research participants. Tape-recorded interviews, field notes, video tapes and any important documentary evidence should be secured in, for example, a locked drawer or filing cabinet. Any electronic material should be stored in a password protected environment. It is imperative that confidential information is kept in a place that can only be accessed by the research team. You should be careful if you transfer your raw data to external drives or if you email data among the research team in case they get lost or stolen. You may also be required to keep data for some time after your research project is complete. Again, it is important that this data is archived in a secure place.

Many countries now have data protection laws about how people store personal information (names, addresses, date of birth). If you are working in the UK you should be guided by the Data Protection Act 1998, which is discussed in more detail in Chapter 4 on research ethics. If you are intending to store personal information about your research participants, you should check through the guidelines as you may need to register as a 'data user' (Arksey and Knight, 1999: 135). If you are working in another country, you should investigate what data protection laws are in place.

Transcription

Transcription is the production of a written version of audio or visual material. Researchers often prefer to have a typed textual copy of their interviews to work with (Gibbs, 2007), as it is easier to approach analysis and dissemination if the data are captured in this way. It has to be remembered that transcription is always only partial and selective (Rapley, 2007). Transcription involves a change of medium (spoken to written), and as you transfer audio material into text you can only capture what has been spoken and not the 'setting, context, body language and feel' (Arksey and Knight, 1999: 141). This means that any transcription can only ever be one of many interpretations. It is up to you to decide how detailed your transcription needs to be, although it may be worth noting that transcribing data is both time-consuming and expensive and this needs careful consideration before any final decisions are made.

Verbatim Transcription

A verbatim transcription is a document recording the exact words that have been spoken and who spoke them. You would usually number the lines of a transcription, so that when you start to work with your data, you can easily retrieve the quotes that you want to use. You would then have the name of the person who had spoken (this would not be their real name but an appropriate pseudonym, as any identifying material should be removed at the transcription stage), or some identifier (for example: I for interviewer, R for respondent). It is common to start a new line for each turn in the interview (see Box 10.1). You should be systematic in how you carry out your transcription. How will you represent a pause, or when someone speaks over someone else, or when someone shouts? There are existing transcription conventions to help you to do this (see, for example, Silverman, 2001; Rapley, 2007). Box 10.1 provides an example transcript.

Box 10.1   Example transcript – interviewer and respondent discussing crime

I: So, do you feel safe within the community?

R: Well to be honest, it depends on where you are and urm what time of day it is, I mean well sometimes at night you see loads of lads and stuff hanging around and you always think that well they are up to no good you know maybe drinking and taking drugs, I mean sometimes it's probably harmless but sometimes you think to yourself are they going to do something to hurt me.

I: Do you think there is a problem with crime in the area?

R: I suppose it tends to be well with the younger lads, you know they have nowhere to go on a night and end up just hanging around the streets, drinking, smoking and well last week one of my neighbours was telling me that a 14 year old lad was arrested for selling drugs, I mean what is this area getting like, I suppose it's scary in some ways (laughs).

I: Have you ever been a victim of crime?

R: Not me personally, thank goodness but I know well plenty of people in the area who have I mean some people get their cars broken into, houses burgled and the graffiti on the local community centre wall is well awful and makes the area look scruffy (sighs) well disgraceful isn't it really.

Working with focus group interviews can be particularly difficult, as you will have to try and differentiate between the different voices in the recording. During focus group interviews, it is not uncommon for people to interrupt each other and talk over others. This can make it hard to transcribe or even to hear what the participants are saying. You should be prepared to spend longer transcribing interviews that involve more than two people. This is why those using focus groups should always have someone with them taking notes of the conversation which can help with the identification of voices.

If you are doing conversation analysis (see below), you are likely to want to use more complicated transcription methods, for example, those which can capture changes in intonation, stress and pace.

Gist, Summary or Partial Transcription

In some cases it is perfectly acceptable not to transcribe the whole of your data. It might be appropriate to record the gist or the sense of what the interview is saying, or to write a summary of what the interview is about. This is common in policy research (Gibbs, 2007). Alternatively, you may produce a partial transcription. Here you combine a verbatim transcription of key sections of the interview with a summary of the rest of the data. It should be borne in mind that summaries and gist transcriptions can disguise 'the complexity and subtlety of the interview' (Arksey and Knight, 1999: 146) and may not provide the level of detail that you require.

Transcribing Visual Data

If you are working with visual data, transcription becomes even more difficult. Here you are working not only with spoken text, but with other non-verbal interactional work: gaze, touch, gestures, posture, positioning and action (Rapley, 2007). If you were carrying out a study into how the new open-plan office design in your organisation has been received, you would need to explore ways of noting peoples' reactions and interactions within the environment. There are different ways in which this behaviour can be recorded: written description, notation, drawings, screen shots (Rapley, 2007). The approach that you adopt should be able to best capture the information that is most useful for your project, and most feasible in terms of time and money. Visual data analysis is a difficult task and there is still a need for developing suitable methods of analysis. Further guidance on visual data analysis can be found in Flick (2009) (see also the further reading guide at the end of this chapter).

Working and Reporting Transcriptions

Rapley (2007) distinguishes two types of transcription that occur at different stages of the research process. The first he calls a 'working transcription'. This is the transcript that you use on daily basis. It will be covered in metadata: analytical comments, memos and descriptions. It is likely to be quite detailed. This transcript will be updated and added to as you notice different things as you listen again and again to your interviews. This 'working transcription' is different to the 'reporting transcription', which is the version you will use when you write the report on your research project. The 'reporting transcription' will include sufficient detail to support your argument. You may at this stage 'clean' your transcript, removing, for example, fillers such as 'erm'.

Who Does the Transcription?

There are real benefits to doing your own transcription. If you begin the transcription soon after conducting the interview, it is likely to be fresh in your mind and therefore easier to pick out what is being said. The process of listening to and having to write out the words also means that you get very close to your data. As we have already noted, however, transcription takes a long time, especially if you have not done it before. It has been estimated that an hour long interview will take four to six hours to transcribe (Gibbs, 2007). You may feel that it is a better use of your time to pay a professional to do this.

Whether you employ someone to do this work or not, you will need to factor in some time to check that the completed transcript is accurate. This could be as simple as reading through the transcript to ensure that it makes sense. You might prefer, however, to read through the transcript as the tape is playing to check for any inaccuracies and correcting them as you go along.

Starting Data Analysis

It is hard to pinpoint exactly when data analysis in qualitative research begins but it is unlikely to be at the point when you sit down with a pile of neatly typed transcripts in front of you. As you sit in an interview situation and you listen to your participant's responses you will probably be thinking about what those responses mean, as you conduct further interviews you might well be comparing and contrasting, as you transcribe the data you might start to attach interpretations to what you are writing.

As we have already indicated, there are many approaches to qualitative data analysis. The one that you adopt will be dependent on your research design, which is in turn shaped by how you see the world and what you deem to be true (your epistemological and ontological view, see Chapter 2 for a discussion of these concepts). Different approaches to data analysis will ask you to look for different things. In this section we will introduce just four broad approaches: grounded theory, semiotics, conversation analysis and framework analysis. These are tasters and if they interest you, we advise that you find a book dealing directly with them.

Grounded Theory

Grounded theory aims to develop theory inductively. This means that there is no starting hypothesis, instead theory is built through the observations of that research project (and not preconceived ideas). Those observations are constantly compared to each other and any emerging patterns are noted and coded, and categories generated. Further rounds of data collection are conducted to refine the initial categories in light of new findings. Data collection continues until there are no new codes emerging and categories become stable. These categories form the basis of a theory which can then be tested in different settings. In grounded theory, analysis and data collection are inextricably connected in a process of finding, analysing and theorising (Arksey and Knight, 1999). For example, Gardner and Abraham (2007) used a grounded theory approach to analyse semi-structured interviews around commuters' reasons for driving to work. They were able to identify five core motives from their data: journey time concerns, journey based affect, effort minimisation, personal space concern and monetary costs.

Semiotics

Semiotics is the study of signs. A sign is a unit of meaning and it can be a word, gesture, picture, smell, sound – in fact, anything that means something to someone. Semiotics shows 'how signs relate to each other in order to create and exclude particular meaning' (Silverman, 2001: 198). A sign is made up of two parts: the signifier (the thing) and the signified (the deeper meaning to which the signifier refers). Signs can have denotative meaning (describing their function) and connotative meaning (describing their socially constructed or personal meaning). The aim of semiotics is to 'uncover the hidden meanings that reside in texts' (Bryman, 2004: 393). Semiotics is a useful approach to analysis as it deals with both linguistic and visual data. If you work in an organisation that is looking to update its publicity materials, a semiotic analysis of the current materials (leaflets, website, television advert, posters and so on) might provide a good starting point for your subsequent improvements.

Conversation and Discourse Analysis

Conversation analysis focuses on how we communicate with each other to produce 'orderly social interaction' (Silverman, 2001: 167). It is based on the assumption that conversation is socially structured; it needs to be understood contextually; and that you come to understand by working closely with very detailed transcriptions (Babbie, 2004: 364). Conversation analysis often focuses on turn taking, sequencing, choice of words and speech organisation. Conversation analysis is important because it can show that 'the work of being an ordinary member of society is made up of masses of tacit, taken-for-granted knowledges and practices' (Rapley, 2007: 86). You might want to choose to investigate the ways in which service providers interact with their customers. Conversations between a librarian and a library visitor could be recorded (with their consent) and analysed in order to show the negotiations, explanations and interpretations that make up library decision making processes.

Framework

This approach to analysis was developed to be used for applied policy research. There are five stages to Framework: (1) familiarisation (establishing an overview of the data); (2) identifying a thematic framework (identification of key concepts emergent from the data and those which informed the research aims); (3) indexing (systematic application of the framework to the data); (4) charting (taking the data from its origination and collating it under the theme, giving an overview of the data as a whole); (5) and mapping and interpreting (identifying the key characteristics of the data and interpreting what they mean) (Ritchie and Spencer, 1994). To give one example: Grewal et al. (2006) used Framework to analyse 40 in-depth interviews with older people. The analysis revealed five key concepts associated with quality of life: attachment, role, enjoyment, security and control. The analysis suggested that quality of life was reduced by the loss of ability to pursue the attributes rather than the attribute itself. The aim of the project was to look for ways to develop generic measurements for quality of life which, following their research, they argue should be capability rather than preference based.

Coding Your Data

Creating Codes

Irrespective of which approach to qualitative data analysis that you adopt, the starting point for analysis is likely to be coding. As Richards and Morse (2007) note, codes at their most basic are labels for your data. Labelling metaphors are, of course, an over-simplification. Your coding, as Richards and Morse (2007) rightly highlight, does more than just tell you what kind of jam you are eating; it is part of the theorizing process. Coding involves identifying and categorizing the parts of the data that you believe will be useful for your research. How you choose to code your data depends on what research questions you are asking. In Table 10.1, an example is given of which codes that may come out of interview data.

When working with data it is important that researchers read all of their transcripts, familiarising themselves with their content prior to assigning specific codes. Approaches to coding will be varied. Gibbs (2007) suggests that the following are all aspects that could be coded:

Table 10.1   Example transcript with codes

Statements	Codes
I: So, do you feel safe within the community?	
R: Well to be honest, it depends on where you are and urm what time of day it is, I mean well sometimes at night you see loads of lads and stuff hanging around and you always think that well they are up to no good you know maybe drinking and taking drugs, I mean sometimes it's probably harmless but sometimes you think to yourself are they going to do something to hurt me.	*young people* *under age drinking/drugs*
I: Do you think there is a problem with crime in the area?	
R: I suppose it tends to be well with the younger lads, you know they have nowhere to go on a night and end up just hanging around the streets, drinking, smoking and well last week one of my neighbours was telling me that a 14 year old lad was arrested for selling drugs, I mean what is this area getting like, I suppose it's scary in some ways (laughs).	*young people* *drugs/criminal activity/young people under age drinking*
I: Have you ever been a victim of crime?	
R: Not me personally, thank goodness but I know well plenty of people in the area who have I mean some people get their cars broken into, houses burgled and the graffiti on the local community centre wall is well awful and makes the area look scruffy (sighs) well disgraceful isn't it really.	*criminal activity*

- specific acts or behaviour;
- events;
- activities;
- strategies, practices and tactics;
- states;
- meanings;
- participation;
- relationships/interactions;
- conditions/constraints;
- consequences;
- settings;
- your reflections.

Gibbs' (2007) list is not, of course, conclusive and there are many other ways that you can approach your coding, but the list provides a starting point. Your approach to coding might be concept-driven. This means that you develop your codes based on the literature you have read. This approach is deductive. In contrast, your codes might be data-driven meaning that they emerge from the data. This approach to coding is inductive (see Chapter 2, for more discussion of these approaches). However, it is common for researchers to adopt both approaches, combining both inductive and deductive approaches when coding their data.

Either way, you should be systematic in your approach to coding. You could adopt the following strategy: carrying out initial coding, re-read the data, look for overlapping codes and combine codes where necessary and then check the validity of your codes on new data. Richards and Morse (2007) offer three different kinds of coding, each with a different focus: descriptive coding, topic coding and analytic coding. These approaches increase in sophistication and you could very well use all three approaches in one piece of analysis (Table 10.2).

Table 10.2   Different kinds of coding

Descriptive coding	Codes capture the factual details of the data (for example, gender, age, context). These codes require little interpretation and are used primarily for retrieval and retaining contextual features.
Topic coding	Codes aim to identify all data on a particular topic so that it can be grouped together. This approach is useful early in analysis as it helps you to see what is in the data.
Analytic coding	Codes aim to categorise and question the data. Here you are trying to understand what the topic codes mean.

Source: Richards and Morse (2007).

As Table 10.2 suggests, as coding becomes more sophisticated you are moving away from simple description of data to analysis. This analysis could ultimately lead to concept development and theory building.

How to Code?

The simplest way to go about coding is to do it manually. It can be as simple as highlighting parts of your transcript with a coloured pen or a sticky note. You can annotate your transcript with notes or write memos on index cards. You can organise your data by cutting up your transcripts and organising the extracts into different piles (always remembering to keep a copy of the original format so that you keep the important contextual detail of any quote). A basic word-processing package can also facilitate coding. Here your highlighting can be done on screen and the different codes can be copied and pasted into new documents. While the word processing approach brings many benefits such as the speed and ease with which you can put the same extract into different codes, some researchers really enjoy physically sorting their data as it helps them to see the patterns more clearly.

As your project becomes larger it is more difficult to do manual data analysis as the data management aspects of large datasets can become very problematic. There are a number of qualitative data analysis software packages on the market that can support you if you are working with a lot of qualitative data. It is worth remembering that the software package will not do the analysis for you – that is your job. What a good package will help you do is to organise, manage and sort your dataset. Some well-known software packages include: NVivo (previously called Nudist), ATLAS.ti and The Ethnograph. These programmes are very useful for supporting data storage, coding and searching. Many packages are now designed to help you analyse not only textual but also audio and visual data. Lewins and Silver (2007) offer an overview of qualitative data analysis packages.

If you have not used qualitative data analysis packages before, you are working on a small budget and you do not have a lot of data to analyse, you may decide that it is not worth investing in a specialist software package. The amount of data that you have and the complexity of the project will influence whether you decide to use specialist software and such packages are only beneficial to analysis when the data is large and complex. However, if you do decide to go down this route you will find that you will be able to ask questions about your data that would be impossible if you were working manually. Another alternative route to consider is using more readily available software packages, which tend to be more basic, that is, programs such as Microsoft® Excel® in which you can develop charts with themes and sub-themes related to the respondents. Using these kinds of packages tends to be cheaper, easier to use and generally more accessible.

One mistake that new researchers make is to believe that coding is the totality of their data analysis. Coding is better seen as a way of organising the mass of qualitative data that you will have collected in the data collection process so that you can start to see what underlying messages there are within your data. Data analysis should not just be about giving back the data of your respondents in different words or in a different order. Analysis should go beyond description, it is about interpreting what has been said in terms of the research questions and existing literature.

Interpreting Your Findings

As you begin the process of interpretation, you might begin by looking at the categories that you have developed through the process of coding and see whether there are any patterns within the categories allowing the categories to be combined. You may want to explore different ways of representing these connections. You might, for example, use a diagram, a model or a network (Richards and Morse, 2007). You should choose the approach that helps you best to 'see' what the data is telling you.

As you combine the coding categories, you should be asking yourself questions about what you are doing. The questions should relate to your research questions or the policy problems that you are investigating. For example: are there any dominant themes that exist across all of the data? Do these themes mirror what you already know about the area (from your reading)? Can you identify any connections between your categories? How strong are the links? How different or similar are the categories? Does one thing seem to lead to another thing happening? How does what you have found compare to what had already been written about in the literature? Are there any exceptions to what you are proposing, and why are they there? The answers to your questions will be the foundations of your interpretation. It is these questions that will ensure that your analysis is not just 'getting a sense' of the data, but making sense of it and creating new meanings through your treatment of it (Sandelowski, 1998: 376).

You should keep a note of your thinking during this process, perhaps through memos (Richards and Morse, 2007) or in your research diary as this will record the development of your ideas. As discussed in Chapter 2, research is never neutral and we need to be aware of our role in the meaning-making process. A white, male, doctoral student and a woman who had recently gained indefinite leave to remain in the UK, for example, would analyse data from an interview study on female asylum seekers' experiences in the UK very differently. Reflecting on these influences and understanding how they shape your interpretations is important and needs to be recognised. A research diary can help you to become aware of these issues.

It can feel daunting when you move away from the text and start to add in your own views as you may worry that you are misinterpreting what your respondents have said or done, but, as Bryman notes, stepping into this uncomfortable zone is necessary because: 'your findings acquire significance only when you have reflected on, interpreted, and theorized your data' (2004: 411). And when you are there, you will find that it is one of the most creative and satisfying aspects of the data analysis process.

Reporting Your Data Analysis

It is likely that, having spent a lot of time on your data collection and data analysis, you will want to ensure that your research has the greatest impact it can (see Chapter 14, for more information on different ways of disseminating findings). In order to do this, you need to spend some time thinking about the best way to communicate the key meanings clearly and comprehensively. Just as there is no single way to carry out qualitative data analysis, there is no single way to write it up. As Sandelowski (1998) notes, you have to choose which story you are going to tell and how you are going to tell it. Sandelowski (1998) offers three framing devices that might be of use in the presentation of your findings (see Table 10.3).

It is your decision, based on your understanding of your research and your readership, which approach you choose. It is imperative, however, that the order puts across your story in way that engages the readership and relates to your research questions.

However you choose to organise your write-up, you are likely to include some extracts of your raw data to illustrate and evidence your story. Extracts

Table 10.3 Framing devices for how to present findings

Time	The write-up reflects the unfolding of time in the participants' lives (or indeed the researcher's). It shows what happened first, second, and so on and is useful in showing how certain events are linked temporally.
Prevalence	The write-up is organised around central tendencies and ranges. The most prevailing themes within the data could be covered first, with deviations later addressed. This approach helps to emphasise convergence and divergence.
Sensitising concepts and coding families	Here concepts from theory are used to help structure the data. If you are looking to generate your own theory, you might draw on one of the 'coding families' used in grounded theory.

Source: Sandelowski (1988).

from your interviews, focus groups and/or field notes will really bring your report to life. Shorter quotes should be given in the main body of text, while you should set larger quotes apart from the rest of the text. You could also label the quotes in some way: this might be with a number, or with a pseudonym (see Box 10.2).

Box 10.2   Example of analysis – criminal activity

The data from the interviews suggest that there is varying criminal activity within the local community ranging from vandalism and car theft to burglary. Several of the respondents commented on how they had felt threatened by 'lads and stuff hanging around' and some of them had experienced criminal activity first hand or knew someone who had within the area. One respondent stated that:

> Not me personally, thank goodness but I know, well, plenty of people in the area who have I mean some people get their cars broken into, houses burgled and the graffiti on the local community centre wall is, well, awful and makes the area look scruffy (sighs), well, disgraceful isn't it really. (Rebecca)

Thinking about the presentation of your data analysis is not wasted time. Indeed it is 'essential not only to maintain the integrity of the qualitative enterprise, but also to the widest dissemination and utilization of qualitative research' (Sandelowski, 1998: 382) and should be given as much consideration as other aspects of the data analysis process.

Conclusion

This chapter has given you an overview of qualitative data analysis and provided information about how qualitative data can be analysed as part of a practitioner research project. Given the effort that goes into data collection, it is likely that you will want to know the best way to deal with it. There are, however, no hard and fast rules about how qualitative data should be analysed. What we have tried to do in this chapter is to emphasise that, whatever approach you choose, you should be clear about what you are doing and why. It is important to work systematically and this means that you should keep your data under control through careful storage and consistent recording. This will benefit not only yourself as you will be more organised, but also your participants as their personal data will be properly protected. Specifically, you should now have a detailed understanding of the different approaches to transcription and the process of coding data using software packages and manual methods of analysis. Additionally, you should be able to understand the process of interpretation and the importance of coding. Finally, this chapter has supplied guidance on making sure that you report your data in the best possible way for your intended audience to get the most from it. There is no recipe for qualitative data analysis; you have the freedom to choose the approach which suits you, your project and your readership. What is important, however, is that you can articulate why you have chosen the approach you have and that you can justify why is was the right choice.

Further Reading

Flick, U. (2009) *An Introduction to Qualitative Research*, 4th edn. London: Sage.
Gives an overall introduction to qualitative research including guidance on approaches to analysis, including the analysis of visual data.

Gibbs, G. (2007) *Analyzing Qualitative Data*. London: Sage.
Gibbs has produced a very user-friendly guide to analysing qualitative data. It also includes detailed information on approaches to transcription.

Lewins, A. and Silver, C. (2007) *Using Software in Qualitative Research: A Step-by-Step Guide*. London: Sage.
This book will be invaluable if you choose to use software in your analysis. It overviews some of the packages available to purchase and also describes how you can work with them.

Rapley, T. (2007) *Doing Conversation, Discourse and Document Analysis*. London: Sage.
Rapley's book focuses on three specific approaches to data analysis: conversation, discourse and documentary analysis. It is from the same series as Gibbs' book and is written in the same clear and informal style.

ELEVEN

Different Kinds of Quantitative Data Collection Methods

Jason Leman

By the end of this chapter you should be able to:

- choose the mode(s) of surveying that will best suit the requirements;
- identify ways to increase response rates;
- recognise the uses and drawbacks of technology in surveying.

Introduction

Quantitative research is relatively familiar to the public. From the nationwide census to market researchers on the high street, quantitative research is a common method of gathering data and feedback. However, this type of research is much more than the questionnaire that you receive. The bulk of the work happens before and after the point at which the questionnaire is delivered to the potential respondent. If the development work has been successful the respondent will find the questionnaire clear in its aims and straightforward to answer, and the responses received will answer the research problem posed. This, and the following two chapters on quantitative research methods (Chapters 11–13), aim to increase the chances of a good outcome for your survey.

As shown in Figure 11.1, the process of quantitative research can be described as a set of questions. The aim of this chapter is to answer the question 'How do you ask?'. This covers the process of quantitative data collection techniques, highlighting and comparing a variety of methods and possible pitfalls. Quantitative research is relatively easy to carry out, but also easy to get wrong. This chapter aims to steer the practitioner-researcher in the right direction, so that the study will benefit from an awareness of the limitations within which quantitative research operates and follow good practice to get the best out of it.

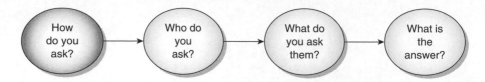

Figure 11.1   The quantitative research process as a set of questions

The next chapter (Chapter 12) covers sampling and survey design, thereby answering the questions 'Who do you ask?' and 'What do you ask them?', while Chapter 13 covers data collection and analysis, answering 'What was the answer?'.

How Do You Ask? Methods of Surveying

There are several different methods of quantitative data collection to consider, each with their own advantages and disadvantages. In most instances, practitioner-researchers will be to some extent constrained by cost. Response rates are important to consider if you want your survey to be statistically valid, meaning your conclusions could be generalised to the population you are researching. Each survey method will generate different levels of response. Each method also varies in how much time it will take to gather responses and how much it will cost per response. Table 11.1 provides a very rough guide to what you can expect.

Table 11.1   Comparison of different survey methods

Method	Expected response rate	Time for collecting 500 responses[c]	Cost per response
Postal	Typically 20% to 60%	2 months	£2–10
Online	5% to 15% lower response rate than postal[a]	1 month	20p to £5
Face-to-face	5% to 15% higher response rate than postal[b]	3 months	£10–150
Telephone	5% to 15% higher response rate than postal	2 months	£5–50
Personal/pick-up	Variable	1 week – 2 months	£1–5

Sources: [a]Shih and Fan (2008); [b]Sitzia and Wood (1998).

[c]Assuming the questionnaire is already designed and an average response rate.

Survey Modes

Different methods of presenting the questionnaire to the respondent are referred to as different *modes* of questionnaire. For example, the same questions could be given out over the phone to a respondent, online via a secure website or face-to-face in the street. Sometimes, surveys will use more than one mode, known as a *mixed-mode* survey.

Because a respondent will be filling out the questionnaire in a different way, the answers they give will not necessarily be the same. People tend to be more positive in responding to an interviewer (face-to-face or on the phone), probably because in any social situation we like to think we are pleasing other people and do not want to give negative answers. With an online or paper-based survey, the respondent may not be trying to please anyone with their answers, but also may feel less obliged to give a considered or honest answer (Roster et al., 2004).

What any practitioner-researcher should be aware of is that each mode has its own particular challenges and advantages. While the questions should remain the same, survey instruments should not be copied wholesale from one mode to another, but tailored so that they make the best use of the medium.

Self-completion Questionnaires

Self-completion questionnaires are appealing for gathering large numbers of responses for relatively low costs and are especially suited to simple questionnaires.

If the research topic requires a questionnaire that is long and complex with many open questions, presenting that as a self-completion questionnaire may be inappropriate, as it may seem difficult and/or time-consuming to complete. Unless done as part of an interview, there will be no interviewer present to make clear what the instructions or questions on the questionnaire mean, or encourage the respondent to complete the questionnaire. If a person fills out the question-naire incorrectly or incompletely then it is likely to be impractical to contact them afterwards to check what they meant at the time.

Self-completion questionnaires also require a certain level of literacy, although efforts can be made to simplify the language used. Respondents can also read questions in any order, with a risk they then respond to questions in the context of questions asked later in the questionnaire.

Going Postal: Mail Questionnaires

We can receive mail questionnaires directly through the post or enclosed in a publication such as a newspaper. Postal questionnaires have the advantage of being cheaper than paying for the time of an interviewer to ask questions, but the response rate is generally lower than face-to-face interviewing and responses can trickle in for some time after a final reminder.

If you are sending out a questionnaire by post then you have no control over exactly to whom it goes and how they are going to fill it in. The questionnaire could be filled in at teatime with a group discussion of the questions, be passed from one house-holder to another, or be filled in at the pub. Conversely, where sensitive issues are involved it is an advantage that questionnaires can potentially be filled out without another person being present, allowing for complete anonymity.

If respondents have to pay for returning the questionnaire this will *greatly* reduce response rates. It is recommended you arrange for a freepost return address through the Royal Mail Response Services. Once you have confirmed a design for the envelope you can pass this to a printing company for printing. When the question-naires are returned you should number each one (a number stamp makes this easy) and, if the survey has an identifier, make a record that the survey has been completed (see Chapter 12, for further details on database management).

Sending the questionnaire to a named person can increase the response rate, but does rely on having an up-to-date database with good information. Reminder mailings that ask the person to complete and return the questionnaire if they have not yet done so are invaluable for increasing response rates in postal surveys. A letter or postcard after two weeks and a full reminder including the questionnaire after a further 10 days is standard. Alternatively, send one full reminder after three weeks.

The Personal Touch: Handing Out Questionnaires Yourself

For pilot questionnaires or small-scale surveys, for example, in a class or small organisation, the easiest method of distribution may be to hand out question-naires yourself. It appropriate, you could also collect them in person, which is a very quick way of gathering information. It is important to consider what effect your presence has in this event. For example, if a manager handed out a survey to staff asking for feedback on their employment, it would not usually be appropriate for the manager to be present while staff were filling out forms or to personally collect the forms. An anonymous method of distribution and response, such as including a stamped addressed envelope or using an anonymous collection point, would be more suitable.

If you are carrying out an interview and want the respondent to complete a fol-low-up questionnaire, it is common practise to leave a questionnaire with the interviewee to complete and return by post.

The Drop Off: Pick-up and Complete

Another way of carrying out small-scale surveys of service users or employees is to leave the questionnaires at a pick-up point. For example, if within a clinic or hospital waiting room that users pass through, questionnaires could be sited in a clearly signed holder. Questionnaires could also be distributed by a member of staff to users to complete. The completed questionnaires would then be returned to staff or into a secure box in the waiting room.

Structured Interviewing

Interviewing can vary widely in complexity and depth. Open ended interviewing is covered in Chapter 9. The guidelines around engaging the respondent with the research, clarifying questions where appropriate, and working to be neutral apply in structured interviews also.

As we cannot clone standard interviewers who will ask questions and record answers in identical ways, there is bound to be a level of error introduced by the interviewer. The interviewer themselves might vary how they ask questions, decide to 'help' the interviewee, and vary in their behaviour to the interviewee. Also, the response of the interviewee might depend on their perception of the interviewer, for example, perceptions of ethnicity or class. Working closely with interviewers and good piloting of questionnaires can minimise their influence on the results, but the practitioner-researcher should be aware that results will be a production of both interviewee and interviewer.

It is important that interviewers are trained in general interview techniques as well as the specific requirements of your project. A briefing session is needed to cover the aims of the project and talk about the interview script (also called the interview schedule). Encourage interviewers to practice the interview so that you can answer any questions or resolve any difficulties they might have at the time. The briefing helps ensure the interviewers have the resources and information they require.

If you would like to manage or recruit interviewers yourself, you need to be aware of interviewing techniques and protocol. Issues such as safety, identification and paperwork are just as important as interview technique. More information on this can be found on the Market Research Society website (http://www.mrs.org.uk). Hiring interviewers from a company, or using a company to carry out the interviewing, will be costlier but involve much less researcher time and effort. You will still need to carry out a briefing, but the company should handle all other aspects of interviewer management.

On the Street

Street interviews are advantageous in being much quicker to organise and easier than household interviews. For this reason they are cheaper, sometimes even cheaper than telephone interviews. They are most suited to short (around 5 minute) and simple interviews on non-sensitive issues. Groups such as shoppers, particular age groups, service users or residents of a particular neighbourhood can be easily accessed through street interviews. Long or complex interviews would not be suitable, nor where you need to get a statistically reliable answer based on a randomly selected sample.

Household Interviews

If a household interview is short, the interview can be carried out on the doorstep. For longer or more complex surveys, interviewing within the home is preferable.

When interviewing households, the interviewers should be provided with a contact sheet containing a list of addresses they are expected to achieve, with space to write notes on visits to the address and the outcome of the interview. In the first entry in the example contact sheet list (Table 11.2), the interviewers has called at 7 Windy Lane on a Monday at 3 p.m. but there was no contact with a resident (NC). The interviewer called again and this time the resident said they were busy but the interviewer should call again on the Thursday. Finally, the interviewer carried out the interview (marked as 'I' in the outcome column).

Table 11.2   Example contact sheet

ID	Address	Notes	Outcome
1	7 Windy Lane	NC – Mon 3 p.m. Busy, call back Thurs 7 p.m.	I
2	12 Windy Lane	Telephone refusal	R
3	19 Windy Lane	NC – Weds 7 p.m. NE – out of quota	NE

There are standard categories to record the outcome of household interviews on contact sheets:

I   Interview

P   Partial interview, interview stopped before half could be completed

NC No contact made with resident, if they did not answer the door, or if contact made with a builder or an au-pair for example

R   Refusal to participate in the study

O   Other non-response, for example the householder is ill, or cannot speak English, or the completed questionnaire is lost

UC Contact made at address but unclear if people are resident at address

UN No contact made at address, for example interviewer cannot find house

NE Not eligible, for example the house is vacant, the address is a business, or there is no resident within the age and gender quota required

For interviewers, contact sheets are invaluable in tracking their work. For analysis, the contact sheets enable the practitioner-researcher to work out the response rates for the survey (see Box 11.1).

Box 11.1 Response rates for interview surveys

Response rate = $(I + P) / (I + P + NC + R + O + UC + UN + NE)$

Co-operation rate (number of interviews as a proportion of all those contacted)

$$= (I + P) / (I + P + R + O + UC)$$

Contact rate (Proportion of all cases where some contact was made)

$$= (I + P + R + O + UC) / (I + P + R + NC + O + UC + UN)$$

Refusal rate (Proportion of people refusing to take part)

$$= R / (I + P + NC + R + O + UC + UN + NE)$$

Source: Lynn et al. (2001).

Telephone Surveying

Telephone surveying offers an intermediate solution where face-to-face surveying is too costly but surveying by post has too low a response rate or is otherwise inadequate. Telephone surveying has its own set of challenges. In addition to the particular issues related to sampling, which are covered in the next chapter, there are a few things that are important when administering a questionnaire over the telephone:

- Rehearse beforehand and make sure you have what you need to hand.
- Decide beforehand whether to leave a message about the research on an answering machine or with another person.
- Establish credibility in the introduction by explaining clearly who you are and what you want, along with a realistic estimate of the length of the call.
- Record if the respondent declines the interview.
- Try to be open, friendly and conversational.
- Explicitly state if the discussion is to be recorded and gain consent. (Robson, 2002; Roster et al., 2004)

You will need to call back many people in the sample, as they will often be busy or not available. You can expect to get 25 per cent of responses on the first call, rising to 75 per cent after five calls, although this does depend on the availability of groups of people included in your sample (Hill, 2002). For example, older age groups are more likely to be at home during daytime than people of working age; younger groups would yield a lower response rates than older groups however often you call. Also, the increase in cold-calling has meant that people are increasingly hostile to telephone interviews.

Calling at an appropriate time can increase the response rate, so try to consider when your respondents are likely to be available. Take into account whether you are phoning homes or workplaces, and the times that people are likely to be sitting down for meals or putting children to bed, and therefore unlikely to welcome disturbances.

Interviewee Questions

If the interviewee has questions about the research or the subject that the interviewer is unable to answer, this can damage the credibility of the interviewer and the research itself in the eyes of the respondent. If the research is on a sensitive topic it is good ethical practice to provide information on where the respondent can turn for further information. If the interviewers are provided with a standard briefing note, or information leaflets to hand out, covering the reasons for the research and more information on the issue, then they will be better placed to handle such questions.

Quality Control

If you are using interviewers and want to ensure that they are carrying out the research properly, it is good practise to contact around 5–10 per cent of respondents. You can do this by including a question asking for the respondents address or phone number for checking purposes. For household interviews, the researcher can either make a selection of those households who have responded or request a contact number as part of the interview. This process can also be useful to check respondent's views about the length, content, and overall carrying out of the survey. This is not required where the interviews are recorded.

Online and Computer-based Surveys

There has been a rapid growth in the use of online surveys in recent years, offering a potentially cheap and fast way of administering a questionnaire. However they are not always the most appropriate methodology. The technical support might be costly, chasing respondents to achieve a good response rate can take as long as other survey methods (Fricker and Schonlau, 2002), and they are not suitable for sample populations with limited or no access to the Internet (for example, low income households). Even if you are sure your sample is likely to be online (that is, younger, better off people), technical problems can lead to a data loss or duplicate data, and a complex good looking survey can mean those with older software or computers being unable to access it.

As noted earlier, response rates for online surveys tend to be lower than for paper-based surveys. With an online survey, you are likely to receive the majority of responses in the first five days, with subsequent reminders after that topping up your response rate (Cooper, 2007). An email, postal or telephone contact encouraging completion will increase response rates for an online questionnaire, and offering an online option may increase response rates to a postal or telephone survey. If you need a high response rate and would like to offer an online survey then it is recommended you use such a mixed-mode approach (see below).

The standard process for carrying out an online survey involves setting up the survey, contacting the sample via email, post, or telephone to notify them of the survey, and reminding non-respondents. For example, as a practitioner-researcher you may wish to undertake a survey of health practitioners. Then, you could publicise the survey in advance through communications from their professional association, and send an email with a link to the survey. Reminder emails to non-respondents can be sent every week (varying the day of the week on which it is sent) and further communication from the professional association can be requested, adding pressure on potential respondents until the survey closes usually one month after the initial email. While these methods can ensure a better response rate from online surveys, be aware that the quality of databases containing email addresses can be poor as non-work based email addresses change frequently and are often misspelled.

As with other survey modes, if the sampled person trusts that they are part of an 'official' process, they are more likely to take part. Think about what email address the sample is being contacted by, and what site the survey is being hosted on (Jia-ming and Pei-ji, 2007). Data protection is an important issue for online surveys, especially if people may be submitting confidential information on the form. Check that the hosting of data from an online survey is secure, and that any email addresses sent to a third party will not be used for any purpose other than emailing contacts.

An important aspect of online surveys is the length. In transferring content from paper to online, web designers typically try to cut the word count in half. People are used to browsing the Internet and completing tasks quickly. To present them with a very long web-based form is likely to result in a low response rate, unless there are specific motivators, such as it being a requirement of employment or there being a significant incentive.

Accessibility and Technophobia

When planning an online survey, no assumptions should be made about the level of ICT awareness or engagement in any group. For example some university students can be unsure of using online forms, while some senior citizens can be very confident. Many people have limited access to computers and the Internet, particularly in lower income households. This will have serious implications for the sample and respondent groups (as noted above). Also, although ICT skills may be increasing, there is likely to always be a proportion of any sample that will not feel comfortable with sending private responses through online surveys. It is important that most users can access the survey without problems and with a minimum of ICT knowledge required.

What Type of Online Survey Do You Need?

There are numerous different ways to carry out an online or computer based survey. You need to consider the resources that you have, such as your budget, your own technical expertise and the technical expertise available to you.

It is common with small-scale online surveys is to use an online survey service, where you design a form on a website that then hosts the survey and gathers responses. You can also download software that you can use to construct questionnaires. This is a more technically demanding option as you will need to host the software on a web server to do this. If you are confident in developing online forms you could even construct the survey yourself.

As a first step, consider what your requirements are, compared to what is on offer. There is a world of services available online (which can be found via search engines), many of which will have free trials and some willing salespeople. Check out any company before you make a commitment, and look for recommendations from others who have used the services. If you work in a large organisation, find out if the organisation already has software you could use, or people who have already run a similar survey. For example, this may have been done in human resources and/or public relations departments.

Mixed-mode Surveys

Sometimes just using one method of data collection will not satisfy the balance of cost and response rate required. For example, a practitioner-researcher needs to get feedback on changes to a swimming club service provided to children. The service has email or phone contacts for current and previous service users. Due to a small budget, the researcher decides to only contact these parents rather than potential users, and invites parents to fill out an email survey, phoning only those who do not have an email address.

With the example above, the difficulty of mixed mode surveys should be clear. Telephone interviewing typically has a much higher response rate than online surveys. Furthermore, telephone responses tend to be more positive than online responses because the respondent is engaged in conversation with a person. Yet, given the practical limitations of money and/or time, mixed mode surveys can be the most appropriate method to use.

It should be noted that some combinations are particularly suitable to mixed mode approaches. An online survey that has a paper reminder, or a paper survey that offers the option of completing online, is a common way of improving response rates. In any case, consider who will be reached by your chosen methods and who will not.

Expected Response Rates and How to Increase Them

An issue to consider when choosing survey method is what response rate that can be expected. Rough estimates for different methods are provided in Box 11.1. There can be no guarantee on response rates and if a certain response rate is required the practitioner-researcher should be realistic about the amount of resources that could need.

Your research topic might be the most important thing to you, but a subject of little initial interest to the people in your sample. You are more likely to get a response if someone is interested in the topic of the questions. However, getting response only from those interested is a common cause of what is known as *sample bias*. If you are trying to reach people who are not engaged with your topic then you would need to plan your research accordingly. In general, response rates over 50 per cent are recommended for statistical validity. However, this may not be possible with methods such as postal or online surveys. The lower the response the higher the likelihood of sample bias, so if a statistically valid response is required then consider the survey method you are going to use.

Be realistic about the people in your sample. If they are pressed for time with numerous requests to complete surveys already (for example, as is increasingly the case in schools) they are less likely to take part. At the outset, let the respondent know roughly how much of their time the survey will take, either indicating time or number of questions or information needed.

When considering how to get a good response rate, consider what would motivate the people in your sample to respond. If you are piloting your survey or carrying out interviews or focus groups as a first stage in the research project, ask respondents about how they would like to participate in a survey and what would motivate them.

One of the most common reasons for people failing to fill out a questionnaire is the belief that it will not have any benefit for them or the 'greater good'. It will help to make clear what context the survey is part of, how the information will be used, and feed back a summary of results. This 'closing the loop' is especially important in surveys of staff or service users. However, if several previous surveys have had no effect on an issue, the potential respondents will be likely to view any claims of action with scepticism. If surveying a service or organisation, involvement of staff or users in piloting and designing the survey process is likely to help engagement in this case.

Incentives can play a part in increasing response rates; especially around topics the person might have no great personal motivation to engage with. However if the survey is about a topic that people feel good will towards, for example a survey that will practically help the NHS, then an incentive may have little, or even negative, effect.

Incentives can be offered for every respondent. However, this is generally only practical for small-scale or well-funded surveys. A more common incentive is the prize draw, where every participant has the chance of winning one or more prizes. It is good practice to offer an alternative to a prize, for example cash or donation to charity. Incentives can also be ones that use resources available to the client in a way that encourages the people in the sample to respond. For example, a swimming pool may offer free lessons to a school in return for that school taking part in a detailed study. It is worth thinking creatively about what incentives you may be able to offer, particularly if resources are an issue, and you may wish to consider options like sponsorship, if this is appropriate (for example, advertising a company on the questionnaire or displaying a logo in exchange for prizes). Be aware, however, that some respondents may be concerned about private sector involvement in questionnaires on certain issues (see Chapter 9, for more information on incentives).

Response rates typically vary between different groups of people. A typical respondent to a survey of the whole population would be an older woman, ethnically white British, well educated and from a higher social class. Yet the motivations to respond to a survey are different, and different survey modes will tend to reach different demographic groups. The survey format, questions and incentives can be tailored to a particular group to raise response. To achieve a representative analysis, the responses can be weighted in proportion to the sample you want your survey to reflect.

It has been found advantageous, where possible, to alert people to a forthcoming survey beforehand. This especially applies to household interviews where an interviewer will be calling at the household in person or interviewing over the telephone. The letter will inform people in advance and so help remove initial suspicions, give interviewers confidence as part of an 'official' process, and eliminate the surprise of a cold call. For online surveys or workplace telephone surveys an advance email or letter can also improve response rates (De Leeuw et al, 2007; Robson, 2002). If within an organisation or service, the practitioner-researcher can also alert people through publicity, for example, putting up posters or disseminating flyers alerting people to the survey.

For self-completion and Internet surveys, visual design is particularly important. This is covered in the next chapter.

Conclusion

Generally the choice between one survey mode and another is made on the basis of appropriateness for the people being asked, available resources and desired response rate. It is easy when planning research to aspire to all interviews being carried out face-to-face with a complex CATI form, however the reality may need to be different, with a resulting drop in response rate. This chapter should have given you grounding in how to make that judgement. In choosing mode it is important is to consider what group you wish to target, the sample of people who are best placed to answer your research question and how many of them you need to respond. Targeting people is part of the sampling process, which is covered in the next chapter of this book.

Further Reading

Bryman, A. (2008) *Social Research Methods*, 3rd edn. Oxford: Oxford University Press.
Bryman has produced a short, practical guide to social research using surveys along with a more comprehensive guide that covers these topics.

Buckingham, A. and Saunders, P. (2004) *The Survey Methods Workbook: From Design to Analysis*. Cambridge: Polity Press.
This is a comprehensive guide to questionnaire-based research, especially interviewing, from design to analysis, pointing out pitfalls to avoid with real examples of research.

Gray, D.E. (2009) *Doing Research in the Real World*, 2nd end. London: Sage.
Gray has written a comprehensive and practical guide to carrying out research with many examples and pointers towards good practice.

Robson, C. (2002) *Real World Research. A Resource for Social Scientists and Practitioner-Researchers*, 2nd edn. Oxford: Blackwell.
Robson provides an extensive guide to research covering both qualitative and quantitative methods for social scientists and practitioner-researchers.

TWELVE

Quantitative Data Collection

Jason Leman

By the end of this chapter you should be able to:

- identify the group of people you want to survey;
- work out how many people in this group you need to survey;
- compare different methods of sampling and choose the most appropriate;
- apply sampling methods with an awareness of the issues arising;
- design questions that will produce the answers you want; -
- handle issues such as anonymity and confidentiality;
- identify questions that may be difficult to analyse;
- properly evaluate questionnaires through piloting.

Introduction

As noted in Chapter 11, quantitative research is easy to carry out, but also easy to get wrong. This chapter aims to steer you in the right direction, set out the limitations within which quantitative research operates and good practice to follow so as to get the best out of it. In addition, this chapter aims to highlight the possible pitfalls you will encounter when aiming for reliable and valid survey results. It begins by considering the common methods of sampling (deciding who to ask) and then moves on to questionnaire design (what to ask). These steps in the quantitative research process are illustrated in Figure 12.1.

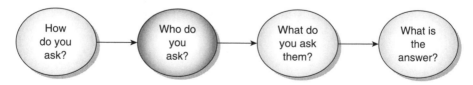

Figure 12.1   The quantitative research process

Who Do You Ask? Sampling

Who Would You Like To Ask? Defining Your Population

Once you have specified your research question, you need to select for which population this question is relevant. This is the *theoretical population* of people, groups, companies and so on you are interested in making conclusions about. What is appropriate is defined by your research question.

In this chapter, we will use the example of research into the possibility of offering well-being and counselling services at a local leisure centre. There are several key factors that you could consider in defining the theoretical population depending on the research questions:

- Geographic factors, for example, any research conclusions only apply to the population of a particular town, or to people located near transport links.
- Demographic factors, for example, the conclusions only apply to people with low income, or over 60, or from a religious community.
- Usage factors, for example, the conclusions only apply to people who use a service.
- Awareness factors, for example, the conclusions only apply to people who are aware of a service.

Who Do You Really Ask? How Large a Sample

Although we would like to ask everyone in our theoretical population for their attitudes or experiences, in practice we need contact details and a means to ask them. You may decide that you can only practically sample from the residents of the town where the leisure centre is located, and then only those who are recorded on the electoral register. This subset of the theoretical population is called the *sample frame*. When researchers talk about results being statistically significant, this is in relation to the sample frame.

Sometimes a sample frame cannot be defined. For example, if you want to offer a service to homeless people at the leisure centre, you would find that it would be very difficult to draw up a sample frame of all homeless people in the town. The sample frame could be defined as the users of an existing homeless service, but such a service is likely to only serve an unknown fraction of the homeless population. In this case it is doubtful if the sample frame would then be a reasonable reflection of the theoretical population, therefore *non-probability sampling* would be used, where the sample frame can be undefined.

In theory, the survey could include everyone in the sample frame, a *census sample*. This is often done where the numbers of people are small or where the numbers of people surveyed does not add considerably to the cost. Then again, just because you can include everyone in your survey does not mean that you should. By means of well thought-through and applied sampling methods, findings based on a sample of the population can be nearly as accurate as a census survey but to a much lower cost. We can usually only ask questions of a limited number of people. This is a smaller sample of the sample frame. Often the sample size is dictated by the resources available, with implications for what can be done with the results.

Generalising to the Population

When choosing how large your sample should be it is important to consider whether you want to generalise your survey results to the sample frame. For many purposes, for example a pilot study, a descriptive survey relating to a single service, or a survey providing contextual information as part of a wider project, you may not need a representative sample. Qualitative analysis of quantitative data, that is, looking at the figures and interpreting them without being statistically rigorous, can be informative if there are no particular reasons for your sample to differ from the population under study (Green, 2001; see Chapter 13, for more on descriptive analysis).

If you want to ensure a statistically significant sample, refer to the further reading at the end of the chapter. Whether or not you are planning to test your conclusions statistically, you should be aware of the impact sample size has on the validity of the conclusions you might make. In generalising we are assuming that the attitudes or experiences of our sample will be representative of the people we want to study. For example, you may receive 380 responses to a randomly sampled survey about interest in the provision of extra services at the leisure centre. Let us say that half the respondents state they are interested. Assuming that everything about the questionnaire and sampling is right, you can be 95 per cent confident that between 47.5 and 52.5 per cent (a 5 per cent margin of error, around 50 per cent) of the whole population of the town would state they were interested in the services. That is a good level of confidence for social science research.

You may then now want to analyse responses from people who are disabled. This leaves a sample of 20 responses, of which 60 per cent say they are interested in extra services, which might lead you to conclude that people who are disabled are more interested in using the services. Such a conclusion would need to be qualified because even if the sample frame only contained 40 people who are disabled, a sample of 20 people leaves a big margin of error and a low confidence level. Even if you are not making claims about statistical validity, drawing conclusions that may affect decisions made about the disabled from the descriptive results could be wholly wrong.

Table 12.1 contains examples of statistical significance for different sample response sizes (shown in the body of the table) and sample frame sizes (shown at the top). For any research the practitioner-researcher needs to consider how sample size affects the validity of results, especially if they are influencing services or conditions for a wider population. There are some simple online tools

Table 12.1 Sample response and generalisability to the sample frame

Generalisability	Margin of error (%)	Confidence level (%)	Sample frame 40,000	4,000	400	40
Very high	±1	99	11,750	3,000	390	40
High	±3	95	1,050	850	300	39
Medium	±5	95	380	350	200	37
Medium	±5	90	270	250	160	35
Low	±10	90	70	70	60	25

to use for determining sample sizes, use a search engine to find a 'sample size calculator'.

When you have decided on the sample size needed, the next factor to consider is the *response rate* of the survey method you are using. You will need to increase the sample size according to how many people you expect to respond. For a postal survey or a survey carried out through face-to-face interviews in households it is quite common to quadruple the sample size you require for statistical purposes (that is, to survey 4000 people in order to get 1000 usable responses). This is because you may get just a quarter of the people responding due to non-response and invalid addresses (see the section on survey modes in Chapter 11 for more on response rates).

Who Do You Pick? How to Sample

There are essentially two methods of sampling – probability sampling and non-probability sampling. Probability sampling is taking a random sample (all the people you *will* ask) of the sample frame (all the people you would *like* to ask). Non-probability sampling covers everything from asking the first people you meet on the street to asking certain numbers of people within groups defined by age, gender, ethnicity and so on. In general, probability sampling means you can better generalise your results to the population you want to study, while non-probability sampling is more suited to particular research objectives such as teasing out age, gender or ethnicity variations in service usage. Much depends on the overall project design, the resources you have, and what type of analysis is being performed on the answers (see also Hague et al., 2004; Babbie, 2007).

Probability Sampling
The basic form of probability sampling is a *simple random sample*, where people from the sample frame are randomly selected. This is a very robust method of sampling and can be easily done for some populations, such as households, employees and students (see Box 12.1).

Box 12.1　Sampling packages

Statistical packages such as SPSS and SAS can easily produce a random sample from a list of addresses or other details. A random sample can also be simply obtained in any spreadsheet. Put the list into the spreadsheet and in the first empty column generate a random number for each entry. In applications such as Microsoft® Excel® and OpenOffice Calc this is termed a RAND() function. Paste this function so each address is assigned a random number. Sort all the addresses by descending value of this number. The entries will now be randomly sorted. For a sample of 200, select the first 200 on the list; for 500, the first 500 on the list, and so on.

In our example, you may want to assess interest in extra services at the leisure centre between people living nearby and people living further away, and decide to survey households on four streets adjacent to the leisure centre. A random sample might get a greater proportion of responses from some streets than others. To address this you could employ *systematic sampling*. The sample frame is divided by the sample size to get a *sampling interval*. If the four streets have 100 houses and you want to sample 25, the sampling interval would be four. You could randomly pick a number from one to four, start at that number on the sample frame, and then sample every fourth house. This will provide the same proportion sampled on each street. However, if there is any regular pattern in the sample frame, for example, every fourth house being detached and the rest terraced cottages, then error can creep in.

A more robust method would be to randomly sample the same proportion of people on each street. You could decide to sample a quarter of the households on the four streets. For the 40 houses on one street you could randomly sample 10 from that street, for the 8 houses on another street you could randomly sample 2, and so on. This is called a *stratified random sample*, and is often used when surveying different areas or populations to make sure each area or population is represented proportionately in the final sample.

Box 12.2　Postcode address files

If a researcher wants to sample households, for a postal survey for example, they will need a list of addresses in the area. These are termed 'postcode address files' and are available from the Royal Mail in the UK. The data is also supplied as part of several programs that combine postcode data with Census data, market research data, and so on.

Using the postcode address file (Box 12.2) and a map, you might then pick four neighbouring streets that are around 2 kilometres from the leisure centre and four neighbouring streets from around 3 kilometres from the pool and sample every address in the streets selected. This is known as a *cluster sample* and is often used for household interview surveys as it reduces the travelling time needed for interviewers. The method is also used for studies on demographic clusters, for example studying the bottom fifth and top fifth earners in an organisation. This method has a higher sampling error than other methods because the sample chosen might be unrepresentative of the sample frame. For example, the households on the four streets selected might have better transport links or house people with a lower socio-economic status than other households at that distance from the leisure centre.

A more robust method would be to randomly sample 16 streets from 2 and 3 kilometres from the pool, and then randomly sample a proportion within each street. This is termed a *multi-stage sample* because you have taken a simple *random sample* of streets and then a *stratified systematic sample* of households on those streets.

Non-probability Sampling

Most non-probability sampling is not generalisable and is best suited to descriptive work or pilot surveys. Where non-probability sampling is to be made generalisable, the researcher-practitioner needs a good awareness of the statistical issues involved. An example is the *quota sample*.

Quota sampling is where a couple of key characteristics, such as age and gender, are controlled for in choosing respondents. For example, a quota sample of 200 would be drawn, where, for example, the proportion of males and females in different age categories are the same as the proportions for the whole population. The interviewer would then ask a screening question about age and gender of a potential interviewee and only interview if they need to fill the quota for that interviewees' age and gender (Worcester, 1996). A range of demographic questions, such as on income and education, can also aid assessment of how representative the sample has been for other variables. To properly generate generalisable results from such a survey is a complex task and the practitioner-researcher would need advice on the appropriate statistical weighting.

A *judgement sample* relies on the judgement of the interviewer. This could be useful for a quick pilot of a survey tool but would not be useful for most analytical purposes. Another type of sampling that is commonly used in the very initial phases of piloting is the *convenience sample*. As the name indicates, the researcher just selects the most convenient sample available, for example, colleagues or people using a service at that time.

A particular difficulty in social research is accessing groups who are either very small compared to the overall population or difficult to access, for example, amateur musicians or illegal immigrants. In these cases it is usually impossible to construct the sample frame as there is no complete list of people within the group. The practitioner-researcher can rely on contacting people at a social event, activity or government programme. This *targeted sampling* is useful for groups who might not usually have much contact with one another outside of a particular event. However, many groups of interest have members not engaged in any accessible public activity.

To counter the problems with targeted sampling, the practitioner-researcher can ask respondents in the targeted sample for contact details of acquaintances with shared characteristics in relation to the research question, that is, that are also illegal immigrants or amateur musicians. The researcher then follows those contacts up, and after surveying asks them for further contacts and so on. Called *snowball sampling*, this method is most useful in studies where the statistical validity is not important. It is based on using the social networks of the target population, and can also be used to explore how these networks are structured.

A related method is *respondent-driven sampling*. This method relies on cards being passed on by respondents to others in the target group, who then approach the interviewers themselves. It is thought to explore social networks more fully than snowball sampling and could produce statistically valid samples (Salganik and Heckathorn, 2004). The advantages and disadvantages of probability and non-probability sampling are summarised in Table 12.2.

Telephone Sampling

If you want to carry out a telephone survey, there are some particular issues to do with selecting a sample. Some marketing data (see Box 12.2 on postcode address files) comes with phone numbers attached to addresses, however, the quality of this data can be variable. It is not recommended to pick numbers from

Table 12.2   Advantages and disadvantages of probability sampling versus non-probability sampling

Sampling method	Statistical strength	Notes
Probability		Need a complete sample frame
Simple random	High	Suitable for large scale surveys
Systematic	High/Medium	Easy to get proportionate samples
Stratified	High	Robust method for proportionate samples
Cluster	Medium	Good for quick household interview surveys
Non-probability		
Quota	Medium	Can be statistically valid but need advice
Convenience	Low	Good for piloting questionnaires
Judgement	Low	Good for social networks and hard to reach groups
Snowball	Low	
Respondent-driven	Medium	Another good method for social networks

a phone book, because certain demographic groups are more likely to be unlisted and that will affect the validity of your sample. It is recommended to get a properly sampled telephone database. Unless you are targeting respondents unlikely to use a landline, mobile phone numbers should be avoided, as that will *oversample* households with both a mobile phone and a landline, and increase costs (Nicolaas, 2004).

Household Sampling

For household surveys, to pick which member of the household to interview the preferred method is asking to interview the person in the household with the most recent birthday – the question is simple, non-invasive and produces a truly random sample. However it will involve much more time and expense as interviews often have to be arranged for another time. You should also be aware that sampling addresses will also tend to *oversample* individuals in single person households.

The time and cost demands of household interviews are high. If you are weighing up the costs of having more interviews or a fully random sample, the choice should usually be towards doing more interviews and simply interviewing the first person who answers (Kennedy, 1993).

What Do You Ask Them? Questionnaire Design

As illustrated in Figure 12.2, we now move on to what to ask, that is, questionnaire design. Questionnaire design is the most important aspect of survey research. If the sampling goes wrong, or the response rate is low, at least you will have some data, albeit not generalisable. If the questionnaire is poorly designed, you will either receive very little data, or get data that is useless because you cannot properly interpret it.

At all times it is important to keep your research question in mind. What are you asking, and what is the simplest way to find out the answer? A challenge of questionnaire design is adapting what might be complex theoretical questions into a research tool that is accessible, of reasonable length and easily understood by the general public. As people receive more surveys the phenomenon of survey fatigue becomes common; practitioner-researchers should be aware that the longer the questionnaire, the lower the meaningful response may be.

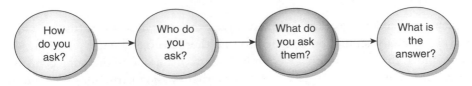

Figure 12.2   The quantitative research process

Reliability and Validity

A major barrier to getting meaningful responses is that people react to numerous psychological cues, can change their mind quite fluidly, can misinterpret questions easily, and so on. These are the twin issues of reliability (will different people understand the question in the same way?) and validity (do answers to your question really mean what you say they do?) (see Chapter 3, for more on reliability and validity).

It is recommended that where possible, researchers use questions from previous studies that have been tested for reliability and validity. However, the reality of practitioner-research is that the demands on the research may make this impossible, and so items (questions) and scales will have to be constructed. The practitioner-researcher needs to take care over the design of the survey, properly piloting the survey to check that what you think people are answering, is actually what they are answering (Pannell and Pannell, 1999). Caution should also be used in comparing results to prior research where new questions have been used.

A few basic rules should be kept in mind:

- never ask unnecessary questions;
- never ask for data you can readily get from elsewhere;
- keep it as short and simple as possible;
- explain the meaning of questions concisely – avoiding ambiguity;
- always pilot a questionnaire, even if just with friends or colleagues.

Self-completion Questionnaires

Self-completion questionnaires are those given or sent to a respondent for them to fill out. Respondents may not read a covering letter or email, so the survey itself should have a clear title, short introduction to the survey and instructions on how to complete. Having a survey that is clear, well laid out, logical in flow from one question to the next and visually attractive to the respondent will increase response rates and improve quality of response.

To aid accessibility, type should be at least 10 pt sans-serif font, preferably 12 pt. If the survey is using colour, it is important that survey text will still be clear. Overall, when deciding on the format, accessibility should always take priority.

Interviewer Scripts

When an interviewer is carrying out a survey, the interview script (list or schedule of questions) should be designed so that there is no ambiguity or confusion. Remember that your interviewers might know little about the subject of the research; the purpose of the script is to give them basic instructions for them to follow so they can get the information needed. Directions for the interviewer should be in capitals, what they read out to the respondent should be in sentence case. When choice lists or scales are offered to the interviewee, it is good practice to have a showcard – an A4 laminated piece of card with a large font version of the options on a scale – that the interviewer can show the respondent during the interview.

The interview script should aim to be neutral and informative. A question or statement that is too long might lead to interviewers paraphrasing and in effect asking a different question from that intended; equally a question or statement that is too short might not give enough information and lead to interviewers providing their own interpretation. Attention needs to be taken of the educational and language competence levels of interviewees. Going through the directions and language used in a draft script with an experienced interviewer or someone used to conversing and working with the particular social group (such as elderly or English as second language speakers) can be very useful, as they may have a good awareness of problems that might arise.

The initial request for an interview is best left unscripted as that is a useful way for an interviewer to establish a rapport with the potential respondent, however, it is important to ensure that establish a rapport does not involve leading the respondent towards certain responses (for example, by sounding blasé about the subject of the research and thus encouraging flippant responses). Flexibility is also good for household interviews, with regard to whether the interviewer carries out the interview there and then, or makes an appointment (Groves and McGonagle, 2001). An example interview script is provided later in Figure 12.4.

Piloting Questionnaires

A vital part of questionnaire design is piloting. This can help ensure that questions are worded correctly and that respondents navigate round the questionnaire correctly. The pilots can also help ensure that people understand the questions in the same way as each other (reliability), and their answers mean what you take them to mean (validity); although it is very difficult to practically prove this (Heath and Martin, 1997).

A typical piloting of a questionnaire might first involve a convenience sample pilot with colleagues and friends to remove any obvious errors. Then a full pilot study would be carried out. To ensure the survey will not encounter particular difficulties it should be piloted with around 50 respondents. This does depend on your sample frame, as for some populations it will be difficult to pilot on more than a few respondents. Limitations of time and resources can also make piloting difficult, but the more feedback you can get before carrying out the full survey, the more issues with wording and routing will be ironed out.

It is good practice to ask respondents to fill in a short questionnaire about the pilot, covering how long it took, whether it was clear, and whether they did not like any of the questions. You can also improve the usefulness of ad hoc pilots by asking people to set aside an appropriate time to complete the questionnaire and being on hand to discuss what they were thinking about when answering a question. Be sure to review all the responses and your notes in revising the survey. Carrying out a pilot analysis of the data collected can also help raise issues with question or scale design.

If the changes made to the questionnaire after the full pilot are significant, for example, introduction of new questions, changing of scales, merging of questions, there should be another full pilot with these changes to the survey instrument. If this is not possible, a minimum of an ad hoc second pilot with colleagues or friends should be carried out.

Anonymity and Confidentiality

If a survey is anonymous then the respondent will not be identifiable in any way on the survey, therefore they can respond without being concerned about repercussions. It should be made clear what is happening to the data and that along with the responses being anonymous, no information would be released that could identify an individual.

Stating that a survey is confidential is often mistaken by respondents for stating that it is anonymous. Confidentiality is part of adhering to the Data Protection Act, which states that the results and statistics of any research should not identify any particular individual or group. The Market Research Society Code of Conduct also has clear recommendations for the handling of data. If the information being collected is not anonymous, it should be made clear to the respondent who will see the data, especially if the data is being forwarded to people outside of the research team. Chapter 4 explores these issues in more detail.

Question Design

The general questions you will ask in the questionnaire should be largely defined by desk research and qualitative research prior to the quantitative survey. This section will cover how to design questions and scales that will give useable answers, before moving on to a more general discussion of question design.

Routing and Navigation

If a respondent is asked a question that they do not know the answer or to, or it does not apply to them, they may still give a response. To avoid such meaningless responses you will want to select a particular group of respondents, for example, if they work in a particular job role or have had experience of a particular service. This requires a routing question, which serves as a provider of data in its own right, but also to direct respondents or interviewers to relevant sections of the questionnaire. See Q1 on the example self-completion questionnaire (Figure 12.3) that routes respondents around two questions if they do not apply, or the screening question on the interviewer script that will only continue the interview if the respondent is on a low income band (Figure 12.4). Note that the example avoids duplicate values by having £9999 as the upper bound on one option and £10,000 as the lower bound on the next. The question also covers all possible options and also includes a 'prefer not to say' option, a common response to questions concerning income.

Routing should be as simple and clear as possible; always remember that a response incorrectly entered can be removed, but a response that is not there because the respondent was routed around it cannot, and should not, be constructed from subsequent responses.

Scale Questions (Ordinal Level Questions)

Scales come in two basic forms. The scale can come with each possible response labelled (Q4 on the self-completion example, Figure 12.3), or with only the end-points labelled (Q5 on Figure 12.3). Scales with four, five or seven points are common, although anything from three- to 12-point scales are used.

The labelled scale is often called a Likert scale. It can provide clear descriptive analysis such as '75 per cent agreed or strongly agreed with this question'. This type of scale is an *ordinal measure* (see Chapter 13, for more information on this), where there is some kind of rank to order the responses.

The second example, with only endpoints labelled, is known as a *semantic scale*. This can be treated as an *interval measure*, where we assume that the respondent is assigning equal intervals between each point on the scale. Although not strictly statistically correct, a typical analysis can use means, for example, 'For those on low incomes, Question A had a mean response of 4.24, higher than the overall mean of 3.76'.

Where it is possible that an answer may not apply to a respondent, it is advisable to have a 'Not applicable' or 'N/A' option at the end of the scale. If it is likely the respondent might not be able to answer a question, then a 'Don't know' or 'D/K' option (as in Q4, Figure 12.3) might also be advised. The two can be combined into a 'N/A or D/K', as the answers will need to be discounted from analysis in either case.

When the scale is constructed of opposites, such as agree and disagree, it is common to have a neutral middle value, such as 'neither agree nor disagree'. If a middle option is used then it is strongly recommended a 'D/K or N/A' option is also provided, to try and guide respondents who are unsure or find the question not applicable away from marking the neutral option. If you do not include a middle option then try and guide respondents who are undecided away from randomly ticking a point on the scale, for example by stating in the instructions, 'if you cannot decide whether you agree or disagree with a question, please leave the question blank or mark "Don't know"'.

Single-choice Lists

Along with from defining what questions to ask, the purpose of much of the qualitative research prior to a quantitative survey will be to define appropriate categories that answers may fall into. Having categories or attributes to measure that are not meaningful to the respondent will return meaningless answers.

Single choice lists can be a simple selection of possibilities, for example, how the respondent travelled to use a service. Qualitative research could explore the most common types of transport, and also pick up distinctions within transport, such as 'Bus, paying concessionary rate' and 'Bus, paying full fare'. It is also important that where the respondent is selecting a single option, they are asked to indicate what is usually or mostly applicable (for example, Q3, Figure 12.3). To avoid having to include every conceivable method of transport, the question could also include an 'Other' selection with a space to give an open comment, so that respondents can provide their own answer if appropriate.

Multiple-choice Lists

The questions above are single choice questions, where the respondent ticks only one answer. We can also ask the respondent to tick all the answers that apply in a list, a *multiple-choice question* (see Q2, Figure 12.3).

A common difficulty is ensuring that respondents only give single answers for single choice lists and multiple answers for multiple-choice lists. It is good practice to have an instruction directing the respondent where appropriate, as on Q2 and Q3. Note also the visual cue of differently shaped tick boxes (Figure 12.3).

Standard Scales

Standard scales are mostly used to gather demographic data about the respondents. In choosing the scales to use, you should be aware of the data you with which you will be making the comparison. For example, with an ethnicity questions, will you be comparing the demographic profile of your respondents to Census data? If so, you will need to use the same categories.

When asking a question about personal relationships, you should include co-habiting or living with partner as an option: 'Are you: Divorced, Living with partner, Married, Single, Widowed, Other (please specify) …'.

It is good practice to ask demographic questions at the end of a questionnaire, as asking for personal information up front can put people off or change the responses they give. For some demographic questions, such as on ethnicity, the response can be different or change over time as social attitudes change (for example, Craemer, 2006; Mangels and Neves 2007). Although we as researchers need to classify people for analysis, we should be aware that individuals might object to categorising themselves into to the classifications we are offering – the fastest growing response for ethnicity is 'Other'.

Ranking Questions

Ranking questions ask the respondent to rank multiple aspects, for example, ranking the three most important reasons for using the leisure centre from 1 to 3, as shown in B3 on the sample interviewer script (Figure 12.4). The prime difficulty

Croaktown Leisure   **Questionnaire on new services**

Croaktown Leisure is working to expand the range of services available at the centre. This questionnaire wants to get your views on what use at the centre now, and what you might want to use at the centre in the future.

All the information you give is entirely confidential and treated in accordance with the Data Protection Act. The information you give will not be used in any way that could identify you.

IMPORTANT: Please read before completing the questionnaire

As this questionnaire will be read by a computer scanner please :

- Mark not applicable, **NA**, if the question does not apply;
- **mark** or **fill** the circles;
- use **black or blue ink** to complete the form;
- **do not** strike through a block of circles;
- if you make a **mistake - cross through** the option and select the right one.

Q1 In the past month, have you gone to any   Yes O   No O   ▶Please go to **Q4**
sporting or leisure facilities *in Croaktown*?   ▼

Q2 Which leisure facilities you have used in the past month?
(please mark all that apply)

Croaktown Leisure Centre   ☐   Croaktown Golf Club   ☐

Croaktown Skatepark   ☐   Ribbiton Bowling Green   ☐

Other (please specify) _____

Q3 What is the most important reason you use leisure or sports facilities? *(please mark only one)*

Gets me out of the house   O   Improves my sporting ability   O

Improves my fitness   O   To meet people   O

Other (please specify) _____

Q4 In general, would you say:

	Very Good	**Good**	**Fair**	**Poor**	**Don't Know**
my overall health is…	O	O	O	O	O
my level of physical fitness is…	O	O	O	O	O
my mental well being is…	O	O	O	O	O

Q5 Please rate on the scale below, how important leisure and sports facilities in Croaktown are to your daily life:

Not at all important   1   2   3   4   5   6   7   Very important
                          O   O   O   O   O   O   O   **PTO**

Figure 12.3   Example self-completion questionnaire

Croaktown Leisure   **INTERVIEWER BOOKLET**

A1) READ ALOUD THE INTRODUCTION BELOW

Thank you very much for agreeing to take part in this survey. As we explained in the letter, this is a survey about the impact of leisure facilities in Croaktown, especially people who have lower incomes. The information you give will not be used in any way that could identify you. We are interested in people's views, and there are no right or wrong answers. To start with, I will need to ask you a question about your income.

A2) HOLD UP SHOWCARD A AND ASK THE SCREENING QUESTION BELOW

SCREENING QUESTION
Is your annual household income, that is, the combined income of everyone in your household:

	TICK RESPONSE	
£0 to £9,999	O	GO TO **B1**
£10,000 to 19,999	O	GO TO **B1**
Over £20,000	O	GO TO **A3**
Prefer not to say	O	GO TO **A3**

A3) THANK THE RESPONDENT FOR THEIR TIME AND END THE INTERVIEW.

Respondent ID _____

Interviewer ID _____

Start time _____ End time _____

CONTACT PHONE NUMBERS	
Abi	0123 444 5678
Bob	0234 555 6789
Carol	0345 666 7890

B1) FILL IN RESPONDENT ID, INTERVIEWER ID, AND START TIME ABOVE. THEN GO TO **B2**

B2) What leisure facilities you have used in the past month?:
MARK ALL THAT APPLY. DO NOT PROMPT EXCEPT FOR CLARIFICATION
Croaktown Bowling Green _____   Croaktown Skatepark _____
Croaktown Swimming Pool _____   Other leisure facility _____
                                          in Croaktown

B3) HOLD UP SHOWCARD B
I'm now going to ask you to rank the three most important reasons why you go to leisure facilities. What is the most important reason [RANK FIRST], the next most important reason [RANK SECOND], the next most important reason [RANK THIRD].

	RANK		RANK
Gets me out of the house	__	I want to improve my skill in the activity	__
To meet up with friends	__	I enjoy doing the activity	__
I want to improve my fitness	__	To meet people	__
Other 1_____	__	Other 2 _____	__

Figure 12.4 Example interviewer script

with such a question is that many respondents will not rank correctly, for example, giving the same rank to several items, or only ranking one item. These questions work better in interviewer surveys, where the interviewer can guide the respondent through the question, or online surveys where the questionnaire will not allow an incorrect response. An alternative is to ask a question on importance for each item, or ask for the most important item (as in Q3, Figure 12.3) and then rank the items by the frequency of responses.

Question Design and Analysis

At the design stage the practitioner-researcher should always have in mind how they will analyse the results of a question. A common pitfall is to ask multiple questions in one, for example, in asking participants to rate the following statement: 'The Swimming pool has good facilities and access.' This gives an overall rating of facilities *and* access, but no conclusions could be drawn about facilities *or* access and it may frustrate respondents wanting to give feedback about one aspect. Combination questions can be used, but it is important to be aware of the limitations on analysis your question is imposing.

Another pitfall is to offer a statement such as 'the right amount of money is spent on wheelchair access', and ask the respondent to indicate whether they agree or disagree with the statement. If the respondent disagreed with the answer the practitioner-researcher would have no way of knowing if the respondent thought too little or too much was being spent. The practitioner-researcher should think about how they would interpret a positive or negative response to each statement.

Finally, when choosing an ordinal scale, think how you are going to present the data. For example, a question asking how often someone uses a service could be worded 'All the time, often, sometimes, rarely, never'. However, if you need to know what 'sometimes' actually means in practice it may be unsuitable. In this case a better scale would be 'Daily, Weekly, Monthly, Rarely, Never', which still has problems (see below), but is often easier to analyse.

Clarity and Language

Where there might be ambiguity, you can clarify statements. For example, on the scale above, what would someone who uses it three times a week put? This could be clarified by adding a statement, here in brackets, after the question: 'How often do you use the facilities (for example, if you use the facilities more than once a week but not everyday, please put weekly)?' Clarify language and give examples where it might help, but be aware that the questionnaire should not be cluttered, or come across as patronising.

Always try to use unambiguous and clear language. 'It is not uncommon for you to experience episodes of anxiety related to claustrophobia when using the changing facilities' could be reworded as 'Do you usually feel nervous or anxious about being in the changing cubicle?' In the second example, the double negative 'it is not uncommon' has been removed, in general it is better to avoid negatives such as 'not'. The language should also be as simple as possible (see Further Reading at the end of the chapter for tools that help with this). When drafting a questionnaire, have in mind that the respondent could interpret a question quite differently. Prior qualitative research and piloting should help inform what terminology and language is appropriate.

Bias in Question and response

The survey process needs to aim for a detached level of objectivity; otherwise respondents might be sceptical about the aims of the survey and any conclusions could be called into question. This ranges from including leading questions, such as 'Do you agree that our service is good?', to using scales that are likely to get positive evaluations, such as 'please rate our services, on a scale of 1 to 10, where 1 is ok and 10 is excellent', to the distribution of promotional literature along with the questionnaire.

Agree/disagree scales often use non-neutral statements such as 'Too much money goes on wheelchair access'. There is a risk such a question will bias responses towards agreeing with the statement, but it may also elicit more honest views because giving a positive response becomes more permissible. People often bias answers towards what they think is more socially acceptable, what they think the researcher wants to hear, or what would cast them in a good light. To counter some of these difficulties it may be practical to include an opposing statement, for example, pairing the above with, 'Access for people who need help with walking does not get enough funding'. Including opposing statements is also useful in countering the halo effect (see below).

A related problem is the use of loaded words and terms, for example, 'The prices are reasonable for people on state benefits' would be better worded as 'The prices are reasonable for people with a low income' as it (mostly) removes possible negative connotations. In any case, the analysis should be aware of how bias could affect response.

Specific versus Broad Responses

If there are complex issues of importance in the survey, for example, if you are asking about people's attitude to anti-social behaviour in a swimming pool, it would be advisable to have a set of several questions exploring attitudes rather than relying on just one. This is because what might count as 'anti-social behaviour' is broad and could mean anything from loud talking through to physical threats. An array of questions could be asked on risk, or witnessing bullying behaviour. Or, a list could be provided with the respondent being asked to tick the behaviours they have witnessed and how seriously they rate them. Either method would provide a better overall picture of the issue than one statement could alone. This might also apply to where an overall experience, for example of teachers on a course, does not reflect variations between teachers.

However, complex issues need the respondents' attention. Asking detailed questions on many topics will lose the concentration of most respondents, especially if they would have little personal interest in the survey. As referred to earlier, the number of questions should always be kept to a minimum. Long lists of questions may also lead to the *halo effect*, where a respondent answers the whole questionnaire based on their overall impressions of the issue, rather than giving a detailed response to each question.

Conclusion

This chapter should have equipped you to carry out basic sampling and questionnaire design as part of your quantitative survey. Choosing sampling methods appropriate for your survey method and whether you need statistical validity is an important part of designing your survey. You should also have an awareness of pitfalls within sampling so that whether statistically significant or not, you can ensure your research is being carried out with the right people, whether they be random, targeted, or contacted through social networks.

Questionnaire design is at once very simple and very complex. In essence anyone can put together a questionnaire. The key is to put together a questionnaire that will be user-friendly, engaging and that produces useable results. Following the guidelines set down is one thing, but most important is piloting and feedback on the survey tool – without this you are trusting to luck rather than science.

Now you are at the point of carrying out your survey. In the next chapter, we will consider what to do with your questionnaires and data once it starts rolling in!

Further Reading

Babbie, E.R. (2007) *The Basics of Social Research. International Ed.* London: Wadsworth.

Hague, P., Hague, N. and Morgan, C. (2004) *Market Research in Practice – A Guide to the Basics.* London: Kogan Page.

Punch, K.F. (2003) *Survey Research: The Basics.* London: Sage.

These are useful texts on general sampling and provide questionnaire design methods .

Online sample size calculators can be found at:

RAOsoft (2004) http://www.raosoft.com/samplesize.html

MaCorr Inc (2009) http://www.macorr.com/ss_caclulator.htm

(Continued)

(Continued)

Heckathorn, D. (2009) 'Respondent driven sampling'. Available at: http://www.respondentdrivensampling.org/ (accessed 25 August 2009).
Provides links to papers and software on respondent driven sampling.

Cobb, T. (2006) Web Vocabprofile [Computer software]. Available at: http://www.lextutor.ca/vp/ (accessed 25 August 2009) [an adaptation of Heatley and Nation's (1994) Range.]
Has an integral text summary that easily identifies which words are in most common usage, rarer words and words used at academic/professional level. There are many more web resources, find them by searching: common words English.

Finally, the Economic and Social Research Council's Question Bank contains validated and reliable questions on many topics, sourced from many national surveys. Found at http://www.esrc.ac.uk

THIRTEEN

Quantitative Data Processing and Analysis

Guillaumette Haughton and Anna Stevens

By the end of this chapter you should be able to:

- enter data into a suitable computer package for analysis;
- ensure that the dataset is accurate using a series of cleaning techniques;
- merge datasets;
- identify different types of questions and different ways that these should be handled in the analysis process;
- undertake basic data analysis;
- produce simple tables, graphs and charts to present data;
- calculate the spread of data;
- recognise more advanced statistical techniques.

Introduction

This chapter explains what to do with the quantitative data you have collected. It works through the stages of how to enter the data, either manually or using a software program, coding the data and producing a useable dataset. This includes an explanation of how to recognise different types of variables and different ways to handle these, cleaning the dataset and merging separate datasets. The chapter moves on to explain how to analyse the data. This looks at the different ways to present data, including tables, graphs and charts, and simple data analysis. The chapter also introduces some more advanced data analysis and statistical techniques that readers may wish to study further. Following on from Chapters 11 and 12, the techniques presented in this chapter will help you to find out what the answer is to your research question (Figure 13.1).

To be sure that the data can be analysed in a way that will answer your research questions, it is worth planning in advance what you intend to do with the data

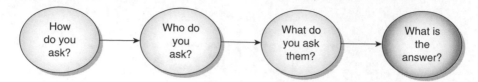

Figure 13.1 The quantitative research process

before you begin collecting it. This will help to ensure that you collect all of the data you require in one go, without needing to go back to respondents with further questions at a later stage, and that you do not collect lots of data that you will not want to or be able to analyse. If you do not prepare your study properly, it can take a long time to gather extra data that was missed in the first instance (and depending on your sampling technique, it may not even be possible), or you may spend a great deal of time gathering or analysing data that turns out to be irrelevant.

Data Entry

Depending on the size and timeline of your survey, data entry may be an ongoing process from the moment the questionnaires start returning. It is important to keep track of the forms. Essentially, this means being explicit in labelling data so that it will be straightforward (if necessary) to check that data that has been entered into a database or spreadsheet corresponds with data on paper questionnaires.

Booking In

When you get questionnaires returned via post or by interviewers you will need to book them into your database. A database of the whole sample should be kept and a unique ID number assigned to each record on this database before sending out questionnaires. This ID number can be printed as a small number at the bottom of the questionnaire so that when returns come back in it is possible to match this with the database. However it is worth noting if the subject area is particularly sensitive an ID number may put off respondents from replying. It is important to reassure respondents of data protection and that their responses will be treated as completely anonymous (see Chapter 4, on research ethics). If the survey is not anonymous, each questionnaire should already have a unique 'sample ID number' (see Chapter 11, on quantitative data collection methods) that ties it to the sample database. If you are expecting any more than a couple of hundred returned questionnaires, it would be worth purchasing a mechanical number stamp. When you have assigned the questionnaire a number, enter the return ID number next to the sample ID number on your mailout database. This way you have a simple way of keeping track of who has replied so far and you will be able to send out targeted reminders.

If you are doing this with bundles of quantitative interview responses in questionnaire format at a time (for example, if you are completing sets of questionnaires, or interviewers are bringing in questionnaires in batches), this will be straightforward to do. However, if responses are arriving in more than one format (e.g. through the post or as email attachments), it may become more confusing. The numbers need to remain unique, and will be easier to manage if they are all consecutive with no gaps. Keeping all returned questionnaires together is essential.

The booking in process also applies to online surveys, where respondents have been identified. Some online tools will do this automatically. If your database needs manually updating with responses, make sure this is done before sending out further reminders. It is not necessary to assign responses a return ID number at this stage.

If you have chosen to use a combination of survey collection methods, such as online and paper surveys, the booking in process is even more important. You may choose to collect the online and paper surveys into separate databases and reconcile the two distinct numbering systems once all responses have been collected or when you are going to send out a targeted reminder letter.

Once all paper questionnaires are collected and allocated a unique return ID number, they need to be put into a database format so that they can be compared and analysed. The data can be entered into a database manually or using optical mark recognition software.

Manual Data Entry

Suitable programmes for manual data entry are standard database packages such as Microsoft® Access® or OpenOffice Base. These programs also allow you to create forms to make data entry easier. Statistics packages such as SPSS, Snap or SAS can also be used for manual data entry. For manual data entry you should not use spreadsheets such as Microsoft® Excel® or OpenOffice Calc. This is because data is not fixed into rows, or cases, and can be lost. The authors would strongly recommend using a different package for data entry. However, we are aware that many users are more comfortable with Microsoft® Excel®. If you do choose to use a spreadsheet package, we would urge that you regularly check that you have not inadvertently lost or rearranged data into the incorrect rows or cases. It is also worth keeping a 'master' version of any data separate to the copy that is being worked with, in case of accidents.

While manual data entry is much slower than scanning for long forms with many checkboxes, it is at least comparable to (in terms of the time requirements) scanning for shorter forms with written comments, or longer complex forms with few actual questions.

Document Management: Optical Mark Recognition Software

An alternative to manually entering data is to use software that scans and enters the data into a useable format automatically. Online survey packages have a function to do this instantly, as the data is already gathered electronically, but paper copies will need scanning so that they can be digitally processed.

Although these packages do speed up the process, they are not a panacea. The process of scanning and checking the survey still takes time, with a 1000 questionnaires taking around 8 days compared to 12 days for manual data entry. Also, scanning is generally less accurate than manual data entry, so the final dataset will need more cleaning (see next section). Scanning is particularly effective for short, simple questionnaires – less so for long complex questionnaires. As most practitioner-researchers will not have access to a document capture system, it is a good idea to outsource the data entry of large-scale surveys.

Open Comments

With open comments it is worth considering whether you need them in a database. Typing in long open comments can be a time-consuming task, taking longer than the rest of the questionnaire. If you want the comments in digital form for analysis, distribution or archiving, they will need to be data entered. It might be advantageous to have the questionnaire scanned for checkbox answers, where answers are a straightforward tick or cross in a box, and then have the comments manually data entered onto a separate database. Then analysis could begin on the quantitative part of the questionnaire without being held up by the longer process of typing in comments. If entering comments into a separate database it is important to record the same return ID number alongside these comments so they can later be matched with the rest of the questionnaire data.

Alternatively, you may have questions with short open comments, for example 'other' answers than the limited options given for a particular question or the general area that a person has travelled from. These may require 'post-coding' (see below), or grouping alongside the rest of the database of answers for analysis. In this instance, they will need to be data entered alongside the rest of the database and coded.

The Coding Book

Whether you manage your data manually or via a software package, you will need to create a coding book for your survey. The coding book is also referred to as a coding frame, and is used to help the researcher 'translate' the survey data into a workable dataset.

The coding book does not need to be a physical book, but ideally a blank copy of the full survey with the coding for each question marked clearly on it. This means working out how many potential answers (or values) there are for each question, and how they need to be entered into the database. The coding book should also include information on the type of variable. There are four levels of measurements.

1. Nominal Level Questions

These are also known as categorical variables. The different responses available cannot be put into rank order and do not have values relative to one another (for an example, see Box 13.1). While these will be given a number value in the dataset, this number bears no relation to the other numbers and comparisons between different values will not be meaningful. Apart from putting them in alphabetical or sense order, it makes no difference what value is given to what variable.

There may be a limited number of responses to a nominal question, but in some cases it may be necessary to offer respondents an additional option of 'other'. It may also be possible for respondents to give more than one answer to a nominal question. A nominal variable may only require one field in a database, if only one response is possible, or it may require a field for each possible answer.

Box 13.1   Nominal level questions

How did you travel to Littleton Nature Reserve today? Please tick all that apply

☐ By car
☐ By bus
☐ By train
☐ By bicycle
☐ Walked
☐ Other, please specify..

Which areas of Littleton Nature Reserve did you visit today? Please tick all that apply

☐ The Bird Sanctuary
☐ Woodland Zone
☐ Pond and Marshlands
☐ Gravel Quarry
☐ Visitors Centre and Gift Shop
☐ Cafe/Picnic Area

Dichotomous Questions

These are nominal questions where only one of two responses is possible (see Box 13.2). These types of questions are sometimes used to direct respondents to skip questions that are not relevant to them (known as 'routing').

Box 13.2   Dichotomous questions

Gender

☐ Male   ☐ Female

Did you visit the bird Sanctuary today?

☐ Yes   – please go to next question.
☐ No   – please skip the next question and go to Question 8.

---

2. Ordinal Level Questions

Ordinal variables are also known as rank variables, because they can be rank ordered – 1st, 2nd, 3rd and so on (see Box 13.3). This type of questions includes scales, such as Likert scales (see Chapter 12, for more information on this). When ranking variables, such as the order that political parties came in an election, we cannot say the difference between the 1st and 2nd rank is the same as the difference between the 2nd and 3rd rank. Comparisons can be made between the different variables in an ordinal question using the rank order. Ordinal variables should be entered into a database as one field, and a number allocated to each possible answer. The number would be entered into the appropriate database cell instead of the full answer.

Box 13.3   Ordinal level questions

How often do you visit the swimming pool? (tick one box only)

☐ Every day
☐ 4–6 days per week
☐ 2–3 days per week
☐ About once a week
☐ Less than once a week
☐ Less than once a month
☐ Never

Which age group do you belong to? (ring one age band only)
Under 16 16–24 25–34 35–49 50–64 65 and over

How satisfied are you with the changing facilities at the swimming pool?

☐ Very satisfied
☐ Fairly satisfied
☐ Neither satisfied nor dissatisfied
☐ Fairly dissatisfied
☐ Very dissatisfied

---

3. Interval level questions

These types of questions are sometimes referred to as 'true measures', as the difference between the values given is meaningful and the values are evenly distributed units (see Box 13.4). For these types of measure, while differences between the values is meaningful, ratios are not, as there is no meaningful zero point. Interval level questions may concern ideas such as temperature, where there may be a 'zero', but 60°C is not twice as hot as 30°C . It is worth noting that Likert scales are not an interval variable, but that they can sometimes be treated as such. Typically, the full number would be entered into the database for these questions.

Box 13.4   Interval level questions

In which year did you first visit the Littleton Nature Reserve?

_____

---

4. Ratio level questions

Ratio level questions are also a type of 'true measure' (see Box 13.5). The difference between values is meaningful, *and* there is a meaningful zero point, which means that ratios (and averages) between values are also meaningful. As with interval questions, this type of variable would generally be entered as the full number into the database. Figure 13.2 provides a flow chart helping you to categorise the variables.

Box 13.5   Ratio level questions

How long did you spend in the swimming pool today?

_____

How far in miles did you travel to the swimming pool?

_____

Setting Up Your Database

This section will explain how to set up the database using Microsoft® Access®, as this is part of the Microsoft® Office suite, which often comes with Windows® packages and is therefore readily accessible. Also, the data can at a later point be converted from Microsoft® Access® into Microsoft® Excel® or SPSS or other formats which offer more options regarding data analysis. You will need some experience of Microsoft® Access® to do this. This section refers primarily to manual data entry, which is the cheapest and most widely accessible option for small research projects. Nevertheless, the principles of creating the database are similar whatever format or method is to be used.

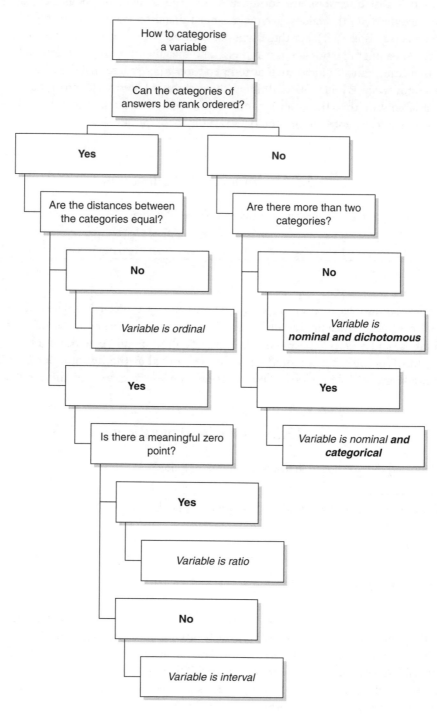

Figure 13.2   Categorising variables

To set up a database in Microsoft® Access®, each possible variable for each question needs its own field, and the coding book should list each field label. The labelling between coding book and database should correspond exactly so that there is no confusion. Each field label should relate back to the question, and if separate fields are required within a question – for instance, if a respondent can give multiple answers to a question – it needs to relate to each element of the question (see Box 13.6).

Box 13.6   Database fields and values

Q1 – Have you been to Littleton Nature Reserve?

Answer	Field Name	Value
Yes	Q1_been	1
No		2

Q2 – Which areas of Littleton Nature Reserve did you visit today? Please tick all that apply

Answer	Field Name	Value
The Bird Sanctuary	Q2_1	0 = Did not visit today (i.e. not ticked) 1 = Visited today
Woodland Zone	Q2_2	
Pond and Marshlands	Q2_3	
Gravel Quarry	Q2_4	
Visitors Centre and Gift Shop	Q2_5	

Q3 – How did you travel to Littleton Nature Reserve?

Answer	Field Name	Value
By car	Q3_1	0 = Did not use (not ticked) 1= Used
By bus	Q3_2	
By train	Q3_3	
By bicycle	Q3_4	
Walked	Q3_5	
Other, please specify	Q3_6	
	Q3_oth	Type in written response

(Continued)

(Continued)

Q4 – Which age group do you belong to?

Answer	Field Name	Value
Under 16		1
16 – 24		2
25 – 34	Q4_age	3
35 – 49		4
50 – 64		5
65 and over		6

To create a table for data entry, select 'Create Table in Design View' in Microsoft® Access®. Referring to the code book, enter in the field names. The fields will form the columns, and each individual questionnaire (or case) will form a row. Once all of the fields are in place, the data can be entered from each questionnaire. If the questionnaires are data entered in the order they were booked in (return ID number 1, return ID number 2 and so on), then the first field can be auto-numbered in Microsoft® Access®. Enter the appropriate number or text into each cell in the row for the questionnaire, tabbing across to the next box and completing them in logical order. If a question has been left blank then the cell should also be left blank – filling these cells with '0's or any other number or symbol will risk skewing the analysis. When entering data, it is best to go through and enter everything as it is completed on the paper questionnaire. Areas of the questionnaire where routing has been followed incorrectly should be amended as appropriate in the following cleaning phase. Open comment fields can be standard text fields, which can take up to 255 characters, making them suitable for short responses and comments. Although Microsoft® Access® can take much longer comments using the 'Memo' data type, larger comments are better entered into an Microsoft® Excel® format alongside the corresponding ID return number. This can at a later point be merged into the original dataset in another format (such as SPSS) if the longer comments need analysing alongside other recorded variables. If you are proficient at Microsoft® Access® or OpenOffice Base, you could amend the forms capability to make data entry easier.

Cleaning the Data

Once all data is entered into a database, the data requires cleaning. How much cleaning is needed will depend on the survey – a long complicated questionnaire with lots of routing is likely to need significantly more cleaning than a short straightforward questionnaire. Typically, surveys administered by interviewers will be more accurately and clearly completed than those respondents complete themselves, and data which has been inputted manually will be more accurate rather than scanned data, as scanning software can miss marks made on the questionnaires and will often misread written sections.

To begin cleaning, you should first save a separate copy of your dataset, so that the original is kept intact in the event that anything happens to the version you are working in, and to refer back to in the future if necessary. In your new dataset, you will need to work methodically, question by question to ensure the data is as accurate as possible. This involves a series of checks that need to be carried out (see Box 13.7).

Box 13.7   Data cleaning checklist

A cleaned dataset should meet the following criteria:

- ID numbers are all present and correct.
- No duplicate cases exist.
- Data is within expected parameters.
- No data is missing.
- Routing has been followed correctly.
- Routing has been recoded as 'N/A' where appropriate.
- Data is within the expected range.
- 'Other' responses are all appropriate.
- Spelling (including place and street names) is correct, and written responses make sense.
- Written responses have been post-coded as appropriate.
- A chosen sample meet quality checks.

ID

The return ID numbers must be unique, so it is important to first ensure that no ID numbers are duplicated or are otherwise incorrect. If all of the entries are in order, it should be simple to spot any errors. Any missing ID numbers should be entered. Check that the number of cases matches the number of questionnaires booked in – if there are fewer then some questionnaires have been lost or not entered; too many and some questionnaires may have been entered twice.

Sorting Data

A very useful tool in data cleaning is the ability to 'sort' the dataset by any column on responses. This is done by right-clicking in the variable name cell at the top of the column (or holding CTRL and clicking the mouse for Mac users). From the drop-down menu which appears, choose 'sort ascending'. This will put all of the rows of responses in order according to the responses for that question. The column will start with any blank cells and work down to the highest number in the column. 'Sort descending' puts the responses in the reverse order. As all cases are recognisable by their unique ID number, it is best not to use this function until you have checked that all of the ID numbers are accurate, as this may leave you with rows of data that you cannot identify. Sorting data columns makes it easier to check that all values in the column are present, and to check that they fit within the expected parameters.

Duplicate Case Checks

Thereafter, identify any duplicate sample IDs. This should have been picked up in the booking in process with a paper based survey, but with online surveys duplicate entries can be common. Sort the dataset by sample ID to check for duplicates (alternatively you could use a query, or match the dataset to the mailout database). It is worth keeping an eye on the dataset as you work to spot any instances where a case appears to be duplicated – if this seems to be the case, refer back to the paper surveys to check that a questionnaire has not been accidentally entered twice or answers transposed from a different questionnaire by mistake.

Missing Checks

Check if any responses have been missed – this will be straightforward if respondents could give only one answer, as a missing answer will leave an empty cell. For questions where multiple answers are possible, this will be clear from a row of '0's (that is 'no's). Refer back to the paper version to check this – if a question has been missed by the respondent it should be left as a blank space. Replacing a non-response with a 'no' will give inaccurate figures, as there is no way of knowing whether a missing response should have been a 'yes' or 'no'.

Routing Checks

Where there are routing questions, respondents need to follow the correct routing for the following questions. Where a respondent has answered in a way that means they are not required to answer the next question, that question should be blank. If the respondent has answered this question, you may wish to refer back to the paper questionnaire to ensure that the question did not apply to them. If a respondent has incorrectly answered a question that they were routed to miss, you should remove this answer from the dataset.

Recoding for Routing Questions

Where respondents were routed to miss a question, this should be marked into the dataset with the figures '99', which is used to signify 'Not applicable'. This helps to distinguish between non-responses and places where you did not anticipate a response.

Range Checks

Check the numbers that have been entered fall within the expected range for the question. If a question has seven potential responses, a response of '8' is not appropriate, and needs to be checked back to the paper questionnaire.

'Other' Answers

Check through all of the 'other' responses for questions where this option was available. In some instances these will have wrongly been selected by respondents when there was an appropriate choice in the list given (for example, in a survey of respondents use of transport a respondent may have written in 'bus' or 'no. 53 bus' in the 'other' column, rather than checking the 'by bus' option). These responses should be removed, from the dataset, and corrected in the appropriate column.

Spell Checks

Where a written answer has been required, these need to be checked for spelling. Check by eye, or export the text to word (right-click in the column and choose gazetteer 'copy' from the drop-down menu) and use the spell check function found under tools. A local A–Z gazetteer can be useful for checking street names or areas particularly if the area is unfamiliar to you; Internet search engines such as Google Maps (http://www.maps.google.co.uk) and Streetmap (http://www.streetmap. co.uk/) can also be useful for this. If an answer does not seem to make sense, refer back to the paper questionnaire to make sure that it has been entered correctly.

Post-coding Responses

Post-coding is so called because it is coding that is done after the survey has been conducted, while questions that only had a certain number of possible answers would be coded before the questionnaire was distributed. After carrying out a questionnaire, you may want to code answers that have been written in by respondents. First, look at the different answers that have been given and try to categorise these – they may be saying the same thing in different ways, so you will want to group similar responses. Make a note of all of the categories you identify, and assign a code number to each possible category. Add a new column to the dataset (right-click and choose 'insert column' from the drop-down menu), and in this column enter the new codes for the responses. You will need to assign a group to each answer (although you can have the group 'other' if there are a small number of responses that do not seem to sit with any others). An alternative method is to create a column for each category and mark the appropriate column on each row. However, if you want to use the coding for anything more than sorting the comments you will need to combine this information into one column. The new codes should all be added to the coding book.

Quality Check

Keep an eye on the responses for each question as you clean the data, and consider if the responses seem reasonable and as you expected. If responses seem very different to those you envisaged then there may be a problem with the dataset. Checking the responses against the paper questionnaires can confirm if this is the case. It is a good idea to do a complete check of a proportion of the cases against the paper questionnaires in any case. Generally it is good practice to check approximately 10 per cent, randomly selected from across the dataset. This clearly depends on the scale of the survey however: for a large number of questionnaires you may choose to do a quality check on less than 10 per cent (and equally for a small number of questionnaires you may want to check more than 10 per cent). If you find a lot of discrepancies between the paper questionnaires and your dataset when carrying out the quality check, you may need to re-enter the data.

Merging Datasets

If you have entered some of the data in a different format – for example, open comments in an Microsoft® Excel® spreadsheet with data in an Microsoft® Access® document – it is possible to merge all of the data into one dataset. This can be a complex process, so you should consider whether this is something that will be important to your analysis. If you intend to look at the open comments alongside some of the other information given by respondents, for example, the age group of the respondent, then it will be necessary to merge the datasets. However, in most instances you will find that this is not necessarily a useful thing to do. So rather than look at open comments in relation to age group, you may instead choose to compare the age group of the respondent to their levels of overall satisfaction, and then look at the open comments to guide your broad understanding of why some people are satisfied and others less so.

It is not within the scope of this chapter to give instructions on how to merge datasets, as the details varies between different programmes and versions, but programmes provide instructions in their help functions and manuals. Still, as a more general point, we recommend you save a separate version of the dataset before merging datasets, so that you have an accurate version to refer back to should any problems occur. Also, before merging datasets you should ensure that:

- both datasets are sorted by their ID numbers in ascending order;
- both datasets have the same number of cases, that is, that all cases are present in both datasets; and
- there is a row for each case in both datasets, even those for which there is no data present.

Archiving

It is good practice to store the questionnaires and dataset for some time. Five years is a typical guideline, but there may be other requirements given by any funding or supporting bodies, or if you intend to publish your findings, so it is best to check this in each individual case. Archiving your data also enables you to revisit the data in the future, if you feel there is more to be had from the data than the current research requires. For example, the funding body for your research may wish to have an overall analysis of patterns of usage or behaviour in a given context, but a practitioner-researcher may wish to revisit the data to explore variations by, perhaps, social class, region or ethnicity through cross-tabulation (see below). You need to be aware, though, that there may be issues about data ownership to think about before you publish any findings.

Data Analysis

Simple data analysis can be done in Microsoft® Excel® or in statistical programs, such as SPSS. It is easy for the analysis phase of a research project to get out of control, so it is useful to begin by sitting down and thinking again about what the goals of research are and what you want to get from the analysis. You should also consider the time that is available for the analysis and ensure your goals are realistic within this time frame. While it is good research practice to only ask for data that you intend to use in your analysis, it may not be possible to fully analyse all of the data and explore all permutations. It is best to begin by analysing what is most important to your research, and expand into wider areas that seem interesting as time allows. With a plan in place, you can avoid wasting time producing endless tables and graphs that will not be used.

Be wary of drawing conclusions from data analysis at an early stage. It is important to bear in mind that initial analysis may not reflect a full and true picture that might be developed from full statistical analysis of the data.

It is also important to remember that small numbers of question responses should not be used to produce percentages – if a response rate for a question is below approximately 35 respondents, then a percentage should not be used, as the response rate is too small for percentages to be reflective of a trend. In this case you should only report the actual numbers, for example '21 of our 33 respondents believed that ward cleaning services had improved over time'.

Calculated figures should be rounded to an appropriate number of decimal places, and this should be applied consistently (so one table should not use two decimal places if all other use one). While you may wish to keep figures un-rounded for your own purposes, this step is essential for reporting. Also, the funder of the research may have a preference.

Frequency Table

The most common form of quantitative data presentation is a simple frequency table, and it is likely that you will have a large number of these (for an example, see Table 13.1). A frequency table will look at one question from the question-naire, and give the frequency of each possible response to the question and the percentage of respondents that gave this response. Frequency tables are a good point at which to begin analysing the data, as they quickly give an overview of the findings to familiarise yourself with the data, and provide a good starting point to explore the data in more depth.

Table 13.1 Frequency table of age group of respondents ($N = 138$)

Age group	Frequency (n)	Percentage
Under 16	12	8.7
16 – 24	5	3.6
25 – 34	23	16.7
35 – 49	44	31.9
50 – 64	36	26.1
65 and over	18	13.0
Total	138	100.0

Cross-tabulations

The other type of table you may wish to produce is a cross-tabulation. This is where you look at one variable in comparison to another. These tables are useful to see where there may be differences in responses for one variable in relation to another variable. For example, in Table 13.2 you can see that younger visitors are more likely than older visitors to visit the pool every day. If you want to make a particular point such as this in a report, you can make in clearer by using per-centages in each column rather than just counts, as in Table 13.2. Be wary, how-ever, of drawing conclusions about the importance of differences between groups in analysis such as this. You need to be clear that these differences are statistically significant (this is explained further below).

Table 13.2   Cross-tabulation of number of visits by age group (N = 319)

Visits per week	Under 16		16–24		25–34		35–49		50–64		65 and over		Total	
	n	%	n	%	n	%	n	%	n	%	n	%	n	%
Every day	18	23.7	9	17	16	32	1	4.5	4	8.3	2	2.8	50	15.7
4–6 days per week	7	9.2	12	22.6	13	26	3	13.6	11	22.9	6	8.6	52	16.3
2–3 days per week	23	30.3	6	11.3	5	10	8	36.4	18	37.5	14	20	74	23.2
About once a week	15	19.7	13	24.5	8	16	2	9.1	7	14.6	25	35.7	70	21.9
Less than once a week	2	2.6	8	15.1	2	4	6	27.3	3	6.3	7	10	28	8.8
Less than once a month	5	6.6	4	7.5	6	12	1	4.5	1	2.1	13	18.6	30	9.4
Never	6	7.9	1	1.9	0	–	1	4.5	4	8.3	3	4.3	15	4.7
Total	76	100	53	100	50	100	22	100	48	100	70	100	319	100

Graphically Presentation of Data

As well as tables, numerical data can be presented in graphs and charts. This can be a good way of breaking up large chunks of text in reports and adding interest to presentations, and it can be an effective way of presenting information and drawing attention to certain features that may be less evident in a table format. If you present data in a chart or graph, you must choose an appropriate style for the type of data. A number of different types of charts and graphs can be produced quite simply in Excel, using the chart wizard. This has a step-by-step guide to help you to produce the diagram from the figures.

When producing graphs you also need to be aware of the media they will be used in, for example, whether they will be printed or displayed on a computer. Although computers can produce complex graphs using many colours, we recommend you to aim for the simplest way of presenting the data. Be aware that readers may be colour blind or have poor eyesight, and that the graphs may be printed in greyscale by those without a colour printer to hand. The requirements of readers should also be considered. For some reports the graphs might be best presented in the simplest and most uncluttered way. For others, for example, where the graphs might be used as reference, exact figures or percentages within the graph would be useful. Make sure that all charts are clearly labelled and that the values are defined.

Bar Graphs

Bar graphs are most suitable for simple counts of variables. General tips for how to produce bar graphs in Microsoft® Excel® is provided in Box 13.8. Typically, data is shown in separate columns, usually vertically, but also sometimes horizontally, against a value axis (see Figure 13.3). Because the data is in distinct bars, the different variables do not need to bear any relation to one another, which is why it is suitable for nominal and ordinal level data.

Box 13.8   Tips for bar graphs in Microsoft® Excel®

- Graphs with vertical bars are called column graphs.
- The clustered sub-type will do single bar and grouped bar graphs.
- The stacked subtype will do composite bar graphs.
- In Microsoft® Excel® 2003 or earlier:

  o Double-clicking on the bars will allow you to set your preferences for bar display.
  o Under the Options tab you can set the ratio of the bar width to gap between bars.

- In Microsoft® Excel® 2007:

  o Right-click and select 'Format Data Series...' to change how the bars look.
  o Click on the table and use tabs under Chart Tools to change the design or layout of the table.
- MS Excel can also use additional custom graph types such as 'range bars' or graphs that use pictures.

(Labwrite Resources, 2005)

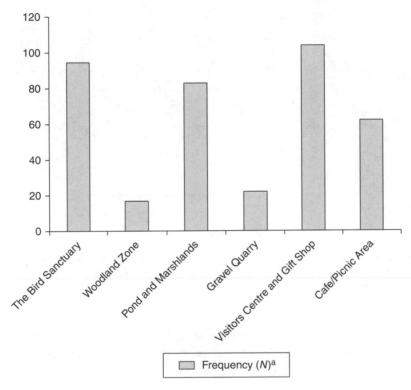

Figure 13.3   Bar graph of areas of Littleton Nature Reserve visited by respondents
($N = 138*$)
Note: [a]Respondents were able to visit more than one area of the site.

There are two other common variations on bar graphs that can be used: a grouped bar graph and a composite bar graph. A grouped bar graph is where two or more bars are shown for each variable, which have some relation to each other (see Figure 13.4). The bars may show change over time, for example, the percentage of visitors to each area of the site over different seasons. Present the different bars within each variable in different colours/shades, so that it is clear for

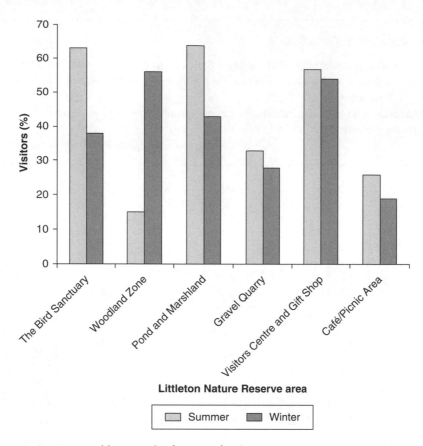

Figure 13.4   Grouped bar graph of areas of Littleton Nature Reserve visited by respondents in different seasons (summer visitors n = 213; winter visitors n = 114)

the reader which bar shows which variation of the variable. With this type of graph, it is often most appropriate to show percentages, as simple numbers of respondents may not be directly comparable. For example, a survey in summer may have a much higher response rate than one in winter, so all of the bars showing numbers for winter will be considerably smaller than for those showing summer figures. However, using percentages could show that, for instance, although visitor numbers overall are lower in winter, the woodland zone is more popular among winter visitors than summer visitors.

A composite bar graph (Figure 13.5) can also be used where there is more than one piece of information for each variable, again using different colours, but in this instance within one bar. These are useful for showing the sum of the information, as well as how it is broken down over the different groups. They can also be used to display the proportions of a whole (for example, a graph can display the levels of satisfaction for each zone within one bar, so that it can clearly

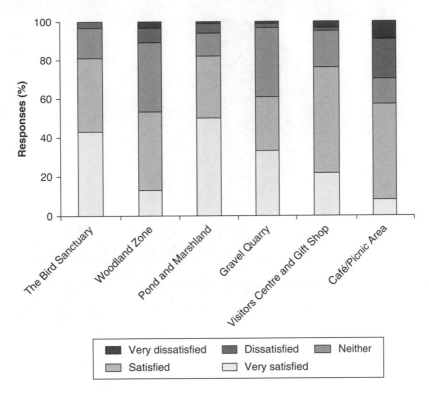

Figure 13.5   Composite bar graph of respondent satisfaction with areas of Littleton Nature Reserve (N = 138)

be seen that one zone rated much higher levels of satisfaction than another proportionally).

Pie Charts

Pie charts can be used for similar types of data to bar graphs and histograms. The data is shown proportionally in a circle, with a representative fraction of 360° shaded to represent the data (see Figure 13.6). They are a useful way of visually representing the composition of one variable proportionally. Pie charts are a useful way of comparing data visually. Variations on this are 3D pie charts and doughnuts (which have a hole in the middle). These are technically the same as a standard pie chart, but stylistically different. The Excel chart wizard can be used to construct these easily.

Line Graphs

Line graphs are used to show data over two continuous variables, which are plotted on the x- and y-axes in an even distribution (Figure 13.7). This may be, for

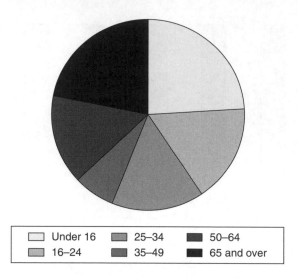

Figure 13.6   Pie chart of visitors by age group (N = 138)

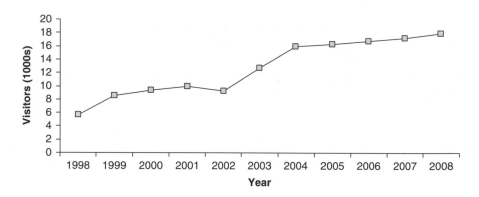

Figure 13.7   Line graph of visitor numbers to Littleton Nature Reserve over a 10-year period

example, total visitor numbers to the Littleton Nature Reserve over a number of years. The points for which data is available are marked at the intersecting points, and a line is drawn to connect the points along the graph.

Spread of Data

As well as displaying the data in graphical form, it can be useful to perform calculations to show the spread of the data. Commonly used statistics are the three different types of average, range of data and quartiles.

Average: Mean, Median and Mode

An average can be calculated in three different ways, and is likely to give three different results.

Mean

The mean is what we commonly understand as 'average'. This is the most common measure of the spread of data and is useful in many circumstances. All the numbers in a series are added together, and divided by the number of numbers in the series. So, the mean can be calculated as shown below.

Series: 5, 4, 15, 23, 8, 11, 9, 21, 17, 25, 45, 2, 13, 16, 6, 13, 24, 19
Sum of numbers = 276
Number of numbers = 18
Mean = 276 / 18 = 15.3

Median

The median is another type of average, useful where a few very high or low values would make a mean value meaningless, for example, measuring average income when there is a great difference between the highest and lowest income. To calculate this, the numbers of a series are put into numerical order, from smallest to largest. The middle point of the line is the median figure. Where there is an even number of figures, a mean of the central two figures is generally taken to be the median.

Series: 5, 4, 15, 23, 8, 11, 9, 21, 17, 25, 45, 2, 13, 16, 6, 13, 24, 19

Series sorted into numerical order:
2, 4, 5, 6, 8, 9, 11, 13, 13, 15, 16, 17, 19, 21, 23, 24, 25, 45
Number of numbers = 18

Series midpoint:
2, 4, 5, 6, 8, 9, 11, 13, <u>13, 15,</u> 16, 17, 19, 21, 23, 24, 25, 45
Median = (13 + 15) / 2 = 14

Mode

The mode is the number that appears most often in a series. Similar to the median, the mode can find an average without very high or low numbers skewing the outcome. The mode is also useful when wanting an 'average' from non-numerical data, such as participants favourite swimming stroke. The mode can be calculated by looking at the number of times each number occurs in a series.

Series: 5, 4, 15, 23, 8, 11, 9, 21, 17, 25, 45, 2, 13, 16, 6, 13, 24, 19
Occurrence
– Number occurs once: 2, 4, 5, 6, 8, 9, 11, 15, 16, 17, 19, 21, 23, 24, 25, 45
– Number occurs twice: 13
Mode = 13

Range

The range of a series of numbers is the difference between the highest and lowest figures, which shows how broadly distributed the numbers are. So:

Series: 5, 4, 15, 23, 8, 11, 9, 21, 17, 25, 45, 2, 13, 16, 6, 13, 24, 19

Series sorted into numerical order: 2, 4, 5, 6, 8, 9, 11, 13, 13, 15, 16, 17, 19, 21, 23, 24, 25, 45

Highest number = 45

Lowest number = 2

Range = 45 − 2 = 43

Range is 43.

Outliers

Outliers are figures that are very different to the rest of the figures in a series, and are likely to skew the findings if they are included in calculations around the spread of the data. So, for example, the average length of time that visitors to the Littleton Nature Reserve Gift Shop spent may be in the range of 2 to 45 minutes, but one visitor may have been attending a job interview, and so spent 96 minutes in the Gift Shop. This is over twice as long as any other visitor, so this figure is an outlier. If you consider a figure to be an outlier, it should be left out of a statistical calculation, but your report should mention that this figure has been omitted from calculations as an outlier, and explain why.

Standard Deviation

The standard deviation is the measure of the spread of figures in a dataset and thereby provides a better understanding of the distribution of the data, which is useful when undertaking more advanced statistical analysis. The standard deviation is measured in relation to the mean value – if the figures are all very close to the mean value then the standard deviation will be small (if all of the figures are the same as the mean then the standard deviation will be 0), whereas if the figures are widely dispersed and much greater or smaller than the mean then the standard deviation will be large.

It is possible to calculate the standard deviation for a dataset, and many textbooks and websites can assist you to do this. Alternatively, you can paste your dataset into an MS Excel® worksheet and use the function option to choose the formula 'STDEV' to apply to the selected figures. This will simply calculate the standard deviation for you.

Quartiles

Another measure of spread that can be used is quartiles. These split an ordered dataset into four equal groups to give three values which lie at the 25th, 50th and 75th percentiles of the distribution.

Series: 18, 17, 15, 12, 9, 8, 7, 7, 4, 6, 12, 10, 8, 19
Series sorted in numerical order: 4, 6, 7, 7, 8, 8, 9, 10, 12, 12, 15, 17, 18, 19
Number of values = 14

The value that lies at the 50th percentile is the median. To calculate the position of this the following formula can be used (where n = number of values):
0.5 × (n + 1) = position of 50th percentile
0.5 × 15 = 7.5

Therefore the 50th percentile lies between the 7th and 8th position, that is, the values 9 and 10. Since there are two values the mean of these is taken to be the 50th percentile:
50th percentile = median = (9 + 10) ÷ 2 = 9.5

The value that lies at the 25th percentile is the lower quartile. This is equivalent to the median of all the values that lie below the 50th percentile. Using the above formula:
0.25 × 15 = 3.75

Therefore the 25th percentile lies between the 3rd and 4th value, which is 7.
4, 6, 7, 7, 8, 8, 9, 10, 12, 12, 15, 17, 18, 19

The value that lies at the 75th percentile is the upper quartile. This is equivalent to the median of all the values that lie above the 50th percentile. Again using the above formula:
0.75 × 15 = 11.25

Therefore the 75th percentile lies between the 11th and 12th value, since the value is 11.25 it is one quarter away from the 11th value and three quarters away from the 12th, which is 15.5.
4, 6, 7, 7, 8, 8, 9, 10, 12, 12, 15, 17, 18, 19

Significance

Statistical analysis of data can appear to tell us a lot about the data that has been analysed, but it is important to be confident that the results are statistically significant. Statistical significance means that the results are unlikely to have been by chance and they are really reflective of a pattern that exists. Calculations of statistical significance involve complex mathematics, but there are books, websites and statistical packages that can help you with this if you want to know more about this subject and to calculate the significance of your results. It is important to use common sense when looking at the results from data analysis and make a decision about whether a statistic produced is meaningful, or it is a result that could have come about simply by chance.

Significance Tests

Often in social science we want to investigate if any relationships exist between variables involved in the study. For example, we may want to look at any variations in responses by gender or by age. Once analysis has been carried out how much confidence can we have in our findings? The size of the sample is usually relatively small compared to the population so how certain can we be that the findings represent the whole population? The answer is that we can never be 100 per cent certain, in any research project there is always going to be margin for error. However there are methods we can employ to determine the level of error. Researchers often use the term statistically significant, which can be defined as:

> how confident we can be in using a finding taken from a sample to generalise to the population as a whole. (Connolly, 2007: 158)

Table 13.3 provides a cross-tabulation for which a significance test can be done. An outline of the process that should be followed when carrying out tests of statistical significance is set out in the five stages below with an explanation of the terms. This is called hypothesis testing. This gives an overview of the concept of statistical significance and of how to approach analysis in this way. Such techniques may not be required for the scope of your study, but even if you do not perform significance tests it is essential that you are aware of the fact that relationships that you identify in your data may be down to chance.

Table 13.3   Example of a cross-tabulation for which a significance test can be done

	Male		Female		Total	
	n	%	n	%	n	%
At least one visit per week	90	68.7	156	83.0	246	77.1
Less often	41	31.3	32	17.0	73	22.9
Total	131	100.0	188	100.0	319	100.0

1. State the Null Hypothesis

At the outset of analysis the assumption should be that no relationship exists between the variables under investigation, that is, it should be assumed that the observed difference is due to chance alone (Durrant and Staetsky, 2008). This is called the null hypothesis (denoted H_0).

> Our example: The null hypothesis (denoted H_0) states that there is no relationship between frequency of visits and gender.

2. Set the Level of Error

A commonly used term in statistics is the p-value. This is used to establish how much confidence we can have in our findings. Normally this is set at 5 per cent, which means we can be 95 per cent confident that the findings in the sample reflect the trend in the whole population (Connolly, 2007). This percentage is converted to a probability and then denoted as 0.05. Findings are generally considered statistically significant if the p-value is smaller than 0.05.

> Our example: Set the level of error at $p < 0.05$.

3. Select the Appropriate Significance Test

There are a variety of tests of statistical significance, which can be carried out on quantitative data. The most appropriate test to use depends on the type of data that you have (whether it is on a nominal, ordinal, interval or ratio level, whether the data is categorical or continuous, as set out earlier on in the chapter). An explanation of the various statistical tests that can be used is beyond the scope of this chapter, however refer to the list of further reading at the end of this chapter.

> Our example: Use the Chi-Square test since the variables are categorical, this is a commonly used test in survey data.

4. Carry Out the Test to Calculate the Significance Level

This can be done using statistical software such as SPSS. To understand the process it is useful to read up on how the tests are calculated before using software to generate statistics. Again, helpful resources for how to run a significance test can be found in the list of further reading at the end of this chapter.

> Our example: Use SPSS to find out that $p = 0.003$.

5. Evaluate the Significance

Use these findings to make the decision whether there is sufficient evidence to reject the null hypothesis. If p is less than 0.05, the results are generally taken to be statistically significant and the null hypothesis can be rejected. This process can be illustrated using the example below. Table 13.3 shows the frequency of visits to the swimming pool per week broken down by gender.

> Our example: The p-value is smaller than 0.05. This means that the null hypothesis can be rejected and it can be concluded that there is a statistically significant difference between how often females visit the swimming pool compared with males.

Conclusion

This chapter has provided hands-on guidance on how you can work with the quantitative data that you have collected – from the initial phases of entering data, coding data and producing a dataset via data analysis through to the presentation of findings. We have emphasised the fact that different types of variables enable different types of analysis and we have described the ways in which different kinds of data can best be presented. Readers have also been recommended to be cautious when interpreting findings, and we have made readers aware of issues such as statistical significance.

Further Reading

Field, A. (2009) *Discovering Statistics Using SPSS*. London: Sage.
Field provides an easily accessible guide to advanced statistical analysis via SPSS. It explains how to run analyses and how to interpret the outcome.

Vogt, W.M. (1999) *Dictionary of Statistics and Methodology*. London: Sage.
This is a non-technical guide for generalists in an accessible format.

Salkind, N.J. (2008) *Statistics for People Who Think They Hate Statistics*. London: SAGE.
This is a down to earth guide to statistics, which provides an easy to understand explanation of statistical terms and of how to carry out analysis in SPSS.

Norusis, M. (2005) *SPSS 14.0 Advanced Statistical Procedures Companion*. London: Prentice Hall.
Norusis provides an in-depth guide of SPSS procedures and several practical examples to follow.

FOURTEEN

Dissemination

Colin McCaig and Lena Dahlberg

By the end of this chapter you should be able to:

- understand the kind of report(s) that are most suited to their circumstances;
- understand the importance of structure and precision;
- understand basic precepts of research reporting, that is, table layouts, references and the use of appendices;
- understand the need to negotiate dissemination proposals with research funding bodies or sponsors;
- understand the different types of audience to which your research findings may be of interest;
- write short web-page or newsletter-length summaries of the findings;
- understand the different timescales and agendas of the media.

Introduction

Dissemination is the final part of the research and evaluation process, and is equally important for practitioners reporting on the findings of their research to their funders or a wider group, for example, colleagues, research students submitting their work for assessment to academic boards, or anyone that has to present orally often complex findings in front of an audience. The three key elements in dissemination are: content (what to disseminate); audience (who to disseminate to) and delivery (how to disseminate). Any kind of research or evaluation dissemination needs to combine each these aspects to be successful.

The importance of structure, precision, clarity and objectivity of content will be emphasised throughout. The chapter will emphasise that the choice of dissemination form should be determined by its intended audience, that is, the needs of client/funding organisation and any collaborators, the context of the study, and likely readership or group being reported to. This chapter consists of three sections covering different forms of dissemination: written reports; oral presentations; and representations of research in the media.

Written Reports

The Process of Writing

Usually, the written report, whatever form it takes, is the point at which practitioner-researchers finally get to tell the world what they have been up to, and thereby add to the fund of knowledge in the field. Up to that point the research is merely a collection of data organised, if at all, only in the minds of the researcher(s).

> We become conscious of, and gain insight and understanding from our research and, in turn, pass this consciousness on to others through presentations and by writing. (Strauss and Corbin, 2008: 243)

Writing up, in other words, is as crucial to your research or evaluation as the collection and interpretation of data; research has no meaning until it is written up, and often there is no coherent story of *what* you believe the problem to be, *why* you think your research methods will elucidate the issues and *how* your findings illuminate the way forward until you do write it up. The researcher is key to the way knowledge is created from mere data. As Gilbert points out, the way research is written depends on what position researchers wish to take:

> Knowledge itself is a social creation. If you believe something, it remains a mere belief until you can persuade others that it is true; then it becomes knowledge that is shared. (1996: 328)

For Denscombe, the writing up stage is a blend of interpretation, craft and convention. Interpretation, because the presentation is the writer's particular take on the findings of the research. Craft, because of the skill involved in writing the research story from initial problem and research questions to the layout of the final conclusions will often be critical to its ability to have an impact. Convention, because there are certain ways in which reports are expected to be written by those that read them, in terms of the referencing, table layouts and structure, which, again, make it easier for the findings to be well received (Denscombe, 2007).

Given the importance of writing, it makes sense to begin writing up the research as you progress through the various stages of the work; it will save time at the end of the project and make you think about audience and structure from the outset. If you have done any kind of literature review or desk research, write it up in the manner you will expect it to be presented in the final report; the methodology can also be written up, adapted and fleshed-out, if necessary, from your proposal or project plan. Naturally, only the completion of the work will produce summative hindsight, meaning that you may have to rewrite some of your earlier speculative musings (indeed at the very least it will have to be reworded for aspects such as tenses, changing 'doing to did', 'is to was' and so on now that you are preparing a report which will be read historically). The process of rewriting will help to build the story in a more focused and persuasive way.

Structure

Report structure should follow as far as possible the logic suggested by the research questions that formed the focus of your research proposal, though of course it should also addresses issues and other research questions that arose during the research process. Unless you are reporting on just one aspect of the research (for example, the methodology or the literature review) you should always be working within the structure outlined in Box 14.1, regardless of whether the presentation is to be written or oral. Note that in almost all types of report (the exception being some technical reports) you will face space limitations, so in effect editing the data and the supporting argument is something that will have to be considered separately for each version you produce. For practitioner-researchers working to a specific brief these considerations should be discussed with the funding body at a fairly early stage. A large part of this discussion could consider which of the findings are considered most and least relevant (though, as we discuss later, a different audience may be interested in aspects marginal to a funder such as methodology, theory or specific findings). In general, however, reports will have the structure presented in Box 14.1.

Box 14.1   Structure

1. Background context – the problem or issue in question.
2. Justification of the study – why the problem or issue is relevant.
3. Purpose of the research – the purpose and specific research questions.
4. Methods – how the research was done (both data collection and analysis), justification for chosen methods, ethical considerations.
5. Findings – presentation of findings and analysis.
6. Discussion – findings in relation to existing literature and policy.
7. Conclusion – including policy/practice implications and recommendations, if required.

Within this structure, reports should contain a broader discussion of methods, including ethical issues, options not chosen and the reasons why, relating these to the research questions identified in the research proposal or plan and specified in the report. The report should then go onto explain and justify the methods of analysis employed. Research findings based on analysis of the data gathered should be organised in accordance with the original research questions and present any quantitative or qualitative data that supports your statements in the text, in tables, figures or other suitable formats. The discussion section is where your findings can be related to relevant literature and policy in the field. For example, does your research throw a new light on previous research? Does it counter previous findings or offer additional insight? What implications does it have for policy and practice? However, this section is not the place to introduce new findings. If possible, draw conclusions both in terms of research/theory and implications for practice/policy in the field and point up areas for further research. Some funders require policy recommendations. These should be specific and designed to correct perceived problems or address issues with existing policy and practice; there is little value in recommending changes in national funding structures or indulging in ideological attacks on broad government policy if you are reporting to a local audience on a very specific issue.

Style

Practitioner-researchers should use a consistent style throughout the report, and this applies as much to headings and subheadings, table and figure layouts as it does to the kind of language and grammar used and the tense used (past is usually preferred to present, as findings are, by definition, historical at the point of dissemination). There is some debate among researchers about whether to use the first (I) or third person (one/he/she) when describing the research process and findings, as with other aspects of the debate about dissemination it largely depends on the expectations of your audience. The most common approach is the third person unless you are writing up a very personal piece of work where your interpretation of the evidence or your interaction with the subject is key to the research, such as in some action research and in some qualitative research traditions. Denscombe provides an example arguing that it would not be normal to use the first person and write 'I distributed 164 questionnaires and received 46% back … From the research I found that …'. Rather, you would expect to use the third-person perspective and write 'Research involved the distribution of 164 questionnaires; a response rate of 46% was achieved … Findings from the research indicated that …' (2007: 228). The third-person perspective is also seen as the preferred method to demonstrate neutrality, which of course many qualitative researchers would not recognise as feasible or appropriate.

At all times reports should aim to use non-discriminatory language, for example 'people with learning disability' as opposed to 'retarded', and make use of the most up-to-date language for ethnic groups, disability categories, age groups and so on. As categories such as those relating to ethnicity, sexuality and disability are subject to occasional change, it may be useful to liaise with your funders and others in the practitioner community for the most appropriate language in each case. Alternatively, up-to-date and subject-specific categories can be found by using

Internet search engines (e.g. search for 'non-discriminatory language' and 'health', 'education').

Another aspect of the style of reporting is referencing and bibliographies. Your funding body will usually have a preference if it is for a report; publishers and those expecting you to bring research papers to conferences will also have style guides. The most common referencing method is the Harvard system which has some minor variations, but in general authors should be noted in the text by *surname*, followed by the *year of publication* and *page number* (if appropriate) in brackets. A fuller exposition of referencing and bibliography layout can be found in Chapter 6 of this volume.

Authors may also have recourse to using footnotes or endnotes to expand on particular points. Whether notes are at the bottom of the page (footnotes) or at the end of the report is a matter of preference. Journal articles and chapters in books generally have them as endnotes, but reports often have them as footnotes: either way they are best referenced by the insertion of a small number (usually superscript) at the end of the word or sentence accessed in Microsoft® Word via Insert/Reference/Footnote or References/Insert Footnote. In general footnotes should be kept to a minimum otherwise they may to distract the reader from the main point of your report.

Data Tables and Figures

There are two aspects of presenting data tables that are important to report writing. The first is how and where tables are embedded in the text of the report (for example, in the main text or in appendices); the second is table layout, and again this is something that your funding body as the primary audience may have a view on. There are various ways in which data can be presented in tables. In part this depends on the type of data being presented, but again the funding body may well have preferences and it would be wise to discuss this with them before investing, and potentially wasting, time in laying out findings in a different way.

The key points to note are: (1) tables should always be accompanied by some form of commentary explaining their significance; (2) they should be appropriately labelled; and (3) they should follow a logical numbering sequence (such as Table 1, Table 2 and so on). Some reports require both tables of data and figures/charts to illustrate data, either to be used to present and illustrate different kinds of data or to present the same data in two different ways (for example, figures in the main report, tables in the technical annexe). Tables and figures should have independent numbering systems. If you are presenting the same data in both tables and figures, they should have the same title. For example, if you present the data on participants' age in the fifth table of the report it should be called *Table 5: Age of participants*, the corresponding figure should be *Figure 1: Age of participants*, assuming that this is the first figure of the report. If your second figure is used to illustrate the data in *Table 12: Height of participants* it should be *Figure 2: Height of participants* and so on. All tables and charts should be consistent in layout, font sizes and terminology. There should be a clear reference to all tables and figures in the text, as in the following examples (Box 14.2). If tables or figures present secondary data, the source should be clearly stated at the bottom of the table/figure.

Box 14.2   Table layouts

If you wish to present findings on how many respondents to a survey chose options about the most important local government services, you could either present the commentary text before hand, followed by the table, for example.

The importance of local authority services

Refuse collection services were rated the most important by respondents to the survey; around one-third (35%) of respondents believed it the most important service and another 42% rated it the second most important service supplied by the local authority. The provision of street lighting was rated the most important by one-quarter (23%) of respondents, and second most important by another 36%. Leisure services were considered least important by half of respondents (50%) but also considered most important by one-fifth of respondents (21%). Schools were also seen as most important by 21% of respondents, and over half placed schools services at the centre of this importance scale (Table 1).

Table 1   Importance of local services (%) ($N = 635$)

Services	Importance scale				
	1 Highest	2	3	4	5 Lowest
Refuse collection	35	42	8	7	8
Street lighting	23	36	25	10	6
Leisure services	21	15	9	9	50
Schools	21	15	55	7	2

Alternatively, the same text could come after the table, or be presented in a series of bullet points:

- Refuse collection services were rated the most important by 35%; another 42% rated it the second most important.
- Street lighting was rated the most important by 23%, and second most important by another 36%.
- Leisure services were considered least important by 50% but also considered most important by 21%.
- Schools were also seen as most important by 21% of respondents, and over half paced schools services at the centre of this importance scale (Table 1).

Many decisions you may make about content and layout will be dependent on audience, and it is to considerations of the requirements of different audiences that we now turn.

Audience

The intended audience and purpose of the study are important when you begin to think about dissemination. There may often be more than one audience for your work, for example, the sponsor or funding body will be one audience with particular requirements; in addition, you may be offered the opportunity to present your research findings to an audience of fellow practitioners, both in writing and orally (see below), and for this kind of audience you may want to concentrate on certain aspects of the findings, such as the implications for practice; you may also be invited to submit a paper to an academic conference focusing on, for example, the theoretical underpinnings of your research or indeed its methodological implications for other work in the field. It is always important to get comments from colleagues and others on drafts, whatever the intended audience (Robson, 2002; Strauss and Corbin, 2008). If your report is targeted at, for example, parents, it makes sense to ask a parent or parents you know to read a draft version of the report. A report to practitioners (for example, nurses, youth workers) will need to be pitched at the right level of understanding, so it is important to have a draft read by someone with practitioner knowledge who can advise on the appropriate use of jargon and level of understanding.

If you are preparing a report for a different audience than originally intended (for example a version for practising nurses of a report originally written for NHS management) then rather than try to adapt the original it may be easier to rewrite it from scratch. This could imply exploring the research questions of most interest to practitioners and presenting only those findings of direct interest to that particular audience, with a short section laying out the wider context, that is, 'this is part of a wider exploration of X and Y for the NHS Management Group which found that ... Z'. Often funders will expect and encourage researchers to disseminate findings to practitioner groups. The research contract may stipulate that you do so and in such cases they will probably want to have some control on how it is presented, that is, in terms of layout of reports and the use of logos on written reports and oral presentation materials.

Even in cases where the contract has no dissemination obligations beyond a final report, the original funders of the research will almost certainly want to have a say in how and to whom you subsequently disseminate the data they have paid you to collect. Ownership of the report and the data should have been agreed long before this stage; it is important to know what you can use in other ways, for example, at academic conferences, journal articles and so on (Robson, 2002), so it is imperative to clarify this with the funding body at the outset of a project. Most funders will insist on ownership of the dataset, including qualitative interview and focus group data and will want to 'clear' in advance any use you may want to make of the data, usually because they are concerned about political sensitivity. However, once the funder has published the report it is in the public domain and you will be free to interpret the (published) findings in other formats as long as you reference the report in the normal way. It is also normal practice to refer to the funders of any commissioned research when writing for publications, for example, in journal articles you may add this footnote to the fist page: 'This research was funded by the DCFS, project reference RES09:103457FE.'

Different Types of Audiences

Commissioned Consultancy Reports

Commissioned research reports for governmental departments and agencies are likely to need to be concise and highlight key findings and to include practical outcomes such as conclusions and recommendations (where required, often they are not sought). In producing this kind of report there are certain conventions to which the report will be expected to adhere. An example may be the format of the report that could require numbered paragraphs and numbered sections. A brief survey of similar types of report for the type of funder will give an idea of the conventions expected. Potentially more vexatious for practitioner-researchers are restrictions on content and layout. For example, practitioner-researchers producing research for governmental agencies would be well advised not discuss theory in the report, even if it significantly informed the research or evaluation design, as they are likely to be asked to remove such references prior to publication. However, emphasis on setting the report in its socio-economic and political context is usually acceptable; if you have been evaluating the impact of a specific programme and it is clear that the programme was not fully implemented because of political barriers, then stress this as it is relevant to the likely impact of the programme (Robson, 2002).

It would be naïve not to anticipate a degree of political interference in how you write the report, the language you use and the emphasis you put on certain findings, and this can be exacerbated when more than one funder is involved or other stakeholders exercise influence on the project steering group. This often results in a lot of redrafting of drafts reports, which will inevitably impact on the amount of time it takes to produce a version everyone is happy with. This may be further exacerbated by the 'timeliness' imperative. Funders will almost certainly have a date in mind from inception that coincides with, for example, a policy launch conference, an upcoming spending review or the development of a White Paper.

Consultancy reports of this kind usually require an 'executive summary' containing a brief introduction to the research question and methodology, bullet-point or single paragraph summaries of the main findings, conclusions and, where required, recommendations. In some cases the executive summary may be the only part of the report physically published, with the main part(s) of the report and technical appendices made available online.

Internal Reports

These are reports written for the organisation that you normally work for, for example, health authority, local authority, educational establishment or voluntary body. They may not be intended for publication in the usual sense of the word, though the findings may well be circulated among your colleagues and other practitioners, and appear in shorter form on newsletters or web summaries. This may mean that the presentation can be more informal than some other types of report referred to in this chapter. However, it is useful to use a standard format for comparability with other work, so it is important to access any previous internal reports where you may find that the same sort of formatting as for consultancy reports (section and paragraph numbering for instance) is expected.

Short Summary Reports

In addition, funders may request shorter versions of the main (consultancy or internal) report such as separate executive summaries, web summaries, research intelligence summary magazines, newsletters, leaflets, conference posters, feedback to participants and press releases. Obviously space is extremely restricted in this kind of report but at a minimum they should contain: the title of the research report with a URL web link to the full report; authors and/or the corporate name of the research team; a brief introduction to the purpose of the research (that is the issues and key questions); key points of the methodology; main findings and conclusions. If you are producing a short summary report of some kind for a funding body and such outputs are not stipulated in the research contract, you should negotiate additional days for their production.

Conference Papers

Conference papers are less formal than written-up journal articles and, unless gathered together in published conference proceedings, are less easily found by others as they are not formally published in the same way as reports, journal articles or contributions to books. However, authors can disseminate conference papers widely using email, websites and mailing lists of researchers with shared interests. Another advantage is that they can be disseminated almost instantly, on the day if you have printed copies at the conference; by contrast journal articles and book chapters can take up to two years to reach an audience. Before having a paper accepted for a conference it is usual to have to submit an abstract, which is a short summary of the paper covering background/justification, purpose, methods, results and conclusions. Rules relating to abstract format and submission will be included in the conference 'call for papers'.

Presenting findings at academic and practitioner conferences is useful for several reasons. For example, in contrast to consultancy reports, this kind of audience will often welcome findings set in a broader, more theoretical context and the feedback you hopefully receive from your audience (either at the event or subsequently by email correspondence) can help you think about the research in different ways. This is particularly relevant if you are engaged in long-term research and the conference presentation is reporting on progress so far or methods employed. Presenting in this format is also useful in developing your arguments: as Gilbert (1996) notes, writing is not merely an objective setting out of the 'facts', there is often a rhetorical element to it: it is about persuasion, about taking a position and making a case for a new understanding of an issue. Remember, a sophisticated understanding of the audience for the research will make a difference in the way you present your argument, so it is important to pitch the paper at the right kind of conference (see section on oral presentations below).

Conference papers sometimes go on to form a special issue in an academic journal or chapters in an edited book (see below for both). If you have a conference paper accepted you should check if this is a possibility, as you may be expected or encouraged to submit your paper in either form after the conference. This can be an advantage giving you a ready-made publication outlet, but could potentially be a problem if you have already decided to submit your paper to another specific journal.

Dissertation and Thesis-type Reports

Many of the rules relating to postgraduate dissertations and PhD theses will be set out by your institution's research support department and should be freely available and discussed with your research supervisor from an early stage. Although there certainly will be specific conventions, rules and regulations relating to this kind of report, the principles of report writing outlined here still apply.

Journal Articles

Many practitioner-researchers working outside of higher education will not have come into contact with academic journals, however there is no reason why your research should not be written up for publication in this manner. If you do not have experience of this kind of publication, it would be wise to make contacts with researchers in your field at a university. They will usually be both willing and able to advise you in preparing a journal manuscript, perhaps agreeing to co-author an article if that is appropriate, or at least pointing towards the most appropriate journals for your work.

The first step, when preparing a manuscript for submission to an academic journal, is to investigate the type of articles various journals accept. Then, you should look for editorial standards and styles required, for example, to determine whether the journal that you wish to place your paper in is a theoretical journal read mainly by sociologists or a journal read mainly by practitioners, or whether it requires articles to have an international comparative slant. General advice when choosing which journal to approach is to look at your own list of references; if you cite many articles from the same journal, your manuscript is likely to fit within their targeted field. It may also be worth looking at journals' impact factors and standing in their field, as this is an indication not only of their impact but also of their status and how difficult it may be to get an article accepted. Information on impact factor and ranking within the field is often found on the publisher's website.

Once you have decided on a journal, spend as long as necessary ensuring that the article meets its requirements; there are no submission dates and articles can be submitted at any time. Do not underestimate the time it takes to prepare a high-quality journal manuscript. If necessary rewrite the bulk of the material rather than try to adapt the text of a report for a quite different audience, and show it to as many colleagues with experience of having articles published as possible, as well as key researchers in your field. Journal editors and reviewers will expect the research to be theoretically and methodologically grounded, that is, it should demonstrate how it fits into the tradition of published work in the field. Of equal importance to many journal editors is that you follow the instructions for authors exactly. Typically these cover font size and type, page margins, table and figure layouts and positioning in the article, referencing, abstracts and contact details for proof checking as well as length of manuscript and abstract. Many journals have electronic submission systems and may require you to nominate both named and anonymised versions (for 'blind review' purposes). The full 'instructions for authors' can be usually found on the inside back page of hard-copy journals or on the publishers' web pages.

As noted above, getting research articles published in academic journals is a slow process (up to two years) because of the peer-review process and backlogged publication schedules; however this will mean that your work will be seen as more prestigious and be cited more often, thus widening and deepening your audience and making a larger contribution to the research world (see Box 14.3).

Box 14.3   The peer-review process for journal articles

When the manuscript arrives on the editors desk it goes through a number of stages:

(1) Editor checks to see if its content falls within the scope of the journal.
(2) Editor sends it out to two or three reviewers to pick up on weaknesses and to see if they think it warrants. (1) publication; (2) publication with changes (often split into 'minor revisions' and 'major revisions'); or (3) rejection.
(3) Editor sends the manuscript and reviews back to authors together with information on his/her decision.
(4) If the editor has invited the author(s) to revise and resubmit, they make appropriate changes.
(5) Author(s) resubmit the revised manuscript
(6) The manuscript may be sent out for review comments again (in which case the process restarts from (2) above) or the editor may make a decision without further review.

Book Chapters

You may be invited to contribute a book chapter to an edited collection of research findings in your field, which is again an excellent way to disseminate your research. The process usually involves initial contact from the editor(s) of the proposed volume who may have a specific slant or angle they wish the papers to take, for example, a critical analysis of policy in the field so, as with conference papers and journal articles the emphasis will be on the practitioner-researcher to present research findings in a different way to how they were presented in reports for funders. Draft chapters usually undergo some level of peer review supervised by the editors and the volume's publishers will certainly also have stylistic requirements, though final responsibility for the manuscript will usually rest with the editors.

Oral Presentations

As with written reports, you should always construct oral presentations with an eye on the most appropriate content for the specific audience and context, as well as paying due attention to aspects that are specific to oral presentations such as the structure of the talk, overall key messages, interactivity with the audience, use of presentation tools, the anticipation of questions and the importance of accurate timing. Oral presentations can take the form of a delivery of a talk to an audience or take the form of a workshop session where the subject is introduced and questions/issues presented for the audience to work on. Here the presenter will typically combine delivery with chairing the debate. By comparison, there is often a chair of conference sessions, which usually include more than one presentation.

Content

At any of the various kinds of conference where you are invited to talk about your research, such as a national policy launch, regional practitioner event or academic research conference, you will only have time to present a limited version of the whole picture. The norm for oral presentations is between 20 and 30 minutes, with additional time (10–15 minutes) for questions, but at academic conferences this can be much shorter (sometimes only 8–10 minutes in total). Whatever the time restrictions presented by the event, it is essential to present at least:

- the full title of the research report;
- authors and/or the corporate name of the research team;
- a brief background and introduction to the purpose of the research (the issues and key questions);
- key points of the methodology;
- main findings;

- main conclusions;
- contact information including links to the main report, if available.

This will generally apply even if the actual subject of the presentation is just one aspect of the wider research such as the impact of policy on one group of subjects (disabled users of library services at a disability services conference, for example). At such events it would be wise to present the generic information about the research in one or two slides (if using a visual aid such as Microsoft® PowerPoint®) to allow the maximum time available for the specific content. The specific content should follow the same format as other types of report, though of course how it is actually delivered will depend on the audience.

Again, as with written reports it is important to share your work with colleagues and practitioners wherever possible by running through the presentation in front of an audience to check that it covers the main issues, flows logically from the premise to conclusion and can be delivered in the allotted time. It is important to go through the presentation 'to yourself' at least a few times just to check that combinations of words that look sensible on paper do not sound clumsy when spoken aloud and for you to arrange some notes to speak from (unless you are sure you can deliver all the detail from memory). If presenting jointly with colleagues pay particular attention during rehearsals to preparing 'relay baton points' so that the handover from one section to another is a smooth as possible; for example, it is always useful to be able to say 'and now my colleague Jane will talk more about the survey findings' as you swap places on the podium, rather than coming to a complete halt at the end of your section, amid the inevitable shuffling of papers and chairs.

Audience

Clearly, in oral presentations the notions of audience and content are more closely linked than other report formats: once the generic aspects have been covered (see above) you need to select just the elements that will be of interest to your audience on the day. For example, a focus on findings that relate to them is appropriate, so that you could concentrate on the policy and practice issues relating to nurses, rather than doctors, hospital managers or auxiliaries (Strauss and Corbin, 2008). For an academic audience you may find it appropriate to introduce wider social, political and theoretical aspects of the research findings and provide more room to explore and discuss methodological approaches. At a government or agency policy launch you may be expected to stick closely to the methodology and key findings; be warned, at policy launches you will probably share a platform with a representative from the funders who may well try to ensure that you remain 'on message' by intervening when it comes to questions from the audience. In advance of any kind of oral presentation it is important to try to anticipate the nature of the audience (executives, practitioners, policymakers, academics) and pitch your material accordingly and be careful to always aim to use non-discriminatory language (Curack, 2000).

Delivery

Once content and audience have been taken into consideration, there are various ways in which you can approach the oral delivery of the material. The simplest and most straightforward is to have some form of visual aid, such as slides displayed on an overhead projection system with printed handouts for the audience to add their own notes to. This kind of material is most easily developed in and presented via Microsoft® PowerPoint® (though there are of course other programmes), which can be delivered via almost any combination of computer and projector. Almost all venues that are suitable for conference presentations are fitted with the hardware and software to enable this delivery format; however, you may choose to use a flip-chart, sheets of acetates or talk without a visual aid at all. For a discussion of alternative formats see Curack (2000). You should always avoid using visual aids that distract from your overall message, for example, by being too colourful or containing too many images; as a rule of thumb, if they do not clarify your main points then do not use them.

Some principles of oral presentation are the same regardless of the delivery method: ensuring that you have sufficient time to get across you main points; that you have outlined sufficient of the methodology to make sense of how the findings were arrived at; and that your conclusion summarises the relevant key outcomes of the research for the particular audience. Beyond this you still have some leeway for creative and interactive methods of presentation, for example, by asking the audience which motivational factors *they think* would be cited as the most important to surveyed students considering entry to higher education, then revealing the *actual* results. Another variation might be to establish a dialogue between two members of the research team to illustrate polar arguments explored in the research or as examples of barriers to understanding.

It is important not to make the delivery too complex however: the whole point of the presentation is to get across a few simple messages (we were commissioned to carry out this vitally important research; this is what we found; this is important to the research/practice community for these reasons) and anything that distracts from these key messages will weaken its impact (Curack, 2000). Another reason to keep your presentation simple is that often such events do not run to time: other presenters may not turn up leaving you with more time than anticipated; more likely, other presenters overrun and you have to shorten your own presentation. So, while it is important to run through your presentation to check that it fits the predicted time allowance, you should also be flexible enough to both expand on some issues and skip over others, without detracting from the overall message (Baume and Baume, 2000).

Presenters should also to think about the type of questions your presentation is likely to stimulate (this is where you may found out how appropriate your presentation was to the audience). It is always useful practice to ask colleagues who have (it is hoped) read your paper in advance to think about potential questions that may come your way.

Finally, it is important to pay attention to presentational aspects of the presenter(s). It is important to strike a balance between dressing comfortably enough to move from sitting to standing positions and move around the podium or stage, and dressing in an appropriate manner for the audience. It remains a safe assumption that an audience of decision-makers in business suits (male or female variants) will take findings more seriously if presented by similarly attired presenters. In general, academic research conferences remain a dress-code free zone.

The Media

Media reports are a way of disseminating your research or evaluation findings to a much broader and larger audience than is possible via other forms of dissemination. For example, you can reach large audiences in local and national press, television and radio, and a more niche audience through specialist and trade magazines. In addition to spreading knowledge about your findings, media reports will spread knowledge about your organisation and raise both your own profile and that of your organisation. Another advantage of media communication is that it gives immediate feedback. Most funding bodies and other stakeholders appreciate when findings are disseminated broadly and when projects get publicity (see Leeds University, 2009).

Being Approached by Media

Practitioner-researchers dealing with the media (newspapers, television or radio) will most often be involved in either of two types of report: consultancy reports for governmental departments and agencies, or national and international conference papers.

If your research was commissioned by a government department or agency, it is likely that the commissioning body will liaise in advance with journalists at a national level or specialist trade newspapers, such as the *Times Education Supplement* or the *Nursing Times*, in time for them to publish a piece in the week of the report's publication. The department/agency may also have produced a press release, which you may be invited to comment on (or even draft yourself). You should ensure that you are relatively happy with the wording of the final draft of the press release because it will form the basis of the story that appears and the starting point for any questions you may be asked by the journalist. From their perspective the media story would ideally consist of the main points from the press release accompanied by some illustrative comments from a member of the team to show that the research was carried out by independent researchers.

Another occasion when researchers may be approached by the media is just before a conference where they are due to present a paper. Journalists are often given access to interesting looking conference abstracts by conference organisers to generate stories that promote the event. With this kind of approach, researchers will generally be on far safer ground, especially if the presentation is not on behalf of a funding body and the story is not part of the promotion of anyone's policy agenda.

Approaching the Media

There are ways in which practitioner-researchers can be proactive when it comes to the media, for example, by writing a tailored version of your findings for specific kinds of media, writing a press release or making a first personal contact. You can be opportunistic in linking your research to a current debate. Contributing to ongoing debates often increases the chance of getting your research published.

The key question to ask yourself when you are considering to approach media is: 'Is this news?', that is, to consider whether it is the kind of story you see in media, whether it is new or different, and whether it is relevant and interesting to people (British Psychology Society, n.d.). Once you have considered this and think that your story is newsworthy, you need to consider your audience. You may be running an event for local audience, which would be suitable for local press, radio or television. Your research findings may be of interest to other practitioners and therefore suitable for reports in trade magazines. Or perhaps your findings are of interest to a wider audience, in which case national media would be suitable (Leeds University, 2009).

When you approach media, you also need to think about the content of your 'story'. Your research findings or event may be best illustrated with visuals, in which case television would be more suitable than radio or press. If your findings require more background or in-depth explanation, the press may be a better option (Leeds University, 2009).

When you approach the media it is important that you collaborate with your organisation's PR team or press office, if your organisation has that kind of resource. A press release needs to be clear, accurate and concise. All personal contact needs to be handled sensitively.

In news releases you have to present your story in a very short format. Try to summarise the whole story in the first paragraph, without making it too long or complicated. Also the news release should ideally answer the questions of who, what, when, where and why. Furthermore, it can be useful to include a comment from a researcher, organisation manager or stakeholder. Sending a press release to the media does not mean that you story is guaranteed to get published, but at least you have given it a chance. In some cases, the release will be published more or less as it is. More often, you will be contacted by a journalist who follows up the release, for example, for confirmation of facts, extra information, quotes from people involved. News releases therefore need to include contact details (British Psychology Society, n.d.). For hands-on tips of how to communicate research via media, see Boxes 14.4 and 14.5.

Box 14.4 General tips for research communication via media

If you wish to work with the media to disseminate information or let your research throw light on current issues, some general tips follow:

- Know your audience. Understanding your group is key to successful public engagement, for example, in terms of what will capture their interest, what tone to use, what is appropriate.
- Prioritise the main message. Identify what you would like to communicate and place the most vital information in the beginning of your report (such as news release or article), as this will ignite interest. Before an interview, prepare a few points that you would like to make. If it is a debate programme, prepare some questions in advance.
- The key message can be followed by further information and illustrated in examples, for example, built around illustrative examples or metaphors, but avoid dry statistics. In news releases, further information can be provided in bullet points.
- Keep it short and simple. Make sure that the communication is clear, concise and engaging. Avoid jargon, lecturing and qualifying statements.
- If you can, present parts of your research as ready made 'sound bites'. A well thought-through sound bite is memorable and may give your story additional attention at the same time as it may prevent the media from distorting the message by developing their own soundbite.
- Take note of the name of the journalist, the programme/paper and so on. Keep a record of the dates and times of media contacts and a record of conversations with journalists, especially in relation to how the findings will be used.
- Be sure not to pass on any sensitive documents, pictures or other materials to journalists. This is particularly important when the research data belongs to the funding body (in which case its publication by a third party would contravene copyright rules) or where data contains personal information about research participants provided on conditions of anonymity.
- Negotiate the right to approve how the material is used. This requires balancing the desire to have your research publicised with danger of the media misrepresenting your work.
- Remember that everything you say is 'on the record', unless you have agreed otherwise.
- Finally, relax – remember that you probably know the subject much better than the journalist. Take a few deep breaths and some time to collect your thoughts. Make an effort to speak slowly and clearly.

Note: for some of these and other tips, see Leeds University (2009).

Box 14.5 Tips for research communication via specific media

For communication with the press

- If you do not know the answer to the question, you can ask for some time to think through your comment and get back to the reporter at a later stage. Remember, though, that journalists often work to tight deadlines.
- You may be in the position to write the actual piece yourself. If not, request to have final editorial approval before publication.
- If you are writing the article yourself, consider appending a picture along with the text, as this makes it easier for the editors to include the story.

For communication with television and radio

- Wear comfortable but smart/casual clothing and avoid patterns.
- Avoid fidgeting with hands, papers or clothing as this is distracting for viewers and can interfere with sound.
- Look at the interviewer – they represents the audience.
- If you do not know the answer to a question, it is much better to say so than to provide inaccurate information.
- If you are interviewed for a recorded piece to be broadcasted in television or radio and you feel uncomfortable with something you said, you can ask for it to be redone.
- Stay calm, even if you feel provoked by the interviewer or other panellists.

Note: for some of these and other tips, see Leeds University (2009).

Conclusion

You should now feel confident enough to undertake the final and perhaps most important element of the research, its dissemination, in a variety of formats appropriate for diverse audiences. At all times the three key issues are content (what to disseminate), audience (who to disseminate to) and delivery (how to disseminate). This chapter has endeavoured to provide an introduction to all forms and formats, and an understanding of the requirements of those that facilitate dissemination, from conference organisers and publishers through to journalists working in the mass media.

Further Reading

Curack, L.J. (2000) *Oral Presentations for Technical Communication*. Boston, MA: Allyn and Bacon.
Although focused largely on science and technology research environments, this remains the most comprehensive volume on oral presentations available to practitioner-researchers

in all fields. In a series of pragmatic chapters it covers: how to deal with nervousness and anxiety; ways to improve your recall of facts; and other techniques to build confidence in oral presentations. There are chapters on using presentational software and the use of analogies to explain often complex issues. The volume shares the thematic layout of the current chapter by focussing equally on structure and audience.

Denscombe, M. (2007) *The Good Research Guide: For Small-scale Social Research Projects*, 3rd edn. Milton Keynes: Open University Press.
Denscome's book has a concluding chapter on 'Writing Up', which is full of useful tips and strategies, key point boxes and a checklist. The chapter covers: writing for different audiences; vital information to be included; the importance of following established reporting conventions; the Harvard referencing system; style; and structure. Particular emphasis is given to writing up qualitative research and writing up the research methods section of reports.

Leeds University (2009) 'Publicity toolkit'. Available at: http://publicitytoolkit.leeds.ac.uk/info/12/resources/12/dealing_with_the_media
Leeds University has a website with excellent information on how to deal with media. Not all information is accessible to a broader audience, but the accessible information includes a list of helpful and concrete 'face-saving tips'.

Glossary

Abstract – A short summary of papers submitted to conference organisers containing the full title and author(s), some background context and justification, purpose, methods, results and conclusions. Abstracts are usually limited to between 200 and 1000 words. Journal articles also require abstracts, although they are submitted along with the manuscript on completion.

Anonymity – The non-disclosure of research participant identity either through name or other identifying features.

Blind review – The process whereby journal editors send anonymised versions of submitted articles out for review by peer researchers in the field (see also **peer-reviewed**).

Boolean operators – These are used as a fundamental method of combing search terms. They can refine or broaden searches. The three most commonly used operators are 'AND', 'OR' and 'NOT'.

Call for papers – Conference organisers issue calls for papers up to a year in advance of events, containing information on how to submit abstracts and sometimes full articles for consideration. They will appear in email distributions lists, trade newspapers, journals and on the conference website.

Case – In a dataset, one case will be the data from one questionnaire, which is entered as one line of a spreadsheet layout.

Census sample – Sample of the complete sample frame, difficult because a complete list of the sample frame only exists in particular circumstances, such as employees or students.

Cluster sample – Probability sample selecting random areas and then carrying out a census sample within each area.

Coding – Basic labels that are placed on data, categorising parts of the data into groups that will be useful for the research and analysis. Codes vary and can be for example events, activities, meanings and interactions.

Coding book or coding frame – A set of all potential responses to a survey giving each a unique 'code' that allows for analysis.

Confidence level – Probability that the answer will be within the *margin of error*. Typical values for social science research are 90 to 95 per cent, although lower values are used.

Convenience sample – A sample selected utilising existing contacts for ease of access or when a sample is already chosen for a particular project.

Covert research – Conducting research without consent of the research participants.

Credibility – The extent to which research can be seen as accurate or believable, a rating often used in conjunction with validity.

Criminal Records Bureau check – An official check carried out on individuals to ensure that they are not unsuitable for working with children or vulnerable adults.

Cross-tabulation (or crosstab) – A type of table that displays one set of variables in relation to another, for example, age and gender.

Data cleaning – A process in the handling of quantitative data that is intended to ensure the accuracy of the dataset prior to analysis by removing errors and inconsistencies.

Data entry – The process of transferring gathered data into a useable format in a suitable computer package.

Deductive – A deductive approach would accept that the researcher has an idea of what is likely to be found and will more often than not take a certain theoretical stance. In this light data are analysed according to these preconceptions (a priori).

Deductive coding – Developing codes for your data based on previous literature or theories, that is, codes that are concept driven. You may develop codes before you start, assigning passages of the data to those codes.

Descriptive research – Research in areas lacking a developed theory. Descriptive research does generally not have theoretical ambitions, but aims to describe one or a few aspects of a phenomenon in detail.

Desk research – Any research carried out away from the field, such as literature searches and reviews, secondary data analysis and other background reading.

Dichotomous question (or dichotomous variable) – A survey question that has only two potential responses, for example, gender.

Discourse analysis – A specific approach that focuses on social interaction and versions of reality that are achieved through language, words, speech and sequencing.

Empirical research – Research based on observations of reality.

Epistemology – Theory of knowledge; what we can know about the reality and how to obtain knowledge.

Ethics committee – A board of experts who will judge your research proposal from an ethical viewpoint and from whom you must seek approval before you conduct your project.

Evaluation – Applied research that intends to judge the value or merit of a product or a service. Evaluations can focus on the process or the outcome, and they can be formative or summative.

Executive summary – A short summary of the main findings, methodology, conclusions and recommendations relating to the research. Can be a separate publication or form part of the main research report.

Explorative research – Undertaken in areas or on topics where there are gaps in knowledge. The purpose is to gather as much information as possible about a specific topic/area. This information will form the basis on which future research can be undertaken.

Expressions of interest (EoI) – A term for the way in which finding bodies announce to the research community that they want to know who is interested in tendering for a specific piece of work. Usually invites a short summary of your research and financial capabilities.

Focus group – A group interview or themed discussion with about 6–10 participants, which is facilitated by a moderator.

Framework analysis – A specific approach to analysis developed for applied policy research. A framework is used to organise, index, chart and map the data.

Generalisability – The potential to apply research findings in other circumstances and settings than those studied, that is, the study sample is representative for a larger population.

Grey literature – Grey literature encompasses documents that have not been designed for general publication and include items such as internal reports, newsletters; research and evaluation findings and policy documents within governmental departments, voluntary sector organisations, academia and industry.

Grounded theory – Aims to develop theory inductively, meaning that there is no starting hypothesis, instead theory is built through the observations of the research project with no preconceived ideas.

Hypothesis – An assumption about how phenomena are related, which is drawn from a theory and which can be tested in research studies.

Incentives – Can be financial or non-financial and offered to an individual or group of people to recruit participants for an interview or focus group.

Inductive – In conducting inductive research the task in hand requires data to be analysed 'a posteriori' that is, categories for analysis are derived from the data rather than being decided beforehand; the data must speak for itself.

Inductive coding – Codes are data driven and emerge from the data as part of the noticing process.

Informed consent – Agreement from the research participant that they are fully aware of the purpose of the research.

Intellectual property – The name given to different types of knowledge including ideas, tunes, blueprints or databases.

Interval level question (or interval level variable) – A survey question with potential responses that relate to one another and are evenly distributed, but with no meaningful zero point, for example, temperature.

Interview – Themed discussion, normally semi-structured, between researcher and subject.

Interview schedule – Also called a topic guide or interview guide. A list of questions and prompts used by researchers when conducting fieldwork to enable relevant themes and issues to be discussed.

Invitation to tender (ITT) – Document, often in several parts, which outlines in detail what is required of those wishing to tender for the contract of carrying out the research.

Iterative/iteration – Revisiting problems and issues repeatedly (hopefully) with fresh insight

JISCmail lists – Free subscriber distribution list organised around subject areas, hosted by the Joint Information Systems Committee (JISC) in the UK. The National Academic Mailing List Service, known as 'JISCmail', is run by the Joint Academic Network or JANET (http://www.ja.net) and funded by the JISC (http://www.jisc.ac.uk) 'to benefit learning, teaching and research communities'.

Judgement sample – Relying on judgement to pick suitable respondents to a survey, used in street surveys for ad hoc studies.

Likert scale – A scale measuring agreement or disagreement with a proposition, for example, a rating of satisfaction, usually containing five or seven points to enable a middle position between extremes.

Linear/linearity – A research design in which each stage is dependent on the successful completion of the previous stages.

Margin of error – The error of the result, so that the result of a question, x, will probably lie between x plus or minus the margin of error.

Mean – An average value calculated by dividing the sum of a series of values by the number of individual values.

Median – The average of a series of values that equates to the midpoint of the consecutive series of values.

Metadata – Information that describes the content, quality, condition, origin and other characteristics of data or other pieces of information.

Mode – A calculation of an average, which uses the most frequently occurring value in a series.

Mode effects – Different ways of asking respondents questions result in different answers, for example, respondents tend to give more positive answers over the telephone than on a paper questionnaire.

Multi-stage sample – Combining different sampling methods, for example carrying out a random sample of areas, which are then part of a stratified random sample.

Nominal level question (or nominal level variable) – A survey question with several potential answers that do not have a relationship to one another, for example, mode of transport.

Ontology – Perception of reality, for example, whether it is independent of our perceptions.

Open calls – Announcements by funding bodies (public or voluntary sector) that a set amount of money has been allocated over a set period for research in a specified area (usually quite widely drawn).

Open comments – Data from a quantitative survey that is more qualitative in its nature, where the respondent is able to express their response more fully, for example, in comments boxes.

Operationalisation – The process of translating research question into variables, that is, questions in a questionnaire, an interview or a focus group.

Ordinal level question (or ordinal level variable) – A survey question with responses that can be rank ordered but are not evenly distributed, for example, age group.

Outliers – An outlier is a value within a set of values that is very different to the other values (much larger or smaller) and may have the effect of skewing any analysis of the set of data.

Oversample – Where a demographic has been over-represented in the sample, for example, people in single person households are oversampled in household surveys as they are more likely to be selected than any one person in a household with multiple occupants.

Peer-reviewed – The process by which papers (journal articles, book chapters, draft manuscripts and some conference abstracts) are evaluated by other researchers in the field. Often comments are collated by the editorial team and revisions suggested before the paper is accepted. Often this process is blind (the reviewer is unaware of the author of the paper) or double-blind (additionally, the author is unaware of the identity of the reviewers, when provided with their recommendations or feedback).

Plagiarism – The unattributed copying of other people's work.

Population – The number of subjects of the study (sample size), usually used in relation to respondents to a survey or to a particular survey question and expressed as *N*. A sub-set of the sample is expressed as *n*.

Positionality – Where the researcher is honest about the purpose of their research and the agenda (s)he has in pursuing it. Identifying positionality helps to negate any potential criticisms concerning bias as readers know from the outset that work has been analysed through this paradigm. It should also clarify that the researcher is not trying to attempt a non-partisan piece of work.

Post-coding – An instance where a coding frame is developed after a survey has been conducted, which allows for qualitative responses to be grouped in a way that allows quantitative analysis.

Practitioner-researcher – Anyone who undertakes research in order to improve their practice.

Probability sampling – Sampling that relies on having a random selection of people in the sample frame.

Public funding bodies – Any body funded by taxation, for whatever purpose. So for example that would include international, national, regional and local government departments, funding councils and agencies (see also **statutory bodies**).

Purposive sample – This approach to sampling uses specific criteria and participants are chosen because of particular features or characteristics they have.

Qualitative research methods – The intensive study of few cases: the study of difference in kind. Explanation is a matter of understanding and interpreting actions, opinions or experiences by taking the context into account. .

Quantitative research methods – The extensive study of many cases; the study of difference in number. Data is analysed via statistical methods and conclusions are drawn about relationships and regularities between variables.

Quota sample – Where the sample has a quota that restricts the number of people in a category who are interviewed. The interviewer will ask a screening question to assess whether a person fits into the quota.

Range – The distribution between the highest and lowest values in a series.

Ratio level question (or ratio level variable) – A survey question with potential responses that have both evenly distributed values and a meaningful zero point, for example, distance travelled in miles.

Reflexive – Reflecting on earlier findings and/or new information in the ongoing redesign of the research.

Refusal rate – The number of people who have refused to take part out of all those who have been contacted. For example, if an interviewer knocks on the doors of 100 houses, 80 people answer, and 40 take part, the response rate is 40/80 = 50 per cent.

Reliability – If a question is completely reliable, it can be asked of every different population and be understood in the same way. The term captures how trustworthy the study is and has to do with errors in measurement, that is, in the collection and analysis of data.

Representativeness – The sample studied is very similar to the population from which it is drawn, in those aspects that are relevant to the study.

Research design – The underlying logic of the study and the means by which the study will answer the identified research questions.

Research diary – A diary where you can note all activities relating to your research project and record ideas and subjective responses to your research.

Research environment – This term is used to describe the body of research theories and practices common to the field, recent research in the specific area and conferences organised by individuals and organisations that are engaged in research in that area.

Researcher effect – The impact a researcher has on the subjects of the research, for example, interviewees may give answers that they think are expected by the interviewer; in participant observation research, actors may not act in ways they would if the researcher was not present

Response rate – The proportion of people who have responded out of all those who have been contacted by the researcher. For example, if a practitioner-researcher sends out 100 questionnaires, 10 of which are returned to sender as 'address unknown' and 30 returned completed, then the response rate is 30/(100–10) = (30/90) = 33.3 per cent.

Sample – The sample is the selection of people in the sample frame who will be asked to take part in the survey. In some cases this may be the whole sample frame, a census survey, but in most cases it will be a smaller subset of the sample frame.

Sample frame – The sample frame defines all the people in the population you would like to survey, in an ideal world. For many surveys, this will be the population of a large geographical area, such as the UK, or North America. For others, particular groups of people will for the population of interest, such as children between 8 and 13 years of age, or employees in a social enterprise. These comprise the sample frame.

Scoping the field – An initial search to find out what else has been published recently in a given area or what other research is currently underway in your field.

Screening question – A question to select a certain section of the population, for example, all people with incomes below £20,000.

Semiotics – The study of signs. A sign is a unit of meaning and it can be a word, gesture, smell, sound. This approach uncovers how specific signs have an effect on the signified.

Simple random sample – Random sample of the sample frame.

Snowball effect – This is a term used in research to identify the ongoing collection of resources/research participants, that is, like a snowball it begins small and as it is rolled through the snow it gathers momentum and gets bigger.

Snowball sample – The researcher makes contacts with participants in the initial stages of the research project and uses them to establish links and contacts with other people from the target group (that is, sharing the same characteristics) to invite them to take part in the research.

Standard deviation – Standard deviation is the way that the spread of figures in a dataset is measured in relation to the mean.

Statistical significance – Significance measures the extent to which the conclusions drawn from the respondents to a survey match what the answers for the whole of the sample frame would be, and thus how significant the results of data analysis can be said to be:

whether they are likely to be correct or have come about by chance. The main determinants of statistical significance are the size of the sample with relation to the sample frame, and the response rate.

Statutory body – Any public funding body or agency (see **public funding bodies**). They are statutory in the sense that, as agencies of the state they have to operate within a specific legal and moral framework with regard to contractual obligations, relationships with the public and have transparent audit and monitoring regimes. While some non-statutory bodies (such as private companies and voluntary sector bodies) also act in the same way, they are not obliged so to do.

Steering group – Governmental departments and agencies usually create steering groups for research projects that will review the research in progress. They typically contain many of the interest groups in the policy field ('stakeholders' in the jargon) and they may have ideas about how research is disseminated.

Stratified sample – Where a proportionate sample is taken from different areas or demographic groups, for example sampling 5 per cent of people who are disabled and 5 per cent of people who are not disabled.

Survey fatigue – An increasingly common reason for non-response to a questionnaire. It is due to people being asked to respond to increasing numbers of questionnaires or to give feedback, so that they no longer wish to do so for the majority of surveys.

Survey mode – How the survey is carried out, for example via postal questionnaire, face-to-face, telephone, online or a combination of these.

Systematic review – A literature review that locates, critically reviews and syntheses the best available research relating to a specific topic.

Systematic sampling – A type of probability sampling where every nth case on the sample frame is sampled, n being the *sample interval*. Has the advantage of evenly sampling from the sample frame, but is vulnerable to periodic factors in the sample frame.

Testability – The extent to which hypotheses and theories can be tested by questions or observations.

Theoretical sample – This approach moves between sampling and theoretical reflection where theoretical consideration guides the research project until saturation is reached.

Theory – An idea or group of ideas related to a research area from which hypotheses and research questions can be derived.

Topic guide – A list of questions/topics prepared for an interview or focus group (see **interview schedule**).

Transcription – The production of a written version/translation of audio or visual material.

Triangulation – The use of two or more different research methods.

True measure – A type of quantitative question where there is a meaningful difference between the values given as responses.

Trustworthiness – The correctness or credibility of an account or method.

User involvement – Participation of representatives from your targeted research group in aspects of your work.

Validity – How well the research question is operationalised into one or several variables, that is, how correctly the research questions capture the phenomenon studied. If a question is completely valid, the responses to the question will be applicable to the general population by the researcher.

Value – Each potential variation of variables/questions. The term used commonly in quantitative research where a value is the measure of a variable for each case in a dataset.

Variable – A variable is the factor (or value) that is being measured by each question in a questionnaire – it is the factor that can vary.

Variance – Level or extent of measurable variation of factors.

Weighting – Statistical technique in which a data item (such as an average) is emphasised more than other data items comprising a group or summary. A number (weight) is assigned to each data item that reflects its relative importance based on the objective of the data collection.

Working hypothesis – A proposition set out as a *possible* explanation for certain occurrences and behaviours (see **hypothesis**).

Bibliography

Publications

Alasuutari, P. (1998) *An Invitation to Social Research.* London: Sage.

Arksey, H. (2004) 'Semi structured and unstructured interviewing', in S. Becker and A. Bryman, A. (eds) *Understanding Research for Social Policy and Practice: Themes, Methods and Approaches.* Bristol: Policy Press. pp. 268–75.

Arksey, H. and Knight, P. (1999) *Interviewing for Social Scientists.* London: Sage.

Aveyard, H. (2007) *Doing a Literature Review in Health and Social Care.* Buckingham: Open University Press.

Babbie, E. (2004) *The Practice of Social Research*, 10th edn. London: Thomson Learning.

Babbie, E.R. (2007) *The Basics of Social Research*, international edn. London: Wadsworth.

Balnaves, M. and Caputi, P. (2001) *Introduction to Quantitative Research Methods.* London: Sage.

Ball, S. (2006) *Education Policy and Social Class: The Selected Works of Stephen J. Ball.* London: Routledge.

Barron, L. (2006) in V. Jupp (ed.) *The Sage Dictionary of Social Research Methods.* London: Sage.

Baume, D. and Baume, C. (2000) *Making Presentations: Training Materials for Research Students.* Oxford: Oxford Centre for Staff Development.

Becker, H. (1987) *Writing for Social Scientists: How to Start and Finish Your Thesis, Book or Article.* Chicago, IL: University of Chicago Press.

Becker, S. and Bryman, A. (2004) *Understanding Research for Social Policy and Practice: Themes, Methods and Approaches.* Bristol: Policy Press.

Blaxter, L., Hughes, C. and Tight, M. (2006) *How to Research*, 3rd edn. Milton Keynes: Open University Press.

Bolton, G. (2006) 'Narrative writing: reflective enquiry into professional practice', *Educational Action Research*, 14 (2): 203–18.

Boswell, W. (2004) 'The World Wide Web and the Internet'. Available at: http://websearch.about.com/od/whatistheinternet/a/worldwideweb.htm (accessed 15 July 2008).

Breitner, B.J., Ayres, L. and Knafl, K.A. (1993) 'Triangulation in qualitative research: evaluation of completeness and confirmation purposes', *Journal of Nursing Scholarship*, 25 (3): 237–43.

British Psychology Society (n.d.) 'Working with the media: a guide for members of the British Psychology Society', unpublished manuscript.

British Sociological Association (2002) 'Statement of ethical practice for the British Sociological Association'. Available at: http://www.britsoc.co.uk/equality/Statement+Ethical+Practice.htm (accessed 2 December 2009).

Bryman, A. (2004) *Social Research Methods*, 2nd edn. Oxford: Oxford University Press.

Bryman, A. (2008) *Social Research Methods*, 3rd edn. Oxford: Oxford University Press.

Buckingham, A. and Saunders, P. (2004) *The Survey Methods Workbook: from Design to Analysis*. Cambridge: Polity Press.

Burroughs, G.E.R. (1975) *Design and Analysis in Educational Research*, 2nd edn. Oxford: The Education Review.

Campbell, A. and Groundwater-Smith, S. (2007) *An Ethical Approach to Practitioner Research*. London: Routledge.

Cappuccini, G., Harvey, L., Williams, J., Bowers-Brown, T., McCaig, C., Sagu, S. and MacDonald, M. (2005) *Careers Advisory Services and International Students*. Manchester: HECSU.

Carr, W. and Kemmis, S. (1986) *Becoming Critical: Education, Knowledge and Action Research*. London: Falmer

Carspecken, P.F. (1996) *Critical Ethnography in Educational Research: A Theoretical and Practical Guide*. London: Routledge.

Childcare Research Organisation (2009) Available at: http://www.childcareresearch. org/Discover?displayPage=datamethods/fieldresearch.jsp (accessed 18 March 2009).

Chowdhury, G.G. (1999) 'The Internet and information retrieval research: a brief review', *Journal of Documentation*, 55 (2): 209–25.

Clarke, A. (1999) *Evaluation Research. An Introduction to Principles, Methods and Practice*. London: Sage.

Coghlan, D. and Brannick, T. (2005) *Doing Action Research in Your Own Organization*. London: Sage.

Cohen, L., Manion, L. and Morrison, K. (2000) *Research Methods in Education*, 5th edn. London: Routledge.

Connelly, F.M. and Clandinin, D.J. (1990) 'Stories of experience and narrative inquiry', *Educational Researcher*, 19 (5): 2–14.

Connolly, P. (2007) *Quantitative Data Analysis in Education*. Oxon: Routledge.

Cooper, J. (2007) 'Factors affecting return rates to on-line surveys', in M. Trotman et al. (eds) *The Challenges of a Changing World: Proceedings of the Fifth International Conference of the Association for Survey Computing, UK*. Berkeley, CA: ASC.

Costello, P.J.M. (2003) *Action Research*. London: Continuum.

Craemer, T. (2006) 'Can a survey change one's race? An experiment on context effects and racial self-classification'. Paper presented at the annual meeting of the American Association For Public Opinion Association. Available at: http://www.allacademic. com/meta/p17090_index.html (accessed 22 July 2008).

Cresswell, J.W. (2007) *Qualitative Inquiry and Research Design: Choosing Among Five Approaches*. London: Sage.

Crouch, M. and McKenzie, H. (2006) 'The logic of small samples in interview-based qualitative research', *Social Science Information*, 45 (7) 482–99.

Cummins, H. (2006) 'A funny thing happened on the way to the ethics board: studying the meaning of farm life for farm children', *Journal of Academic Ethics*, 4: 175–88.

Curack, L.J. (2000) *Oral Presentations for Technical Communication*. Boston, MA: Allyn and Bacon.

Dahlberg, L. and Herlitz, C. (1997) *Vägen från sjukhuset. Om äldre människors återhämtning efter ortopediska skador*. Falun: Dalarnas Forskningsråd [Dalarna Research Institute].

Dahlberg, L. (2005) 'Interaction between voluntary and statutory social service provision: a matter of welfare pluralism, substitution or complementarity?', *Social Policy and Administration*, 39 (7): 740–63.

De Leeuw, E., Callegaro, M., Hox. J., Korendijk, E. and Lensvelt-Muldersr, G. (2007) 'The influence of advance letters on response in telephone surveys – a meta analysis', *Public Opinion Quarterly*, 71 (3): 413–43.

de Vaus, D.A. (2002) *Surveys in Social Research*, 5th edn. London: UCL Press.

Denscombe, M. (2002) *Ground Rules for Good Research: a 10 Point Guide for Social Researchers*. Maidenhead: Open University Press.

Denscombe, M. (2007) *The Good Research Guide: For Small-scale Social Research Projects*, 3rd edn. Milton Keynes: Open University Press.

Denzin, N.K. and Lincoln, Y.S. (eds) (2008) *Collecting and Interpreting Qualitative Materials*, 3rd edn, Thousand Oaks, CA: Sage.

Department of Health (2005) *Research Governance Framework for Health and Social Care*, 2nd edn. London: Department of Health.

Devine, F. (2002) 'Qualitative methods', in D. March and G. Stoker (eds) *Theory and Methods in Political Science*, 2nd edn. Basingstoke: Palgrave Macmillan. pp. 197–215.

Dick, B., Stringer, E.T. and Huxham, C. (2009) 'Theory in action research', *Action Research*, 7 (1): 5–12.

Doctorow, C. (2008) 'Intellectual property is a silly euphemism', *Guardian* 21 February.

Draper, P. (2000) 'The practitioner-researcher in nursing: a response to Peter Jarvis', *Nurse Education Today*, 20 (1): 43–4.

Drew, S., McCaig, C., Marsden, D., Haughton, P., McBride, J., McBride, D., Willis, B. and Wolstenholme, C. (2008) *Trans-national Education and Higher Education Institutions: Exploring Patterns of HE Institutional Activity for the Department for Innovation Universities and Skills*. London: DIUS.

Duke Universities Libraries (2007) 'Advanced searching techniques'. Available at: http://www.esrc.ac.uk/ESRCInfoCentre/Images/ESRC_Re_Ethics_Frame_tcm6–112 91.pdf (accessed 15 September 2008).

Durrant, G. and Staetsky, L. (2008) 'Survey data analysis courses in applied social surveys 2008'. Lecture, 12–14 November, University of Southampton 2008.

Economic and Social Research Council (ESRC) (2005) 'Research ethics framework'. Available at: http://www.esrc.ac.uk/ESRCInfoCentre/Images/ESRC_Re_Ethics_ Frame_tcm6–11291.pdf (accessed15 September 2008).

Field, A. (2009) *Discovering Statistics Using SPSS*. London: Sage.

Fine, M. and Torre, M.E. (2006) 'Intimate details: participatory action research in prison', *Action Research*, 4 (3): 253–69.

Fink, A. (2005) *Conducting Research Literature Reviews: From the Internet to Paper*. London: Sage.

Flick, U. (2009) *An Introduction to Qualitative Research*, 4th edn. London: Sage.

Flick, U., von Kardoff, E. and Steinke, I. (2004) *A Companion to Qualitative Research*. London: Sage.

Fox, M., Martin, P. and Green, G. (2007) *Doing Practitioner Research*. London: SAGE.

Fricker, Jr, R. D. and Schonlau, M. (2002) 'Advantages and disadvantages of internet research surveys: evidence from the literature', *Field Methods*, 14 (4): 347–67.

Fuller, R. and Petch, A. (1995) *Practitioner Research. The Reflexive Social Worker*. Buckingham: Open University Press.

Gardner, B. and Abraham, C. (2007) 'What drives car use? A grounded theory analysis of commuters' reasons for driving', *Transportation Research Part F*, 10: 187–200.

George, A.L. (1979) 'Case studies and theory development. The method of structured, focused comparison', in P.G. Lauren (ed.) *Diplomacy: New Approaches in History, Theory and Policy*. New York: The Free Press. pp. 43–68.

George, A.L. and McKeown, T.L. (1985) 'Case studies and theories of organizational decision making', in *Advances in Information Processing in Organizations. A Research Annual*, Vol. 2. London: JAI Press. pp. 21–57.

Gibbs, A. (1997) 'Focus groups social research update'. Available at: http://sru.soc.surrey.ac.uk/SRU19.html (accessed 28 July 2008).

Gibbs, G. (2007) *Analyzing Qualitative Data*. London: Sage.

Gilbert, N. (ed.) (1996) *Researching Social Life*, 2nd edn. Thousand Oaks, CA: Sage.

Glanville, J. and Sowden, A.J. (2001) 'Phase 0: identification of the need for a review', in S.K. Khan, G.T. Riet, J. Glanville, A.J. Sowden and J. Kleijnen (eds) *Undertaking Systematic Reviews of Research on Effectiveness CRD's Guidance for Those Carrying Out or Commissioning Reviews*, University of York CRD Report Number 4, 2nd edn. York: University of York.

Goffman, E. (1991) *Asylums: Essays on the Social Situation of Mental Patients and Other Inmates*. New York: Doubleday.

Gordon, G.B. (2001) 'Transforming lives: towards bicultural competence', in P. Reason and H. Bradbury (eds) *Handbook of Action Research*. London: Sage.

Gray, D.E. (2009) *Doing Research in the Real World*, 2nd edn. London: Sage.

Green, E.C. (2001) 'Can qualitative research produce reliable quantitative findings?', *Field Methods*, 13 (3). Available at: http://fmx.sagepub.com/cgi/content/abstract/13/1/3 (accessed 26 July 2008).

Greenwood, D.J. and Levin, M. (2007) *Introduction to Action Research*. Thousand Oaks, CA: Sage.

Greenwood, D.J. and Levin, M. (2008) 'Reform of the social sciences and of universities through action research', in D.K. Denzin and Y.S. Lincoln (eds) *The Landscape of Qualitative Research*. Thousand Oaks, CA: Sage. pp. 57–86.

Grewal, I., Lewis, J., Flynn, T., Brown, J., Bond, J. and Coast, J. (2006) 'Developing attributes for a generic quality of life measure for older people: preferences or capabilities', *Social Science and Medicine*, 12 (8): 1891–901.

Grinyer, A. (2002) 'The anonymity of research participants: assumptions, ethics and practicalities', Social Research Update 36. Available at: http://sru.soc.surrey.ac.uk/SRU36.html (2 December 2009).

Groves, R.M. and McGonagle, K.A. (2001) 'A theory guided interviewer training protocol regarding survey participation', *Journal of Official Statistics*, 17 (2). Available at: http://www.jos.nu/Articles/abstract.asp?article=172249 (accessed 8 July 2008).

Hague, P., Hague, N. and Morgan, C. (2004) *Market Research in Practice – A Guide to the Basics*. London: Kogan Page.

Hart, C. (1998) *Doing a Literature Review*. London: Sage.

Heath, A. and Martin, J. (1997) 'Why are there so few formal measuring instruments in social and political research?', Centre for Research into Elections and Social Trends. Available at: http://www.strath.ac.uk/Other/CREST/p58.htm (accessed 12 July 2008).

Heatley, A. and Nation, P. (1994) Range. Université du Québec à Montréal. [Computer program, available at: http://www.lextutor.ca/range/ (accessed 7 December 2009).]

Heckathorn, D. (2009) 'Respondent driven sampling'. Available at: http://www.respondentdrivensampling.org/ (accessed 25 August 2009).

HEFCE (2006) 'Review of widening participation research: addressing the barriers to participation in higher education'. Available at: http://www.hefce.ac.uk/pubs/rdreports/2006/rd13_06/ (accessed 14 August 2009).

Hill, N. Brierley, J. and MacDougall, R. (2003) *How to Measure Customer Satisfaction*, 2nd edn. Farnham: Gower.

Hoinville, G., Jowell, R. and Associates (1985) *Survey Research and Practice*, 2nd edn. London: Gower.

Humphreys, M. (2005) 'Getting personal: reflexivity and autoethnographic vignettes', *Qualitative Inquiry*, 11 (6): 840–60.

Huxham, C. and Eden, C. (2008) 'Action research', in S.R. Clegg and J.R. Bailey (eds) *International Encyclopedia of Organization Studies*. Thousand Oaks, CA: Sage. pp. 20–4.

Janovicek, N. (2006) 'Oral history and ethical practice: towards effective policies and procedures', *Journal of Academic Ethics* 4: 157–74.

Jarvis, P. (1999) *The Practitioner-Researcher: Developing Theory from Practice*. San Francisco, CA: Jossey-Bass.

Jarvis, P. (2000) 'The practitioner-researcher in nursing', *Nurse Education Today*, 20 (1): 30–5.

Jia-ming, F. and Pei-ji, S. (2007) 'The role of trust in affecting potential respondents to participate in web-based surveys', in *Proceedings of the International Conference on Management Science and Engineering, Harbin, 2007, 20–22 August 2007*. pp. 174–9. Available at: http://ieeexplore.ieee.org/stamp/stamp.jsp?arnumber=4421843& isnumber=4421807 (accessed 26 July 2008).

Jokinen, E. (2004) 'The makings of mother in diary narratives', *Qualitative Diary Narratives*, 10 (3): 339–59.

Jones, R. (2000) 'The Unsolicited diary as a qualitative research tool for advanced research capacity in the field of health and illness', *Qualitative Health Research*, 10 (4): 555–67.

Kane, E. (1985) *Doing Your Own Research: Basic Descriptive Research in the Social Sciences and Humanities*. London: Marion Boyars.

Kelly, M. (1998) 'Writing a research proposal', in C. Seale (ed.) *Researching Society and Culture*. Thousand Oaks, CA: Sage.

Kemmis, S. (2007) 'Action research as a practice-changing practice', paper presented at the Spanish Collaborative Action Research Network (CARN) Conference, 18–20 October 2007, University of Valladolid, Spain.

Kennedy, J.M. (1993) 'A comparison of telephone survey respondent selection procedures', paper presented at the Annual Meeting of the American Association for Public Opinion Research. Available at: http://www.indiana.edu/~csr/aapor93.html (accessed 15 July 2008).

Kilmartin, K. (2005) 'Searching, evaluating and citing information'. Available at: http://www.lib.unimelb.edu.au/postgrad/litreview/criticalreading.html (accessed 15 July 2008).

King, G., Keohane, R.O. and Verba, S. (1994) *Designing Social Inquiry. Scientific Inference in Qualitative Research*. Princeton, NJ: Princeton University Press.

Kitzinger, J. (1995) 'Qualitative research: introducing focus groups', *BMJ*, 311: 299–302. Available at: http://www.bmj.com/cgi/content/full/311/7000/299 (accessed 9 July 2008).

Leeds University (2009) 'Publicity toolkit. Available at: http://publicitytoolkit.leeds.ac. uk/info/12/resources/12/dealing_with_the_media (accessed 23 January 2009).

Legard, R., Keegan, J. and Ward, K. (2003) 'In depth interviews', in J. Ritchie and J. Lewis (eds) *Qualitative Research Practice*. London: SAGE. pp. 138–69.

Lewins, A. and Silver, C. (2007) *Using Software in Qualitative Research: A Step-by-Step Guide*. London: Sage.

Lipsey, M.W. (1990) *Design Sensitivity: Statistical Power for Experimental Research*. Thousand Oaks, CA: Sage.

Locke, L.F., Spirduso, W.W. and Silverman, S.J. (2000) *Proposals that Work: A Guide for Planning Dissertations and Grant Proposals*, 4th edn, Thousand Oaks, CA: Sage.

Lynn, P., Beerten, R., Laiho, J. and Martin, J. (2001) 'Recommended standard final outcome categories and standard definitions of response rate for social surveys', ISER Working Papers No. 2001–23.

Mangels, L. and Neves, L. (2007) 'Racial classification in Brazil: discrepancies between observed and self-identified race', paper presented at the annual meeting of the American Sociological Association. Available at: http://www.allacademic.com/ meta/p182287_index.html (accessed 22 July 2008).

Mark, R. (1996) *Research Made Simple. A Handbook for Social Workers*. London: Sage.

Marsch, D. and Furlong, P. (2002) 'A skin not a sweater: ontology and epistemology in political science', in D. March and G. Stoker (eds) *Theory and Methods in Political Science*, 2nd edn. Basingstoke: Palgrave Macmillan. pp. 17–41.

Marshall, C. and Rossman, G.B. (2006) *Designing Qualitative Research*, 4th edn. Thousand Oaks, CA: Sage.

Martin, A.W. (2001) 'Large group processes as action research', in P. Reason and H. Bradbury (eds) *Handbook of Action Research*. London, Sage. pp. 166–75.

Mauthner, N.S. and Douchet, A. (2003) 'Reflexive accounts and accounts of reflexivity in qualitative data analysis', *Sociology*, 37 (3): 413–31.

Maxwell, J. (1996) *Qualitative Research Design: An Interactive Approach*. Thousand Oaks, CA: Sage.

May, T. (2001) *Social Research: Issues, Methods and Process*, 3rd edn. Buckingham: Open University Press.

Mays, N. and Pope, C. (1995) 'Rigour and qualitative research', *BMJ*, 311: 109–12.

McIntyre, A. (2008) 'Participatory action research', A Sage University paper, Qualitative Research Methods Series: 52. Thousand Oaks, CA: Sage.

McNiff, J. (2002) 'Action research for professional development: concise advice for new action researchers'. Available at: http://www.jeanmcniff.com/booklet1.html (accessed 5 January 2009).

McNiff, J. and Whitehead, J. (2002) *Action Research: Principles and Practice*. New York: RoutledgeFalmer.

McNiff, J. and Whitehead, J. (2006) *All You Need to Know About Action Research*. Sage: London.

McWilliam, E. (2004) 'W(h)ither practitioner research?', *The Australian Educational Researcher*, 31: 113–26.

Mockler, N. (2007) 'Ethics in practitioner research', in A. Campbell and S. Groundwater-Smith (eds) *An Ethical Approach to Practitioner Research*. London: Routledge. pp. 88–98.

Moon, N. (2003) 'External data sources for sampling', MRS Seminar, NOP World.

Murphy, R. and Torrance, H. (1987) *Evaluating Education: Issues and Methods*. Milton Keynes: Open University Press.

Newbury, D. (2001) 'Diaries and fieldnotes in the research process', *Research Issues in Art Design and Media*, 1. Available at: http://www.biad.bcu.ac.uk/research/rti/riadm/issue1/abstract.htm (accessed 7 November 2008).

Nicolaas, G. (2004) 'Sampling issues for telephone surveys in Scotland', seminar. Available at: http://www.bioss.ac.uk/staff/adam/rsse/2003-2004/presentations/gerry_nicolaas.ppt (accessed 15 July 2008).

Norusis, M. (2005) *SPSS 14.0 Advanced Statistical Procedures Companion*. London: Prentice Hall.

Onwuegbuzie, A. (1997) 'Writing a research proposal: the role of library anxiety, statistics anxiety, and composition anxiety', *Library & Information Science*, 19 (1): 5-33.

Oppenheim, A.N. (1992) *Questionnaire Design, Interviewing and Attitude Measurement*, 2nd edn. London: Continuum.

Pannell, P.B. and Pannell, D.J. (1999) 'Introduction to social surveying: pitfalls, potential problems and preferred practices', SEA Working Paper 99/04. Available at: http://cyllene.uwa.edu.au/~dpannell/seameth3.htm (accessed 10 July 2008).

Patrick, J. (1973) *Glasgow Gangs Observed*. London: Methuen.

Pearson, G. (2009) 'The researcher as hooligan: where "participant" observation means breaking the law', *International Journal of Social Research Methodology* 12 (3): 243-55.

Plummer, K. (2000) *Documents of Life 2: An Invitation to A Critical Humanism: An Invitation to Critical Humanism*. London: Sage.

Poulsen, K.B., Jensen, S.H., Bach, E. and Schostak, J.F. (2007) 'Using action research to improve health and work environment for 3500 municipal bus drivers', *Educational Action Research*, 15 (1): 75-106.

Powell R.A. and Single H.M. (1996) 'Focus groups', *International Journal of Quality in Health Care*, 8(5): 499-504.

Punch, K.F. (2003) *Survey Research: The Basics*. London: Sage.

Punch, K.F. (2005) *Introduction to Social Research: Quantitative and Qualitative Approaches*, 2nd edn. Thousand Oaks, CA: Sage.

Punch, K.F. (2006) *Developing Effective Research Proposals*. London: Sage.

Rapley, T. (2007) *Doing Conversation, Discourse and Document Analysis*. London: Sage.

Read, M. and Marsh, D. (2002) 'Combining qualitative and quantitative methods', in D. March and G. Stoker (eds) *Theory and Methods in Political Science*, 2nd edn. Basingstoke: Palgrave Macmillan. pp. 231-48.

Reason, P. (2006) 'Choice and quality in action research practice', *Journal of Management Inquiry*, 15 (2): 187-203.

Reason, P. and Bradbury, H. (2008) 'Introduction', in P. Reason and H. Bradbury (eds) *The Sage Handbook of Action Research*.London: Sage. pp. 1-10.

Richards, L. and Morse, J.M. (2007) *User's Guide to Qualitative Methods*. London: Sage.

Richie, J. and Lewis, J. (2006) *Qualitative Research Practice A Guide for Social Science Students and Researchers*. London: Sage.

Ritchie, J. and Spencer, L. (1994) 'Qualitative data analysis for applied policy research', in A. Bryman and R.G. Burgess (eds) *Analyzing Qualitative Data*. London: Routledge. pp. 173-94.

Robson, C. (1997) *Real World Research. A Resource for Social Scientists and Practitioner-Researchers*. Oxford: Blackwell.

Robson, C. (2000) *Small-Scale Evaluation*. Thousand Oaks, CA: Sage.

Robson, C. (2002) *Real World Research. A Resource for Social Scientists and Practitioner-Researchers*. 2nd edn. Oxford: Blackwell.

Roster, C.A., Rogers, R.D., Albaum, G. and Klein, D.A. (2004) 'Comparison of response characteristics from web and telephone surveys', *International Journal of Market Research*, 46 (3): 359–73.

Salkind, N.J. (2008) *Statistics for People Who Think They Hate Statistics*. London: Sage.

Salganik, M.J. and Heckathorn, D.D. (2004) 'Sampling and estimation in hidden populations using respondent-driven sampling', *Sociological Methodology*, 34: 193–239. Available at: http://www.jstor.org/stable/3649374 (accessed 26 July 2008).

Sandelowski, M. (1998) 'Writing a good read: strategies for re-presenting qualitative data', *Research in Nursing and Health*, 21(4): 375–82.

Schatzki, T. (2002) *The Site of the Social: A Philosophical Account of the Constitution of Social Life and Change*. Pennsylvania, PA: University of Pennsylvania Press.

Shaw, I. (2005) 'Practitioner research: evidence or critique?', *British Journal of Social Work*, 35: 1231–48.

Sheffield Hallam University (2004) *Research Ethics Policies and Procedures*, 2nd edn. Sheffield: Sheffield Hallam University.

Shih, T. and Fan, X. (2008) 'Comparing response rates from web and mail surveys: a meta-analysis', *Field Methods*, 20: 249–71.

Silverman, D. (2001) *Interpreting Qualitative Data*. London: Sage.

Silverman, D. (2005) *Doing Qualitative Research*, 2nd edn. London: Sage.

Sitzia, J. and Wood, N. (1998) 'Response rate in patient satisfaction research: an analysis of 210 published studies', *International Journal for Quality in Health Care*, 10 (4): 311–17.

Smith, M.K. (2007) 'Action research', in *The Encyclopedia of Informal Education*. Available at: http://www.infed.org/research/b-actres.htm (accessed 30 November 2009).

Snape, D. and Spencer, L. (2003) 'The foundations of qualitative research', in J. Ritchie and J. Lewis (eds) *Qualitative Research Practice*. London: Sage. pp. 1–23.

Soobrayan, V. (2003) 'Ethics, truth and politics in constructivist qualitative research', *Westminister Studies in Education*, 26 (2): 107–23.

Stoker, G. and Marsh, D. (2002) 'Introduction', D. March and G. Stoker (eds) *Theory and Methods in Political Science*, 2nd edn. Basingstoke: Palgrave Macmillan. pp. 1–16.

Strauss, A. and Corbin, J. (2008) *Basics of Qualitative Research: Techniques and Procedures for Developing Grounded Theory*, 3rd edn. Thousand Oaks, CA: Sage.

Stringer, E.T. (2007) *Action Research*. Thousand Oaks, CA: Sage.

Sullivan, D. (2001) 'Power searching for anyone'. Available at: http://searchenginewatch.com/showPage.html?page=2156031 (accessed 15 July 2009).

Sullivan, D. (2007) 'How search engines rank web pages'. Available at: http://searchenginewatch.com/showPage.html?page=2156031 (accessed 15 July 2009).

Tedlock, B. (2000) 'Ethnography and ethnographic representation' in N. Denzin and Y.S. Lincoln (eds) *Handbook of Qualitative Research*. London: Sage. pp. 455–86.

Teorell, J. (2001) 'Methods combined: a comprehensive introduction to qualitative and quantitative research in the social sciences', unpublished manuscript, Uppsala University.

The Data Protection Act (1998) Available at: http://www.opsi.gov.uk/Acts/Acts1998/ukpga_19980029_en_1 (accessed 7 November 2008).

Tierney, W.G. (1999) 'Guest editor's introduction: writing life's history', *Qualitative Inquiry*, 5: 307.

University College Cork (2007) 'Information literacy: conducting a literature review'. Available at: http://booleweb.ucc.ie/Information_Skills/litreview.htm (accessed 15 July 2009).

University of the West of England (2007) 'Accuracy of websites'. Available at: http://ro.uwe.ac.uk/RenderPages/RenderLearningObject.aspx?Context=7&Area=1&Room=2&Constellation=44&LearningObject=188 (accessed 15 July 2009).

Vogt, W.M. (1999) *Dictionary of Statistics and Methodology.* London: Sage.

Wellington, J. (2000) *Educational Research Contemporary Issues and Practical Approaches.* London: Continuum.

Whyte, W.F. (1993) *Street Corner Society: Social Structure of an Italian Slum*, 4th edn. Chicago, IL: University of Chicago Press.

Woods, P. (1988) 'Educational ethnography in Britain', in R.R. Sherman and R.B. Webb (eds) *Qualitative Research in Education: Focus and Methods.* London: Routledge. pp. 90–109.

Worcester, R. (1996) 'Political polling: 95% expertise and 5% luck', *Journal of the Royal Statistical Society. Series A (Statistics in Society)*, 159 (1). Available at: http://www.jstor.org/pss/2983464 (accessed 26 July 2008).

Yerrell, P. (2000) 'The practitioner-researcher in nursing: there won't be too many Kilgore Trouts. A response to Peter Jarvis', *Nurse Education Today*, 20 (1): 36–8.

Websites

Labwrite Resources (2005) http://www.ncsu.edu/labwrite/res/gh/gh-bargraph.html (accessed 14 August 2008).

MaCorr Inc (n.d.) 'Sample size calculator'. Available at: http://www.macorr.com/ss_calculator.htm (accessed 7 December 2009).

RAOsoft (n.d.) 'Sample size calculator'. Available at: http://www.raosoft.com/samplesize.html (accessed 14 August 2009).

http://searchenginewatch.com/showPage.html?page=2167961.

Index

validity 15, 34–5, 80, 180, 181
variable 198
voluntary and community sector (VCS) 73

Web resources 88–91
  internet 87
  search engines 87

written reports 220
  audience 225
  data tables 223–5
  structure 221–2
  style 222–3
  table layouts 224
  writing process 220–1